DIFFERENT
YET THE
SAME

The mysterious simplicity of spiritual life

Tony Samara

Preface and questions from Christian Ghasarian

© Tony Samara - Christian Ghasarian - 2021

Cover photo © Ana Palma Ghasarian

Publisher: 'Api Tahiti, BP 4500, 98713, Papeete
Tahiti, French Polynesia
contact: contact@apitahiti.com

ISBN: 978-2-491152-03-1

DIFFERENT
YET THE
SAME

The mysterious simplicity of spiritual life

Tony Samara

Preface and questions from Christian Ghasarian

'API
Tahiti

Table of Contents

Acknowledgements

The creation of 'Different Yet the Same' would not have been possible without the shared vision of Christian and Ana Ghasarian, and the countless others who have committed their time and selfless service to this project. I thank them for their harmonious cooperation so that others have the opportunity to read the words within this book, raise their consciousness and find the wisdom of the heart in each situation.

Preface

Anthropologists try to enter people's system of logic, whether it is culturally very distant or very close to their own. They are trained to ask naïve but – hopefully – worthy questions to make obvious what is not necessarily so. Sometimes, they meet persons with significant lives and they want to explore these lives as they express humanity in its diversity. Sometimes a book can also come out from these specific investigations. The anthropology of spirituality offers interesting possibilities to expose significant lives and significant perspectives on life. This book is indeed about an unusual spiritual itinerary and system of knowledge. Borrowing from Zen Buddhism and South American shamanism while taking a clear distance from these conceptual systems and others, Tony Samara, is a contemporary spiritual teacher whose original approach of consciousness could be considered as beyond psychological and cultural frames.

I approached Tony Samara some years ago while I was conducting anthropological research on New Age spirituality in the United States and Europe. I participated in several retreats he gave in Portugal and other European countries. Very quickly, the anthropologist found much interest in his teachings as it addresses the relativity of cultural models, the authority and influence of ready-to-think social ideas on people's behaviour, the psychological mindset produced by mass programmed aspirations, the universality of human quests and dilemmas, etc. Through a very intuitive system of logic, Tony Samara's constant emphasis on the emancipating potential associated with taking a distance from ingrained certitude and what is normally taken for granted, as well as his cautious position about any dogmatism – be it spiritual or any other – are an important dimension of anthropology aimed at developing an open attitude towards other's differences and to acknowledge their humanity as ours. Behind the diversity of cultural forms and experiences, there is a human sameness.

To explore these themes more in depth and allow his spiritual understandings to be more public, I invited Tony Samara to answer a series of questions I would ask him in order to put these exchanges into a book. He agreed and the recordings took place several times during 2008, and also in 2010. With the simple tone of a conversation, and with many examples, Tony Samara talks about specific moments of his life that helped him understand things, travels and encounters that were important for him, his interest and the limits he found in spiritual approaches such as Zen Buddhism and South American Shamanism that he personally went through, as well as many themes such as the essence of consciousness, spirituality versus religion, energy points in the body, health and diseases, relationships and sexuality, spiritual discipline, students' expectations on teachers, sacred plants, masculine and feminine aspects, attachment to forms, dreams' messages, and so on....

Although there are biographical sequences, the logic of these conversations was more to comprehend Tony Samara's special life situations that led him to develop his current spiritual knowledge. Trying to do what anthropologists usually do – to follow a chronological logic in understanding a person's life – was a useless attempt with Tony Samara as his thinking is not linear but lateral or circular, all past experiences resonating in the present moment. Interestingly enough from an anthropological perspective, he is always coming back to the necessity to unlearn the culturally constructed psychological and social ingrained automatisms preventing spiritual awareness.

With total availability and patience, Tony Samara answered all my questions, even those that kept turning around themes for which I wanted more explanations and this made it possible to enter deeper into the core of his understanding and teaching of spirituality. As the following sentence extracted from the text makes it clear, it was not an easy task for a teacher who very much prefers silence to words for experiencing reality: *"I have never really used words to describe this experience or to describe how I know these things. The knowledge comes naturally and this is actually quite a job to describe it in words, to connect things together and make them comprehensible, because I have to use this other part of my brain that I find very difficult to use consciously"*. Yet, Tony Samara's answers to my questions were all spontaneous, as if in an inspirational flow. Although very direct and clear, the humble form of his teaching and his care to avoid dogmatism appear in his constant use of expressions such as "for me", "in my opinion", or "I feel", to accompany his explanations. With his authorisation, I took off many of these important subtleties and sometimes rephrased his sentences to make the written text more fluid than the spoken language.

A key aspect of his teaching is to invite people to "reconnect" to themselves and to the spiritual wisdom that is always inside of them. Significantly, he constantly uses words such as "recognise" and "realise" to make his point. Notions like "consciousness", "awareness", "unity", "being present", etc., are also recurrent. As his thought is deeply holistic and always putting all aspects in relation to each other, all the themes addressed here are inter-related although I tried to organise them into several chapters. His teaching sometimes borrows concepts that are today well established into people's minds (especially those involved on the path of spirituality), among which the Hindu ones of *"karma"*, *"chakra"*, *"kundalini"*, "third eye", *"maya"* (illusion), as well as more traditional and mystical Christian terms.. Yet, my understanding is that he only uses them to help the reader to make sense of what is said. Words are just words. Like the cultures in which they are used, they shape and frame our reality, enriching and limiting it at the same time. They also give meaning to our lives, produce knowledge and help us to understand and communicate things...

In the informal setting of these moments, children who were playing around, entered at some point into the conversation, and one had an unexpected question, asking if all the thoughts, good ones and bad ones, were the same. Tony's answer was that they are different in forms yet the same in essence. A mysterious simplicity… Explicitly or not, that idea is a recurrent theme in these explanations. As a quintessence of his teaching, it naturally came out as the title of this book. Many other questions could have been asked and will hopefully be explored in another space. The selected and necessarily limited ones in this book still allow to deeply grasp Tony Samara's understanding of spiritual life, and the way he continues to teach his understanding of reality, incarnating what he says with humility and simplicity.

Through a specific spiritual quest and itinerary, made of encounters and experiences in different places in the world, this book explores universal concerns beyond psychological and cultural diversities. I hope the reader will find the same – yet different – relevance in reading it as did the person behind the anthropologist writing these lines.

Christian Ghasarian

Spirituality, Religions & God

My first question will be very simple and basic: what is spirituality for you? You began your own spiritual development very early. Why do some people seem to have a need for spirituality and others apparently not?

This is a big question and even though I do not really think there is a need for spirituality, I believe that we are spiritual. The question is that we do not see or we do not understand this because we are caught up in the intensity of life. The word "spirituality" sometimes helps people to classify our experience in more understandable chapters, not knowing that spirituality is actually everything that makes a human being. For me, a spiritual person is a complete human being, one that has attained a sense of union, and this is what I believe all human beings are born into this world to do, whether they understand it or not.

In the beginning, spirituality may perhaps have a sense of personal union. It can be for example through love towards the family, towards the mother, towards self-development. That love then grows to a point where the babies understand themselves as a part of creation and this later develops into personalities, into traits and into cultural social aspects that divide us from the sense of union that we are born with. In my understanding, that sense remains there but it is hidden behind a veil. We then struggle to create a sense or an understanding of the world through coming back home to ourselves for that union to become manifested in our work, in our relationships and in our sense of community, so that we are not that separated as individuals. That union I am speaking about has more meaning than just the mundane. It makes you see that everything you are doing is much bigger than the little that we can see in the practical everyday experience.

The same goes in relationship. Many people would see relationship as just that, a relationship, but for me relationship is a yearning to come back home to oneself. It is an extension of that search to come back to union with oneself and it is the same with art, music, or philosophy. To me, everything comes back to the fact that we have just forgotten that we are complete and whole. We are then trying to make sense of what we have forgotten in many ways such as through philosophy, through politics and many other interests and activities we find in the world today.

The word "spirituality" is a little bit deceptive because it somehow comes from a cultural understanding that we are separated from ourselves. In this sense, spirituality is another aspect, just like philosophy or politics, which we can look at to become whole. Yet, we do not have to look at spirituality. We have to look at ourselves and at the essence of who we are to come back to that realisation. This is basically my understanding of spirituality.

In this perspective, spirituality is not something to develop or to have. It is just being.

Exactly. This is why, for example, some people think that I believe in religion. I may be using the word "religion" in the wrong way but for me the difference between coming home to oneself and religion is that religion believes that there are certain aspects that need to be fulfilled for a person to be complete. These ideas are portrayed in belief systems, in rituals, in things that you have to do, in morals that you have to follow, and in situations or cultural understandings that you have to be part of to become "spiritual". For me, this is a hindrance to true spirituality because it covers up what is really there.

Do you consider that the religious setting of moral beliefs, principles and laws, although they are supposed to lead humankind to a higher state, are missing some essence behind or beyond them?

Yes. I do not really know what religion is, as when I look at it, its history and its background, all I see is suffering. This make me have a very strong resistance towards fanatically religious people who want to impose belief systems unto others as a means of salvation. If this is what religion means, then I think that it is the absolute opposite of spirituality, which is universal and all encompassing towards every aspect of life be it human, plant, animal or mineral.

If you mean that religion is the misunderstanding of the spiritual people who began the religions such as Buddha, Jesus, Mohammed or whoever started the different religions or that it is an institutionalisation of spirituality to create a framework to make it simpler for people to follow, then I believe what you say to be true. Spirituality is so deep that most of it is part of the unknown and this implies a much bigger picture. People get lost and need guidelines to assist them to be more spiritual but the problem is that the people who put guidelines often focus very much on the external belief systems and forget the union, or what it means to come back home to oneself.

Buddha's idea was one thing but Buddhists today put a lot of emphasis on rituals and cultural things that are very different from what Buddha would have wanted to happen according to his way of seeing things. If we look at contemporary Buddhism, the rituals often become the central theme. In Tibet and Southeast Asia, Buddhism is mainly preoccupied with prayers, chants and rituals with monks and lamas, and this for me creates more confusion than spiritual growth. The confusion is that people then focus too much on the little things that are not spiritual but more easily understood in Christian terminology for instance.

For example, "being good" usually equates to being spiritual, but being good is such a vague perception of what is "good". For some people it means *acting* out a sense of goodness rather than *being* a sense of goodness. This is what seems to be more present in the Church today, where you see the portrayal of a sense of goodness rather than the coming home to what is real goodness within oneself. There is a certain superficiality in this act which separates us from real spirituality. We believe we are being spiritual by praying or by dressing up in certain clothes, by going to Church on Sunday, by saying the right thing or by doing whatever fits into that religious belief but we do not come back to the deeper aspect which is what Jesus and Buddha spoke about. These aspects of being are much more difficult to understand, and require much more of a human being than simply putting on the act of "being good".

To be good in oneself means that you have to change what is there that prevents the goodness from shining. For a lot of people this is much more difficult than going to pray and dressing up in certain clothes. I am of course painting an extreme picture just to make it clear but when religion is doing that, it is changing spirituality into something that it is not. Certain people then tend to gravitate towards religion and this is a major problem, because even though these people can be normal people, they can also be very sick people. When I say "very sick people", I mean people who want power, who are egocentric or who wish to control certain aspects of their lives that they cannot face themselves. This then becomes fundamentalism or the extremes of some religions today for example, where people misunderstand things within the heart and think that changing the world to be more spiritual means to utilise those negative aspects of themselves.

By criticising everyone as being sinful and bad, fundamentalists separate themselves to be good and the rest to be bad. That is the logic that leads the crazy fundamentalist Muslims to kill those who do not believe in their way. This is so far removed from spirituality as it just allowed people who are not well to hold on to religious beliefs and to change the world to what they believe is better. I feel that in the end, religion has actually created more suffering than good in the world. If you look at the crusades, the witch hunt and whatever else has happened in history, we see that many sick people have become "very religious" and created a lot of suffering that was surely not what spiritual people such as Jesus or Mohammed or Buddha ever dreamt of being part of their philosophy. In that sense, I am very far removed from religion in the traditional way of understanding it.

Among the many criticisms of religion, there is the current idea that it is based on a patriarchal authority working on fear. People's spiritual quest today is more oriented towards personal freedom, an approach that the Christian leaders and the Church cannot admit. This is why they are fighting what they call the "New Age ideology", as they understand it. For them, the New Age movement is each and everybody suddenly pretending to be God and to have all the answers inside. This is in opposition to the Christian understanding of spirituality, according to which Man is a sinner even though he was created at the image of God.

I believe people are leaving the Church in greater numbers today than ever before because they cannot understand it anymore. It has created a dualism in which the masculine aspect is somehow the active principle in life and the principle that we should follow, forgetting that spirituality is not masculine orientated. I am generalising of course, as within the Church they are as many different people, like in any other cultural or social community. However, in my understanding, we have created this dualism in the Western culture without being aware of it because we have embraced the idea that the masculine aspect is somehow more important than the feminine. When I say the masculine aspect, I mean the idea that God is a separate aspect of ourselves.

In this traditional old sense, God is somewhere outside. If you look at paintings in the Christian religion, everyone is looking up towards the sky, as if God – or some of its aspects – were in the clouds or in the ether. This reinforces the sense of dualism where we are separated and where the outer masculine aspect, which then becomes greater than ourself, has to be the salvation and so, in our spiritual understanding, we look on the outside.

We also find this idea in the figure of Jesus, who, in this traditional sense, is somehow almost as far removed from ourself and from our experience as God is. It is the same for Mary, the feminine aspect. God and Mary are somehow "out there" or separate from our direct experience of spirituality, and we have to strive to be good enough to fit into this idea so that we fall into "Grace", and hopefully get accepted by this outer God. In this logic, being good enough to go out there and be equal to that status allows us to leave this horrible world that we are experiencing which is in here, inside ourself.

I think that is a total misunderstanding of reality and I am sure many will agree if they explore deep enough for themselves. I see the feminine principle – which does not mean "women" – as being the most important aspect of spirituality. The feminine principle means that our understanding of the world, of the Spiritual World and of God, or the Divine or the Universe, whatever name you give it, cannot be understood without going inside. We cannot look outside – in the sense of separating ourselves from who we are – to understand that. Going inside does not mean that we are going inside and finding God within. It just means that we are finding ourselves and creating a sense of reality about ourselves that can touch what is divine.

When we reach that perspective, we see that it is impossible for the divine to be inside or outside because it is all encompassing. It is beyond the concept of thought. It is everywhere, beyond the thought, beyond the breath and even beyond the light that comes into our eyes to create an image or thought that perceives what God is. It is beyond all those aspects because it is the unknown. Yet we have a possibility of knowing the unknown by understanding the unknown within ourselves so that that unknown becomes known. We can then touch upon what is known to the unknown within ourselves, so to speak.

This is more often related to mysticism, where people come to a point where they touch what is called "Union", "Knowledge", "Grace" or "Enlightenment", there are many names. This point that one touches within oneself, is what I feel Jesus was speaking about but of course, he spoke about it in parables and it is very difficult to understand it literally. If we try to understand it from the outside, then we imply meanings to those parables that are sometimes not there, but if we understand the words from the perception of knowingness inside ourselves, then those words, those parables, make a lot of sense.

One easy way for me is to come back to the feminine aspect of who we are and this is the spiritual path that I recommend for people in today's world. The feminine aspect can be understood in many ways but one of the easiest ways is to understand the heart. This "heart" is a feeling that goes beyond mundane emotions and coming back to our centre or our heart allows an understanding of the feminine aspect. We can then make that feminine aspect inside of ourselves strong or real enough and more conscious to marry or to come to harmony with the masculine aspect, which is over emphasised in our society. We come to a sense of inner peace when the masculine and the feminine marry or understand each other.

I see this clearly in the essence of all religions: the masculine and feminine somehow come to a deeper understanding of each other. When this happens, we have a sense of inner peace. What I mean by inner peace is the absence of the mind taking over and thinking. Logical dualistic thinking is connected to the masculine aspect of humanity, yet when thinking does not stop but rather transcends itself and becomes thinking from the heart, we have wisdom or intelligence. That spiritual intelligence helps us to comprehend the Divine in a sense that is more real than what the Churches, the Synagogues or the Mosques try to push upon their faithful. This is one very important aspect of the work I do.

Religion has been very criticised because of everything you said, but at the same time, people of all cultures acknowledge the need of being spiritual, as everyone faces death and has to give meaning to life. Yet, because of what religions have done through history, more and more people do not acknowledge the concept of God anymore. Some philosophers even talk about a "laic spirituality", addressing the need and the inevitability of spirituality, but without God. As for you, you mention the divine aspect in us with no emphasis on God...

That's right because God, in my opinion, has too many negative connotations for too many people. The word "God" has been corrupted. This happened because what is understood as God is something so judgmental and big and out there that it has become a hindrance for some people to even acknowledge that reality beyond moralism, beyond believing or beyond being part of a group. I do not know the etymology of the word "God", but for me the word "Divine" is much more explicit to signify that spirituality is a sense of enlargement or expansion beyond the ego, beyond the mundane self, whether people believe there is a divine or not. In this sense, the Divine is a bigger picture that goes beyond these limited aspects and which is attainable through consciousness. When our consciousness moves beyond the egocentric perspective, it evolves into dimensions that are more understandable. This becomes a divine understanding. It becomes a consciousness that is expanded to touch the invisible world, which is where the divine is of course.

I like the word the "Divine" but it can also be corrupted to have certain meanings. For me the word "God" in the Christian sense is somehow like a father figure. Yet I do not see God in that way because for me, that is absolutely absurd. I see God as an intelligence that is the creator of everything. With the word "creator" I mean the fact that we are here and of course this can be explained through evolution in very scientific terminology, which may perhaps be right or wrong. In essence, the question is still not answered: where did all this come from? How did it begin? We can explain it in many ways to get to a certain point where knowledge fails and then we call that lack of knowledge the "Big Bang". From nothing there was a Big Bang and all of a sudden there was something, but the question remains: "Where did that come from?".

That is creation for me, so what I mean by God is the aspect of creation that is unknown, the aspect that started from a perspective going back into history to explore space to try to understand it, or going to physics to try to understand particles, or going to philosophy to understand the non-understandable. It is really about the unknown.

I actually like the way the Sufis speak about the divine and in some of their traditions, they say that by mentioning the word "divine", your mind has already created a picture and you have already corrupted the divinity of the divine, which is beyond that concept. If you look at the ancient religion of the Old Testament, where Christianity started for instance, God becomes what is beyond God, so to speak. I think that it is almost like a mystical tradition where the divine started through a sound or a word. It actually says: "At the beginning there was the Word, and from that sound, light was created and something happened". That is exactly what creation is.

If you look at it in a fundamental way, then of course you are trying to understand it in a chronological order that makes no sense. What it actually says is that if in a mystical sense you can hear the true sound of the divine, beyond the logical reasoning of creating an image of the divine through the mind and beyond understanding what that image is, then that sound speaks directly to your heart.

The divine also sings. I say it "sings" because it is almost like a mystical universal song, something that makes you know in your heart that what you understand is divine. That knowledge does not come from putting a name to the divine. It comes from an experience. This is what people like Jesus, Buddha and all mystics experienced, the knowingness. That knowingness explained everything and was beyond doubt in their mind about what is nowadays called "God", "the Divine" or "Universal Truth". Yet we need to have a name to talk about these things. This is why, of course, we have these great terminologies that are always debated, "God is not this", "God is that", and so forth. God is none of those things as it is beyond even the word that we are using at the moment to communicate the concept.

You do not use the word "God" very often or only with extreme care because apparently believing or not believing in God is not the question for you. Yet, when you talk about the mystery of creation, the mystery of life, your point seems to be that it is divine. Do you mean there is no need to refer to God because life itself is divine and we are it?

Whether you believe or do not believe in God, the Divine, or the Universal Spirit, it makes no difference because you are.

Yet we obviously face the mystery of life, the mystery of the universe, of the creation, and of the unknown...

Yes, but the unknown is only unknown to you. It is not unknown to the divine so the problem is only your problem.

Even though a great scientist like Albert Einstein said that he "could not consider that God was gambling with the cosmos", western philosophies have particularly developed the idea of randomness of things and events. In this perspective, the creation, everything, went into existence without us knowing why, and therefore probably by chance. Apparently, not all the cultures of the world refer to the notion of God, even though they acknowledge the idea of human fate.

Exactly. I think those cultures that do not mention the word "God" have been less polluted by ideology. I am not saying that this makes one better than the other but the fact is that people have fought endlessly over the notion of God and created too much suffering around that idea. Even within Christianity, whether you are Catholic, Greek Orthodox, Protestant, Reformed or whatever, people have walked further away from the real sense of what is God rather than getting closer to it. This is why I think that notion is a waste of time and it also creates fear. I remember as a child how the idea of God was traditionally so negatively portrayed: "If you are not "good", then God will not like what you are doing". The implication is that God will punish you or will not accept you in his or her love if God is not happy with you.

To me, that very idea was so alien to my understanding of things that even though I was brought up in such a culture, I laughed at the whole concept and actually did the opposite. I was very bad and naughty just to test and see if what people were telling me was true, to see if any lightning would magically come out of the sky and strike me or hurt me. I found this to simply be a belief system which made me very sceptical of my surroundings. It invited me to go deeper within myself to understand the truth from my perspective rather than an imposed such as, "God is angry at you" or "God will punish you if you do not follow certain rules or social norms".

It may seem sacrilegious that some cultures do not have the notion of God, but maybe their notion of God is divine in itself, through an experience rather than just simple ideas and talks. For me experience is an aspect of spirituality that I consider essential. Practice is better than anything else. If you practice, then you do not have to speak so much. You can speak a lot about many things, about how spiritual you are, how developed you are, how enlightened you are, how wonderful you are, how God loves what you do, but that only make sense to people because they follow your madness. It makes no real sense to anyone, as it does not touch people in the same way as Jesus did, for example.

By a simple act of smiling or being, he touched thousands and thousands of people, not just during his lifetime but also for centuries afterwards. It is the same with Buddha and many mystics and poets. They uttered certain things and did certain things that touched people beyond notions and ideas. Those cultures which do not believe in or do not use the word God may be much more peaceful than others.

This approach is to be found in traditional Japan's Shintoism, in shamanic cultures and cultures based on the ancestor's cult, which take into account nature and nature's spirits. They, of course, have the notion of invisible power but not necessarily that of God, as we understand it.

It is also interesting that when people do not have a notion of God, they may have a notion of something else that replaces the concept of God, like a father figure. That concept of spirits, although different in the form, is still the same in the sense that it is dualistic. In my opinion, it still makes no sense because you see things outside of yourself. Shamanism is definitely in the same belief logic as it is full of spirits who will punish you if you do not do the right thing. I do not know Shintoism well enough to comment on it except the fact that it emphasises nature, but I think it is an interesting approach as long as you see nature as part of yourself.

If spirituality is inevitable for human beings, are we really separated from animals and nature? For the Christian Church there are humans, created at God's image and there is the animal realm, far below them. Therefore humans are entitled to take control of nature. In terms of dealing with the ecosystem, this belief can lead to pollution and many other problems. It is striking that the Church may even criticise the idea of global ecology, according to which humans are just one species among others, and are therefore responsible for their actions on the earth. For the Church, assimilating human beings to the natural surrounding world is neglecting their divine nature (as they are said to have been created at God's image). Do you consider spiritual awareness to only be a human fortune?

The fact that the Church condemns the idea that humans are simply part of the creation is just horrific. That clarifies my point that there are some really extreme people in the Church who have created philosophies far removed from the essence and from the spiritual teaching prior to the Church becoming an institution. Jesus always treated human beings very kindly but he also treated the earth, including animals, the same. The Bible has been translated into many languages, from Aramaic to Hebrew, from Hebrew to Greek, from Greek to Latin, and from Latin to English and other languages. Anyone who has translated any document to so many languages would understand how difficult it is to hold its essence, especially when it is a mystical teaching.

In its original version the Bible speaks about animals in the Aramaic language that is very poetic and can imply many things, a bit like the Chinese languages, but this is not the case in English or German, which are very particular in their meaning. In the original text I believe it was written that plants, animals, nature, the universal nature on earth and around us, the moon, the stars, were all created in God's image. I use the words in the Christian sense, "created in God's image", because the divine created the world in seven days and loved every aspect. It did not say, "Oh no, I do not like this aspect, then I am going to create another aspect to see if this is better". Actually, the whole of creation was part of the whole picture that was the divine.

Creation took seven days and in the last part of it, Adam was created out of mud and, of course, Eve from one of his ribs. In the Aramaic word, the earth, the mud or the clay, whatever they used, is a symbol of the whole earth, the animals, the stars, and the lakes. It is encompassed in the macrocosm of the earth within us. Therefore we have that responsibility within us for the outside in the same way as the outside has the responsibility for the inside.

The divine created that picture, for example in Adam in the Bible, and then from Adam was created Eve, which is also symbolic but has been misunderstood. Later, Adam and Eve created humanity, the people today in the world, so our responsibility is not to have dominion over everything but to feel that we are the earth, that our body, our physical and spiritual bodies are of the earth, of the Universe. The earth is not just the physical planet earth, it is also all the stars and the moons. Because of the patriarchal and dualistic point of view, we have separated everything into compartments and we do not see that we are part of everything. To say that we are better than animals, plants or mountains, is to not see that we are divine.

In my understanding, the divine is beyond that mundane self which understands divinities in a separate point of view or as something else than ourself. It is our essence and our essence is the essence of everything. We are not just a human being, we are the Universe. We are everything, a microcosm or macrocosm of everything. By forgetting that, our culture has gone wrong.

One of the reasons why I sometimes feel that conservation of nature, or trying to save the earth, is a waste of time is because it comes out from a western concept of disrespect. The disrespect is not the idea of conservation of the earth itself but the belief that our actions are somehow separate from the earth. If we look at other cultures, like shamanic cultures or cultures that are more in touch and in a respectful relationship with the earth, we see that they treat the earth how Jesus did. They have not been indoctrinated to look after the earth and to dominate it because of the masculine mind concept of the earth being separate from ourselves. Our approach is totally ridiculous since if we destroy animals and if we destroy the earth, then we destroy ourselves. There is no doubt about this, but we just do not see it.

We believe that we need to keep moving on in this cultural context that we have been creating for the last five thousands years. To say that animals and plants are not divine makes no sense because if they are not divine, then it is the same as saying that God, or the Divine, does not exist. If you do not see the divinity in a flower, then you cannot see the divinity in your own heart. The flower carries the creation of the divine, just as it is explained in the Bible. As the divine created the flower, how can it be of no use or of less use than a human being?

In Hinduism for instance, nature, with its animals and plants, is very present. On the other hand, Islam and especially Christianity do not put such an emphasis on nature. Do you consider that it is in the translation of the religious messages that nature got lost?

Yes, totally. This happened because unwise people decided to put their own perspective that they believed to be true at that time onto what was experienced and changed it into words to be followed literally rather than symbolically. So yes, there is a historical aspect to this very complicated issue but it is interesting to see that children very clearly love animals. In my opinion, they are closer to the divine than many adults. They are especially very happy in nature. If for example you have a baby who is crying and you walk in nature, then the baby is somehow soothed. The reason for this is because children feel the divinity of the trees, of the plants, of the earth, of the divine, of themselves. They experience a union by going back to something more original than what civilisation has created today, like a home or an apartment that has television and noise. This is why children in native nature based societies are usually happier than in modern cities.

Social scientists point out that there is a very important social dimension of religion that can be used in a power relationship between humans. God can thus be invoked by people to organise and maintain a conservative social life for the benefit of the most powerful ones. At the same time, as you said, religion can also be used the way it is in some places of South America as a "theology of liberation", referring to God to change social life. Yet, these two positions – the conservative and the revolutionary one – are in the same logic according to which the reference to God can have an effect on society. God can thus be a pretext for social order, either an old one or a new one, rather than a necessity for the spiritual dimension of human life...

Yes. My words might be very critical here but some aspects of dogmatism in various churches are interesting because their whole concepts are misunderstood. For me, the sense of the divine being so separated from ourself really represents the belief system of fundamentalist extremism and this creates a big problem. It is so different from some of the mystics or monks who had deep senses of transformation within themselves. Their actions somehow changed the world in a completely different way than from, as you say, creating a social order that fits into all structures and pictures of what is right and wrong. The idea that we need to create an order of things is very Western. Even if you are not historically based on dogmatic Christianism, it is in the Western culture.

Many people do things, whether political, philosophical, religious, or even conservationist and humanitarian acts, out of a sense that they need to create an order, but that order is already a Western concept. They do so without understanding that this order does not come from external powers but from coming back to a sense of peace. When there is peace there is a sense of order, yet as long as there is a lack of peace within oneself, there cannot be order in the deeper sense of things. We can create wonderful ideas about politics, and of course it makes a big difference if it is democratic or totalitarian, but in the end, the democracy or humanitarian aspects of helping and sharing only make sense when everyone feels a connection to that peace.

In my opinion, the real order should be to create a sense of peace for people, rather than trying to change them into an orderly social picture or a perspective of how things needs to be, how to obey, to follow, or to listen to certain rules and regulations. I am not saying to be anarchistic, because it is totally different, but to really follow the heart much more.

We see this with children who have a sense of knowingness when things are not in order. For example, in Western cultures today (which goes back to one of your questions), most people have a nice house and income, food and school, everything people would dreams of in third world countries. Even so, there is a sense of lack of inner harmony or inner peace for most Western people, a feeling that something is not right. Of course this explodes at times in some kind of protest or cultural shift such as the hippies in the sixties, but the problem really is disharmony inside. We are trying to create this order from outside but it is not being replicated on the inside. Something is missing in that creation of a democracy or civilised evolution of a monetary system, sustained by egalitarian values where everyone is supposed to have the same access to wealth.

In that sense, I believe that lack of inner peace needs to be addressed much more strongly. When it is addressed, then you have a sense of order. We see this actually in the Catholic Church, for example when people like Saint Francis of Assisi, the founder of the Franciscan order, and a few others like him, created a certain harmony, a space of harmony around them which did not really have many rules in the beginning, although the order did of course become more dogmatic later. We also see that around spiritual teachers like Buddha or Jesus. It would be amazing to see them in action. You would think that you would need order and discipline around that gathering of people because there were so many different personalities, but somehow, things worked out. There was a sense of order because people were coming back to the order and to the space of harmony that is inside of themselves. In that space, there is no need to stop people from doing certain things because there is a sense of knowingness. People are at peace. There is less violence, less disturbance and fewer disharmonies.

That peace comes with spiritual teachers but also at different times and I think we are entering a point now in our world where this time of inner peace will be stronger. So if any fundamentalist or extremist tries to impose order from an external point of view of God being powerful and judgmental, it will not work anymore. People have been leaving the Church progressively because they are exploring that inner peace inside of themselves and realising it through Grace – meaning that it is coming from an unknown space. It is becoming so strong that it is creating a new cultural understanding of the world, even in politicians who do not understand why they are doing certain things. There will be less need than ever before to create that structure of civilisation that we have today in the world.

It is a slow process but I believe it to be quite possible as people discover that inner peace within themselves. This is my work, to push people to go back home to themselves rather than trying to go outside of themselves to find this structure of peace through social order. When people ask me about what is the best way to bring up children, they are asking for an external picture so that they can follow that picture to do the right thing for their children. Conservative and dogmatic groups will offer them lovely philosophies as to why this is good and how to do it but my way is to say: "Follow your heart". That means coming back to the peace inside of yourself and from that space of peace use your intelligence to address the situation so that it creates harmony, rather than trying to follow an idea.

This is a very complicated way of doing things because it is of course easier to follow a system than to come back to oneself. Yet, I believe it to be the only possible way in the future and the only possible way that has deep significance for the world, beyond just an era of transformation. The Roman culture disappeared because it did not have an inner structure. The Western culture will also disappear if it does not have an inner structure. That inner structure is not the Church, it is the people. The people cannot come back to that structure nor to that peace by following a dogma. They need to return to that peace to understand how to practice it. Dogmas and books do not give you peace. It is you, your expansion to that space where peace is experienced, that gives you the whole notion of how to act out.

When a child is doing something that is annoying you for example, how do you follow a philosophy if your emotions are unable to bypass the space where you get to a peaceful point and can address that situation in this way? How do you follow a philosophy when your emotions go straight away to a sense of irritation, to an egocentric perception of the situation, or to a projection of the picture where you see things that are not really there? By not seeing the child but just your own emotions and your own picture, you forget that he or she is really an extension of your inner peace. If you address things from that inner space, then you are addressing the whole world from the space of peace.

Then there is peace. No more war, no more conflict between people who believe and people who do not believe, no more children who become teenagers and rebel against their parents who do not understand why, no more cultures within cultures that say "We do not want to do this anymore". If we come back to the sense of peace, we have order because we come back to an order that is the heart, which is a natural order of things, which is the way the divine created the world in the first place.

If peace is coming from inside, it should naturally be expressed outside of the person. Yet, some people's convictions can lead them to be proselyte and therefore intolerant to ways that are not theirs.

Exactly. The fundamentalism that is growing today is one of the most dangerous things that we are facing in the modern world because of intolerance. People do not go back to their heart but to a belief system, believing that what they think justifies their actions. If their actions could be understood from their heart, they would see that they are being foolish and schizophrenic.

Again it is an external perspective. God used to establish social order...

Indeed. Nowadays the Muslim fundamentalists for example, absolutely believe that they are doing the right thing, destroying evil – evil being the Western culture – and dying as martyrs to open the doors of paradise for them and save the world. This is an interesting belief system but if they took God out of the picture and put themselves in a real perspective to see what they were doing, they would understand that they are totally fanatical. But it is not only Muslims who do this. They are the most extreme but many people have beliefs that are not inclusive or universal.

When you begin to see other human beings or nature as your enemy, you are killing parts of yourself because the world is you. Whatever you do in the world, you are doing to yourself. If you bomb a railway station because you believe you are helping to get rid of evil, what you are doing is bombing part of yourself. You are killing a part of yourself, which will allow the evil to come up, so it is the opposite of what you want because it is actually the evil that is making you do that. I use the word "evil" just as a joke in the sense that you see things on the outside as being separate from yourself, so you are actually seeing the divine as separate from yourself. What is evil is that you have not encompassed the divine in the complete sense but you are separating it into good and bad. It then becomes a whole mind game that takes you totally out of the sense of compassion, of love and caring.

The whole world does that, on different levels and different ways, to their children, to other people and to themselves. We do it all the time. We do not honour our complete experience but subdivide our experiences into little facets and then we just think, "This is good" or "this is not good".

Our mind is constantly attacking our beautiful being, our heart, and saying, "I'm not good enough!", "Why am I so stupid?" or "Why can't I do this that way?". I call it sabotage when we spend eighty percent of our time sabotaging ourselves rather than thinking in a positive way – that is using the heart as a method of thinking – and saying, "All right, the world is beautifully spiritual and everything is a mirror of myself. Then I encompass every aspect of that mirror and embrace it totally to learn what things that picture is trying to explain to me". Rather than judge yourself, or aspects of yourself, embrace yourself. That embrace will then naturally go towards your children, towards your community, towards society and the world.

Evolution & Mythology

There is a quote from the Bengali sage Ramakrishna that says: "Spirituality is not for empty bellies". It actually seems that the quest for spirituality is bigger among populations in societies that have overcome basic issues of survival. Do you think the very nature of spiritual life was the same among so called "primitive people" in prehistoric times?

I do not believe that we have changed much nor do I believe that we are currently more spiritual than the "primitive man" was. I think what is important to realise now is that the potential that we have today is different than the potential that we had a hundred thousands years ago and this is because of *karma*. *Karma* for me does not mean punishment and does not mean that you have to suffer because you are bad. It is rather that knowledge is being passed down and this knowledge can be genetic and personal.

The genetic has to do with our ancestors who went through various experiences and gained knowledge from those experiences. That knowledge was not only personal as a thought or as a feeling but got passed down in the genetic make-up that we received as children and that we then passed down to our children. Why are things different today than they were ten or a hundred thousand years ago? Because our ancestors have gone through so many experiences and this knowledge has been passed down to us today to act upon, but unfortunately we do not always act upon it. Even though the knowledge and the potential is there to be explored, we do not really listen to it. This is why I feel "primitive people" sometimes were more compassionate and more loving towards each other than we are in today's world.

With all the knowledge that we have, we still live as if we were trying to survive some sort of catastrophe, where something is going to happen and destroy humanity. We are racing to find some destination that is unattainable without taking care of the steps that we take during that time. We do not take care of our most precious items such as nature, the earth and the people around us, or the situations that mean more to people than what they understand.

I think people have been spiritual all the time and have had the sense of the divine in the same way as we do today, yet our expression of it is different and it becomes part of the cultural understanding, unless someone goes really deeply beyond that. Of course it is expressed in different ways today because we live in a modern society very different than ten thousand years ago. In those days people lived in a society were death and life were not what they are today. It was much more dramatic, in the sense that if there was war it was very much about survival.

Yet I do not believe the difference was because of the people but rather because of the eras that they went through. At certain times, the world got so difficult that people acted out their sense of survival in a much more dramatic way.

We actually see that even in the modern world, given the right environment, people will be as primitive as people were hundred thousand years ago. The difference is that they now have the knowledge to create much more harm than a hundred thousand years ago. Fighting is no longer with wooden clubs, stones or swords, there are now lethal weapons that can demolish and destroy the world in a very short time. I do not think that we have changed very much but our potential and the light is much stronger than it ever was. This light is expanding individually for each person but also for humanity as a whole collective being. The *karma* that has been passed down through genetics and through individuals for a long time has created the potential that creates the light much more strongly for people. Today, we have the chance to change, to be what our ancestors have dreamed of and what we dream of, to be much closer to heart than ever before. I think that the people who worry about our days and who say that the world is a place that has become more difficult, worse than before and that it is dying, are not quite right. If you look at it from a spiritual perspective, there is more chance to create the harmony for ourselves and everyone else than it has ever been possible for thousands of years.

As you acknowledge the idea of ancient knowledge and wisdom passed down through history from one generation to another, you also consider that we are probably today in a better situation to develop the spirituality which is inside of us. What do you think of the common idea that some wise people in the ancient times knew many things and have been trying to transmit their knowledge through mythology and symbols?

People knew things before and people know things today. When you speak a language of knowledge, it is not popular. It is not something like music or television that gets attention of the masses. It is something that only a few people will listen to. This is not different today than it was ten thousand or a hundred thousand years ago. If some ancient person sat down meditating under a primitive tree ten thousand years ago and all of a sudden understood that there was no need for conflict, that person would only be sitting under that tree alone, or perhaps with a few people. That person would definitely not sit with all the members of his or her culture as the whole culture is so preoccupied with other things and therefore do not hear that knowledge. Then of course that knowledge may have become in ancient days, for example in South America, what the shaman's mythology is. As the knowledge was so strange, it needed to be conceptualised in a special language, in metaphors, and to be passed down through pictures, symbols and certain rituals.

Do you see mythology as a discrete and simple way to transmit vast knowledge?

For me it is a waste of time to transmit knowledge through mythology because it bypasses direct initiation into who you are. For native people for example, to have the eagle as a mythological creature is wonderful perhaps because it helps you to connect to some aspect that is difficult to connect to without using some form of mythology or symbolism. But why not connect to that directly rather than going through other ways?

Some specialists, most often outside the academic realm but still very popular, like Joseph Campbell, consider that myths actually carry deep spiritual teachings waiting to be understood for what they are. They say that the reading of mythological texts should not be made historically, because then the stories make no sense, but only symbolically. Yet, mythology is an uncertain way to transmit knowledge to a forthcoming humanity, as it can be totally mistaken in the process. Many people think this is what happened with the Bible where Jesus Christ's messages in parables have been considerably misunderstood. There may be a lot beyond the stories of the Greek gods and goddess and so forth.

I think a lot of people read too much into mythology and this can be confusing, especially when your reference points are not in tune with the parables. Jesus, for instance, spoke in a way that was not confusing to him, because he knew what he was speaking about and many people around him understood. It should be very easy to understand something if the language is very clear and true. If you are speaking directly from your heart about an experience, that language should touch people without the need to philosophise or to intellectualise about the experience.

The language of the heart touches people in a way that no word can touch as poetry does but people can also misunderstand poetry and wonder, what is that person talking about? They can also misunderstand music or mythology in the same way. Yet, if you connect to the essence of mythology then the language is pretty clear. Mythology was probably not created to bring confusion but rather because it was the easiest language to describe an experience.

Carl Gustav Jung uses archetypes a lot in that sense. It is interesting but it is better to go directly to the energy than to go via these devices. It is nice and really inspirational to read poetry that helps us to see things in a different way but it is better to listen to the poetry of your heart, which opens an understanding inside, than to the poetry of some person that wrote it ten thousand years ago. Then mythology, poetry and parables are not confusing. They become clear, as you have accessed that point inside yourself.

Could this vagueness in poetry and mythology be a playful human heritage, giving information while hiding it at the same time to inform and trick people in order to let them learn and discover things by themselves?

It can be a game because some people like to be very intelligent. They write poetry that sounds wonderful and looks interesting but the message could be said simpler in one word rather than having to go through so many verses of poetry. This game could come from persons thinking very highly of themselves, and therefore using a very confusing language or it could also be, and it depends of the mythology, that there is no other way of describing things because language is controlled. It is limited in its expression to certain concepts to which people could attach themselves to try to explain something. Mythology does not really interest me until it is useful. The only mythology I know is the mythology that the mind creates through dreams, which become obvious as you work with them.

Dreams as personal mythologies?...

Yes clearly.

Dante's concept of Divine Comedy may be interesting here because people have this kind of experience in *San Pedro* ceremonies where they burst into an unexpected laughter, as they understand things that all of a sudden appear to be very simple and obvious. A feeling of having insights arises as if the knowledge was hidden to the person who has to grasp it through his or her own way...

It is hidden because we have so many layers.

So maybe mythology is part of this divine comedy? Things should not be too clear otherwise they prevent the person reading it from searching a little bit by himself or herself. But this is obviously not your way...

No, because for me the divine is like an open book. There is nothing hidden and there is no searching. It is a matter of letting go of whatever is veiling you from seeing, so to search is an interesting concept. In some esoteric schools searching is about going far away and someone told me about a book by Paulo Coelho, *The Alchemist*, which is about searching and going everywhere, doing this and that, and coming back to wherever. The alchemical journey is an interesting journey but it is unnecessary because there is no gold, there is no divine to find somewhere.

If you are looking for the divine or the gold, then you will never find it. To go through an all-alchemical or mythological process to try to find the divine takes you away from the space where the divine is. So where is the divine? Well, of course, the divine is there! Everywhere. But how do you find it? You do not find it by looking into compartments. You find it by coming back prior to where the "there" is, by coming to the sense of this moment. It is before the concept of "there" even originated, before the concept of "you" originated, before the concept of "individual ego" arose. That is not in mythology, that is in simplicity and humility.

This is where a lot of spiritual paths differentiate their way of work from mine because they like to use these complicated pictures. For instance, someone was telling me about *Kabbalah*. It seemed very complicated and, listening to that person, I was getting a little bit confused. I was wondering, "Why do we need all this to explain something so simple?" Well of course we need all this to explain something so simple because it is not simple to our minds that need to understand it in a complicated fashion. Divine intelligence is very simple to a mind that is open to immerse itself in the understanding and, in a way, it is also very complicated because it is beyond normal philosophy and psychology. It may not appear to be a simple thing but it is simpler than intellectualism.

You do not have to go through the whole system of complication to get to the space of humility and simplicity. That is perhaps what characterises the way of work that I am practising, letting go of all those concepts. I am not saying that they are bad but ... let them go. Listen to the poetry and the intelligence of your own heart and let it speak because that is in itself worthwhile. We do not need anything else. Mythology is interesting if you see that perhaps an eagle in a dream is not just an eagle but carries more to it. Yet for me what is more important is to experience the sense of the eagle that you had in the dream in a conscious way so that you can communicate it in your own language. Or, if you dream of a king, to experience what is like to be a king, not just in the dream but above all in deep inside you. It is a whole experience. It is not about dressing up as a king, or going back to mythologies about different kings and seeing what it means, it is about your own profound experience. A complicated while simple path...

Nature & human Life

During a retreat I remember you saying, "Nature is always here to help us but we do not see it". Another time you said, "Nature is neutral, it is neither good nor bad". Would you say more about your understanding of the place nature takes or can take in our spiritual development?

Nature is beautiful. I think human beings need natural beauty to feel connected to their heart. Art and music can of course be also very beautiful but for me nature bypasses even those aspects into a profound beauty that people who are dying for example, recognise the essence of. It is so peaceful to be in a natural environment, watching plants, animals or insects, interacting with the ecosystem, as it gives us a sense of connectedness and harmony in the circle of life. This is the beauty I am speaking about. I feel that to recognise this on the outside is of vital help in meditation or when we go deeper inside of ourselves. There is a natural sequence of harmony that is always present and very obvious for people in nature, and that is reflected back through the trees, the flowers, the clouds or the water. This is sometimes forgotten in our hectic environment of modern social institutions, work, and whatever we have to deal with to be surviving in the atmosphere we live in today's world.

Nature is important for me because it goes beyond that and reminds us of what it means to be alive in this circle of life. The beauty is beyond just prettiness like the garden that is made to look pleasing for people. It is inherent in everything that creates nature. The beauty of nature is the dynamic force behind it. This is the force that I am saying is "neutral". It is not there saying, "I want to be beautiful to make you happy or to be good to you". It is just what it is. It is neutral in the sense that if we recognise and connect to this force it is helpful. We then recognise that we are able to be ourselves in the more profound sense.

We are able to be part of that more profound aspect of life rather than the dualistic interaction we have in the modern world, where we are judging or having to judge to grow in a certain way and say, "This is good for us and this is not so good for us", acting out of that space. In nature we can relax and go beyond these judgements to simply feel a deep peace, just like sleeping or resting. It is a vital aspect in the work I do, introducing nature and helping people to see it as part of the meditation and not separate from spirituality. This is often forgotten in religions where a temple has constructed structures to remind people about spirituality rather than the direct interaction with nature, which is the essence of my work.

When you speak about nature and its beauty, do you specifically think about mountains, seas, trees and plants, or do you include animals?

Nature is animals, rocks, water, all the elements that constitute the ecosystem and the ecology that creates nature. It is not just plants although they certainly have a deep and important connection to humanity. The plants and the water on earth are much easier to relate to because they have a certain presence that connects us more than animals, which are still are part of the ecosystem but more dynamic. For example a tree is not only beautiful in the external sense but also in the internal sense that is symbolic. It reminds us of the deeper beauty inside, so we recognise the beauty by experiencing it and then seeing it in the tree. It is almost like it touches some part of us that is able to relate to the beauty of the tree. Animals provide a more moving sensation and it is more difficult to focus on. To see a beautiful eagle flying in harmony with the element of air, a butterfly or a hummingbird is similar, but trees for me are vital.

Someone told me about a story in India in a place called Puna. As the traffic is growing and growing, people decided to extend the road so that the cars would not have problems passing each other, they just cut down all the beautiful ancient trees that created shade for the nice roads they wanted to build... This for me shows that humanity has forgotten the beauty inherent in the whole system. Instead of recognising this beauty and perhaps working around it, they only see the beauty of the road, and this is what separates us from the simple beauty of nature.

It becomes unhelpful when people do something negative to nature because they do not see the beauty that is there. When they cut this beauty they have lost a relationship. In the Amazon forest, once trees are cut, children are born into a society where there is no rainforest. They do not know what trees are because they do not have that experience of them. In Puna apparently there are not many trees left because people cut them down very easily for firewood and other uses. It is amazing that they could do this in India where people are supposed to have a deeper relationship to the elements. Even native or "traditional" people somehow forget the elementary beauty.

In today's world, I feel this beauty is not only vital but it is also a reminder of how our culture can move forward without destruction. It strongly reminds us that the trees need to be alive for us to see the inherent harmony of everything and to replicate it in our culture. Rather than creating a road and destroying what is in its way, it would be interesting to work around the whole concept of nature and create a road that is in harmony with nature. Then our children see the harmony in what we are doing rather than thinking about leaving the modern society to go back to a natural space, which is a typical European philosophy.

While nature is destroyed, National Parks are created so that people have a space of nature to go back to and think, "We still have the National Park for the weekend visits and to see how birds and other animals live!" I feel that is again part of individualism where we separate ourselves from nature by controlling it, by pushing it aside and saying: "It's not important for the movement of civilisation". We preserve it but we destroy all the beauty that is around us by building ugly structures and roads that have no relation to the trees, to the water or to the whole movement of the earth.

Is people's will to have plants at home or to take care of a garden an expression of an unconscious desire or need to connect or reconnect to nature?

Totally! Especially when people reach certain stages of their life, they recognise that this is more important. When you have children or when you get older you need a garden. I remember in Croatia looking at a lady who must have been ninety-five. She was hardly able to move but she was cutting roses in her garden and it gave her immense pleasure. I could see in her face that for her, that was like a mystical experience or meditation. She spent hours just touching the leaves, cutting the roses, tending to the bush. It is very important!

Of course when you are twenty-five or thirty, or very busy with work and life, it becomes less obviously important. It is only when you have time or when you are forced to have time to be present in a different way with children, that nature speaks to you. I feel that it is all right when one is young not to be so connected to nature because of course they are many other things happening. However, if it is prolonged, then we forget the beauty that is real and we get caught up in the beauty that is an illusion, such as: "If I have clothes, if I have money or if I go to the theatre, then I experience beauty". Through this attitude, we forget the simplicity of what can be so profoundly healing for everyone, whether we are conscious of it or not.

Most of the times we are not conscious of the healing potential of nature, because being in another world, we just do not see it. Native people are still often conscious of it because they had no other world to distract them from the natural world they are part of to survive, but this is not everywhere, because of civilisation. Since the beauty is part of their experience, they do not recognise it as a distinct thing. They do not say "this is beautiful", because they do not know anything else. As for us, we are separate from nature although it can be much more inherent in our life. If everyone had a garden or at least had a relationship to a part of nature, they would slowly understand what I am speaking about more deeply. They would have an experience where they could understand it, unlike children today. Some children do not even recognise that milk comes from a cow. When you are so far removed from nature, there is of course no direct connection.

I feel that working on a garden is important, especially these days. It can be your own garden or it can be a place in nature. This is what we do, we have a garden in the forest. Sai has his special corner where he knows the strawberries grow. That allows a direct connection with nature – this is very important – but if it is not possible, you can work on what you have. For instance, we have the veranda full of as many plants as we can fit. I ask the children to tend the plants and to gain an understanding of what happens when they do certain things. Sai watered the plants a lot at one point and he realised that they drown. Then he began to inherently feel that plants are also alive and they have to be treated and understood in the same way as you relate to your brother or sister, in a way that is very dynamic. He is always sensitive but now he is much more sensitive to plants and he really understands. This understanding is lost when you live separated from nature.

It is so important, especially for children to spend time in their own garden, or even nurture a place in nature. Perhaps your child could discover a special corner where he knows the strawberries grow, as such allows a direct connection with nature. This is very important, but if it is not possible, you can work on what you have. For instance, if you have a veranda, fill it with as many plants as can fit. Ask your child to tend the plants to gain an understanding of what happens when they do certain things. They can realise that by overwatering the plants that they drown. They can inherently feel that plants are also alive and they have to be treated and understood in the same way others in their family, in a way that is very dynamic. This understanding is lost when you live separated from nature.

I remember people walking in the forest and saying, "Gosh, it has been such a long time since we have seen this, how green the trees are, the smell, and the atmosphere and many things that are important". I love nature and I do not know what it is like to live without nature. Nature is more beautiful that any music, any art or anything that I have seen and therefore to live without it seems to be a very poor way of living.

Compared to the place it has in shamanism, nature does not seem to be very important in Zen Buddhism…

The Zen monastery I lived in was actually in a National Park, in Mount Baldy, California which is up in the mountains, so nature was wilder to some degree. The Japanese way of tending nature is much more controlled. I find that pleasing on some level, like an English garden but I do not find it as pleasing as going to places like Costa Rica where nature has a sense of aliveness which is lost in a garden.

There is a lot of poetry about the beauty of nature but if we look at the animal realm we see predators and predated. So with beauty, the neutral nature includes suffering and violent death…

It is not really violence. It is only violence because we see it from a human perspective, coming from a moralistic and socialised manner of seeing things that makes us judge animals in a certain way. We have a concept that animals are good or bad if they do certain things we believe to be good or bad. Most animals in their natural state, not if they are kept in a cage, have no concept of what it is to be negative, they are living their instincts. Their instincts have developed to survive in an ecosystem, and the ecosystem has created them to survive in a way allowing the ecosystem to continue its own process. Only if you destroy the ecosystem does the whole situation change and the animals can then become negative.

When I used the word "violence" I actually meant pain, such as an animal being eaten alive and obviously experiencing huge suffering. How can this "unpleasant experience" still be part of the beauty of nature?

When an eagle catches a rabbit, it is very painful for the rabbit, there is no doubt. The rabbit is feeling the pain and suffering but on some level it is not painful because the rabbit always knew that it was going to happen. That is part of being a rabbit. It is not like a human being who is out of the ecosystem where war is violence and does not need to happen. On some level, without the rabbit sacrificing its life, the eagle cannot live and then we miss the beauty of the eagle. Then the rabbits would develop too much, like what happened in Australia where they have been introduced and took over to the point of destroying themselves. In actual fact, if you look at it from the perspective of nature and not just from a biological point of view, only the rabbits that need to go, go! This is the beauty and mystery of nature that everything falls into place. It is so uniquely and profoundly part of the mystery of live that it is not painful in the same way as a hunter shooting a rabbit. Most of the time, the hunter does not need to do this. Human beings do not need to inflict pain because they are not in the same way as animals in the circle of the ecosystem as natives are. Native people used to hunt in the sacred way where they are totally part of what is going on.

North American Indians hunted the buffalo with such respect and such love that, from their perspective, they were not killing the buffalo; like the eagle, they were partaking in a whole ritual. In that respect I do not see this as negative. It is quite different when we see hunters like in Portugal or Spain drinking and shooting animals as an authorised game. Even if it provides food, it is not necessary. There is no beauty and no inherent quality in that interaction with nature. It is so different from the whole philosophy of most native people where there is a whole ritual dance behind the way things are done. It is the same with fishing. I saw traditional Polynesian people fishing in a very different way from modern fisherman or fishing vessels from the larger industrial nations of today.

While other people do, I do not see pain in nature. Actually when I see all the things that happen in nature, I just see beauty and I see that it is a wonderful circle that continues. It is not that some parts of it do not need to change, but they will change when humanity changes. Some people may disagree with me but I believe that as humanity becomes more conscious and more loving, nature has a different quality. Evolution has happened the way it has because we needed to go through different stages. That is not negative.

The past has been negative because people have done certain things that were not so good, if you want to use the word "good", but what is good is that they have developed from that stage to this one. Now we do not need to go back to the past nor to the old scenarios, we can move ahead and put more consciousness and love into the ecosystem. The quality of the ecosystem then changes and this is what is wonderful with humanity. We are not only part of the ecosystem but we have an inherent responsibility towards it, which means consciously being part of that ecosystem rather than using or abusing it. I feel that quality is more realised – or possible to realise – today than in the past.

Perhaps native people had to hunt a buffalo but today I am sure the shamans and the elders recognise that the ecosystem has changed, so they also changed their ways and adapted to the new situation. They do not need to do this but they do it because they are conscious of the whole beauty of nature. They recognise that if they do not change, nature will then change and create disharmony for them. On some level I feel that what you are saying with the cruelty has been there because human beings, on some level, have needed that experience. When we change, everything changes. This is the mystery of life.

Some native people are able to walk where there are dangerous animals and these animals do not harm them. As they have a different consciousness, animals and nature responds to that. If we all, as a humanity, change to feel that same consciousness as the native person, then nature changes because it is evolving in the same way as everything, it evolves according to the atmosphere. Now it is evolving because humanity has created a certain dynamic atmosphere that makes nature react in certain ways that are more aggressive than they were in the past. It will continue to be so until our disconnection changes and we become more connected.

But it seems that in pre-historic time animals were even more dangerous and aggressive than today...

Perhaps. I do not really "remember" the dinosaur time very well but I am not sure that what we are told is actually true. I feel the idea that evolution started in a way where everything was very aggressive in a negative sense is actually a mental concept that is sometimes put onto history. We do not know history and can only suggest certain things through bones of animals and so on. What we see creates pictures that we believe to be true but we do not know if that is the total truth. I am not saying that scientists have it totally wrong but that perhaps we would see a very different picture if we were there. If a thousand years from now people would try to get a picture of life today they would perhaps see the world as very aggressive and negative, but there are actually a lot of other things and qualities that may not be obvious to a person a thousand years in the future. There is a lot of love and consciousness but that is quite difficult to see in the bones and remnants of a million years ago.

I actually feel that animals have love. I saw an incredible DVD that someone sent us about some wild cats. The mother of a little animal got hunted down and her baby was looked after by a female lion. It was so incredible that a movie could be made from this whole situation and the baby was like a monkey or some animal that lions would normally eat, but however incredible, that aggressive animal licked it and looked after it. The baby was quite traumatised of course, but on some level the lioness recognised something in another species. I feel that animals have much more consciousness than we normally see as human beings on the outside. It was filmed because it was so different from what scientists believe to be possible between species and from what they dictate as being the law of nature.

Could animals play a role in our spiritual awareness? If yes which one? Is it in direct relationship to them or more in an imaginary representation of them?

I think that all of nature has a role to play in spirituality and animals especially because, unlike trees, we can relate to them as they have lots of senses. To give you an example, I was recently in northern Germany in a beautiful wildness area. There was a farm with ten baby wild boars. I asked the people in charge of the place how could they have wild boars walking to the farm as are they are normally very aggressive. On some level these boars knew that if they just walked around in nature they would not survive because their mother had died.

These little babies were in need of milk, so they walked to the farm! And the people feed them milk and look after them so now they are like dogs, very tame, you can pet them and play with them. I was walking with a little girl and of course she was amazed that these one-year-old animals had lost their wilderness. They were quite big and strong and she was a bit afraid of them, yet, on some level she felt very connected. She was collecting corns and feeding them and, like children are, she was just fascinated with their presence, spending a lot of time looking and being there with them.

A psychologist might say "Ah, this animal is nice for the psychology of the child because it is helping to be less lonely", but I observed that when she was looking at the animals, she was connecting to a wild part that is lost through childhood. As the child grows he or she has to socialise and fit into the structures of society. On some level Shara was relating to the wild boars in a spiritual sense and that quality is difficult to explain but there was more than just a little curiosity; she was fascinated. This is the same fascination that people have when they go to the wilderness in a safari, looking at the giraffes and the zebras in Africa. There is a quality, a mystery that cannot be described in words. It is only when you are there in Africa, watching these wild animals, that you recognise an atmosphere that is lost. Dogs and cats do not have that because they have been tamed, they have adapted to our atmosphere.

Animals are important to me because they connect us to these deeper lost parts of ourselves that were present perhaps millions of years ago in our humanity but that are lost. This little girl was able to be something that she is not allowed to be normally: a little bit wild, a little bit ... something. And the boars represent that spiritually. I do not know what the boars represented to the Celtic people but I am sure they represented something because they were very present in Europe. Like the buffalos for the Native Americans, wild boars were important for Celtic people as Jaguars are of deep importance in the Amazon for example. They represent a quality that is spiritual, like the elephant in India that is important, beyond being a useful animal, through the symbol of Ganesh.

These qualities have been incorporated in Hinduism much more consciously than in Christianity where animals and nature are seen as a lower aspect of consciousness. In Hinduism, the monkey, the elephant, the snake and few other animals, have some significant spirituality. In shamanism, the snake, the eagle and the jaguar, in North America the buffalo, and for the Eskimos the bear, all have a quality that goes beyond just the animal. In the West of course we cannot recognise that because we are normally not surrounded by these wild animals. Yet in the dreams we are still connected to the animals. We have a deep connection even though this connection seems to have disappeared outside. Deep inside we still have an affinity to wild animals.

Is taking care of pets another way to relate to nature?

I think having pets is very useful but the problem with pets is that we normally do not recognise their quality. We want them to fit in to our lives so people buy a dog for Christmas because it is for the children, and then the dog is forgotten and has to fit in or is given away. I feel that the animal simply becomes another material possession. For an old person, or someone that is sick, a dog is very important because there is time to incorporate that animal into your life, but most people have no time. It is not like in the old days where you had dogs and they had a function to guard the farm, to herd sheep or if it was a small dog, to keep the family company as a pet.

Today people have all sorts of strange pets and do not really love them. I think that it is a pity. It is better not to have a pet and instead go to anyone who has one and spend time looking after theirs. People want to have their own dog or cat but there are so many dogs and cats that would love the companionship and they are kept in a house all day and only taken for a walk in the afternoon or in the morning. This is useful but we do not have the moral authority to utilise a dog for our own good, there has to be an interaction.

Early learning & the Zen Monastery

Before addressing how you see the teacher/student relationship, it may be interesting to go back a little into your own personal history. You have met people who somewhat helped you to understand things, and it may still be the case. In order to comprehend how you arrived to what you experience and teach today, would you say a few words about the most important situations and persons that revealed important things to you and helped you along your path on spiritual development? What was the context of your experiences and understandings?

It is difficult because it is not so concrete. It is a bit like falling in love. You cannot really specify facts or cut it down to time frames. I am saying this because in words it may seem that the experience is not so profound and I also do not want to make it sound more dramatic than what it is because it is quite simple and quite down to earth, not at all like some people say that the whole world collapsed, or other such things. As a young child, I did not see those experiences as dramatic or life changing but when I look back, it is much easier to see things in relation to everything else.

I would say that from early life, my spiritual teacher would have been the fact that I lived in very interesting and different cultures than just a simple culture like a typically European culture, as I do now for example. After being born in England, I left at the age of two for Egypt and at the time, it was populated with many different cultures that met there. There were many Greeks, Armenians, Copts, Muslims, Sufis, British and French, and other cultures from the Middle East, like Lebanese and Syrian but now it is very different of course. This was in the late sixties and Egypt was definitely a meeting point of knowledge in places like Alexandria and Cairo for example.

Today it has become much more of an Arabic culture and somewhat fundamentalist in it's orientation but during the time when I was there, it was similar to Persia, which was quite a place of meetings of different cultures, not just on the surface but also within the culture. You could feel and sense this meeting in the underlying culture that is, I feel, missing for example in the Anglo-Saxon culture. England can be very multicultural on the surface, with many people from Pakistan and India, Africa and the Caribbean but it is just on the surface, not in the depth of the culture, which is very English. Where I grew up, that was not the case. There was not one culture. It was definitely a mind and eye opener for me.

What my first spiritual learning was that things could be seen in so many different ways. It is interesting to have an open mind to feel and sense how things can be from so many different perspectives. For me, not to be caught up in one simple way of seeing things, but to be open to things in a social and cultural way was a great teaching. That is very difficult for a child who is socialised in a very strong culture such as our Western one that believes that it is right and superior in its way of seeing the world. Of course, I was a child and did not know how to put that into words or logic, but I put it in my experience of how I perceive the world. My personality, my perception of emotions and several social aspects opened my mind in a completely different way.

There were very poor people there, maybe not as poor as in India but still very poor. Seeing this poverty, which was very much part of the society in the Middle East, made me question things in a way that perhaps, if you are safeguarded from all those things, you do not question. Why are people suffering from poverty? Why are we not loving those people in the same way as I love my family or my family loves me? For a child everything is much more flexible. You do not just say "Oh, they are poor" and you shelf them away from your reality. You deal with it, because that reality impacts on you and your emotions. At least, it did so with me.

This began an inquisitive search, not a consciously spiritual one but a search for the meaning of life – the bigger meaning – that I did not feel was so much part of my immediate family. We were very wealthy and I enjoyed it of course, like any child enjoys wealth, but I did not identify so much with the intellectual background of that wealth because it seemed a little bit superficial. This is why I started looking for other ways, even though I was unable to leave the confines of the security and comfortable zone where my family was living in. Being over-protected, it is not so easy to access other spaces but I did anyway because growing up, I was given a wonderful thing that maybe other families did not allow their children to get: more freedom. Maybe I was actually given that because it was very difficult to control me, I do not know. I was told that I was very wild.

This freedom allowed me to explore and speak to people who normally where not so easy to contact in that context of my life, so I spoke to people, poor people, Copt people, Greek people, and I got to know things in a way that helped me to even ask more questions as I was looking for answers. It just fuelled the drive to know more, to understand things even more. I started reading lots of books. According to my mother, it was my passion to read and explore everything from nature animals, geography, people, and history. I was a little bit too difficult to manage, so they bought me lots and lots of books and it would help. Like a baby sitter, new books would keep me quiet. Yet it was not enough and some other parts of me started to go and explore within.

As I did so, I also felt pain and suffering. That pain and suffering, first being physical, opened up my mind in a different way. I was not so well or healthy as a child. This meant long stays in bed and missing school, which I enjoyed. Perhaps I got sick for that reason because I did not like school and I found it too close-minded. I enjoyed knowledge but not the schooling system so I would stay at home and meditate. Too unhealthy really to run around and play, I would be sitting there or lying in bed, just being in a space of watching myself in a good inner state. Within that space, I realised that there were more interesting things than just the suffering.

When I was very young, I suppose what made me different was that my senses were much more receptive to the invisible world, to a world that is not really tangible in everyday life. By tangible I mean that you eat, you like the food and your belly says, "This is good". When I ate, I was sometimes aware of the energy of the food so I would refuse to eat. My parents thought that it was because I was sick, as I was often unwell, or that there was something wrong and of course, like any concerned parents, they would get upset and angry, as they wanted their child to eat. Nevertheless, that would push me even more into that space of being sensitive to the energies of what was going on in nutrition and food.

I still do this a lot, and at times people says to me, "You have not eaten any food! You need to eat Tony. You are a human being", and she will cook some food for me. I will eat a little bit of it but not very much because I am sensitive to things that are invisible. If you looked at my actions directly, they were sometimes strange because they had no relevance to what was obvious to most people. My eating habits were seen as strange and, in the mind of people around me, seen as if "there was something wrong".

There was another dimension to my being that was very interesting, which I now call "energy" or the "energetic body". I started to explore that and speak about this to my brothers. From that space, I believe that knowledge began to be more accessible to me as a child at around the ages of seven or eight. I would begin to say things that were very strange and unusual, at least within the context of my family. One of the things was: "We must not eat meat". The strange thing was that my family was definitely not vegetarian and would not entertain such an idea in their mind, or even in their habits. These unusual attitudes would come out of nowhere or at least that was the perception of people around me, and they would wonder why I was thinking like that?

When I look at it now, these were initiations into deeper levels of things, which of course were not understood by my parents nor by me. I had to prepare my body to understand them. In a way, this was a type of fasting, not letting the body get heavy with the normal food that parents feed their children, which is what I grew up eating. This is just one little thing. It may not seem like a very big deal but it was because I actually strongly refused to eat. Even if I was scolded and physically punished for not doing so, I was determined not to follow whatever I was being told to do at that time.

That sensitivity was not just with food but also with deception. I would be able to see things that could not be seen. As children have a good imagination, my family thought I was just a very clever and creative child, which of course every child is to a certain level. When I look back, I realise I was seeing things that I can now put together with all my understanding. It was not just a child's imagination, I was actually seeing specific things.

Growing up in Egypt, I was aware of history and picking up on it in a different way. I would be communicating, or feeling that I was communicating, to the fairies and to the ancient culture that was there before the one that is there now. I would tell these stories to my brothers and they would listen fascinated, because it was quite entertaining to them. People thought I was just a good storyteller but I was not really telling stories, I actually saw the things I was describing. The problem is that you cannot communicate these things when you are seven years old. You do not have a concept of what it means beyond what you are feeling and sensing.

I couldn't really tell people that I had seen fairies, as I knew that it was something that went beyond the norms of relating to my parents or to other people, so they called me a daydreamer because often, I would be in a class and the teacher would be speaking and realise that I was "not present.". For twenty minutes I was not there, looking out of the window, "Tony! Listen to what we are speaking about. Be present to the classroom!". Now I realise I was not daydreaming, I was meditating. But meditating, as some people do, by drifting into a space where you listen to other things than the mundane, you go deeper inside. I did not have that word "meditation" or explanations such as, "Sorry teacher, I was meditating for twenty minutes". I just felt bad and I did not know what I was doing.

Following this internal drive that was so strong in me, I was often taken away into this other world. I had to pull myself together and come back to the "mundane space", which really became a conflict at the age of fifteen. I was always balancing into this other world that I was sensitive to, a world which I later found out that my grandmother was also sensitive to, with the 'mundane world' of the society that I was growing up in. It was challenging being present at school and trying to keep people happy by getting good grades.

I tried to push away this other side which did not seem useful as no one except me thought it was important, but I could not. At times, especially at six-seven, there were very strong moments where this "other side of me" took over, so I had a physical crisis. I think at that point I seemed to be very sick. I was taken for many doctors to check up on me and they did not really know what was wrong. Some thought it was just anaemia because I was thin and I did not look healthy, but I was actually very healthy and more energetic than any child around me.

It was not like I was so sick that I needed to stay in bed but I did not look healthy. This was because my energy level was so strong that I was burning up a lot of energy inside, processing these other aspects of myself, similar to what can happen in a retreat. For example, when we sit quietly in meditation, we can be so busy that it requires a lot of physical energy and we are actually doing more work than in normal everyday life. Furthermore, I was so busy in that space that I did not look after myself. I would forget to drink enough water, or I would forget to look after myself in a normal way. My parents would even need to remind me to go to sleep instead of staying up late and ask me not wake up so early! "Rest", they would say. Parents love their children and they just wanted me to be all right. These were my earlier experiences.

Another strong experience was my compassion. I think all children are compassionate, but my compassion went very strongly to obvious points, the first one being to not eat meat. As they are for all children, animals were very important to me and I wanted to be sure that they were well and not harmed. I remember an incident with an animal in Egypt. People that were gardening or looking after a place caught a bird and this bird stole the crops or did something so they wanted to kill it, but I was there to stop this.

I was doing it in many possible ways for a child but energetically, I was so convinced that the bird should not die that these people did not simply push me aside and say, "Silly child, go home and do something else!". They actually listened and took note, which is very strange because normally adults do not really listen to a seven year-old, in Egypt anyway, because there is a deep respect for the elders. The elders know best and you do not tell them what to do. I remember that moment as being just one of the important aspects that was part of the initiation I was going through, where my perception of life really moved quite far from the situation I was in. Over a few years, gradual experiences opened me up more and more.

The other thing that I realised when I was six-seven is that I was very shy, but in a different way. I was not an extroverted person that spoke to people naturally; I was quiet and needed the space for myself. But at the same time, in a group of people, there was so much in me that I wanted to express that I would not sit quietly. I would be active and debating, affirming things such as, "No. This has to be done this way!" Some children would get quite annoyed with me because I would be quite strong. It was like two opposite sides.

These were my first sort of initiations into spiritual work but I would say that my first spiritual teacher was the question "Who am I?". That question was almost forced upon me and I explored it deeply because of the situation I was living in. I had left England at two, before I was old enough to speak proper English and at the ages of two to seven, when you really absorb a lot in the world, Egypt was a very interesting place to grow and explore who I was.

So your learning was not really coming from specific people but from being in a certain cultural context?

Later on in Egypt, I came across very spiritual people that I would believe to be Sufi masters and Coptic Christians. They were not so much teachers teaching lots of people but just being in their presence offered a learning of knowledge.

Was the learning coming from observing their way of life and what they said to you?

I think the essence was more their being, who they were as people. It is difficult to be specific but more clearly, it would be their answers to certain questions. When you are ten-eleven, you ask all sorts of questions: "Why is the world like this?", "What is this?", and "Why is it like that?". Their answers touched more than just logic because they did not come from books they had read. There was something more to just an answer that touched me and I remember the feelings and the joy I would receive out of knowing things on a deeper level than just a concrete one.

Were they men? Women? Did you meet them on the street?

Most of the people that I remember were men. They would be either working closely with us, as gardeners, cooks, or would be friends of the people working closely. I would get to know their children, then go to their home where I would meet some interesting people. This is how I would meet for example the Coptic Christians. I was friendly with some children who took me home and I would meet the whole extended family. Then I would be attracted to someone who knew things…

Just regular people…

Regular people, but you know some cultures are deep and within them there are many amazing wise people. It is not that the wise people have to be well known by the media. They are just wise within their own community and their own little circle. Of course, when you are in the middle of the physical space where that happens, you somehow connect to the people who are in that space. I lived just outside of Cairo for a while after having lived in Cairo. It is a place where there are many different people. As a child, I was not shy. I did not hold back so much. I would go out to people and would feel very comfortable speaking with anybody. What was good is that my family was trusting that it was all right. It is not like today where children are instructed to not speak to a stranger or go up to someone that they do not know. At the time there was much more of a community sense than there is today, where there are reasons why people cannot be so friendly with other people. I lived outside of the city in a village like atmosphere. There were no obvious dangers for young children growing up, except for traffic since it was near Cairo. This was really the beginning of my spiritual work and the first kind of spiritual teachers I had.

After that, when I was twelve, my parents separated and I moved back with my mother to England, which was a much more individualistic culture, so the search went within myself, rather than the outside world being my reference point. I was then questioning many things because of the family situations happening in my life. It became much more a questioning of the emotional aspect of myself and how that fitted into everything. I would not say that was the best time of my life. From the ages of twelve to sixteen was very complicated for me because of many things. I identified very much with the English culture, but I found this culture to be very lacking in the knowledge that I was seeking. Instead, I resorted to reading books and searching within them for answers, which brought me closer to religion and spirituality in the real sense. In the books, people obviously spoke about these things and from there, I met many interesting people in the Catholic tradition, monks of different orders among which the Greek orthodox tradition, and then the Tibetan Buddhists.

I was really searching, so the question "Who am I?" now materialised from more than just a question into a physical search. I understood at that moment that I was searching for some guide or some person who could help me, and decided that Zen Buddhism was an interesting path to follow for many reasons. By this time, my mother had moved my brothers and I to Norway, and I came across the Zen Master who was probably the first physical real person to help me to see things as a teacher and I spent many years working with him prior to being in the monastery.

This was before going to California where this Zen Master worked at that time, and this would be my first direct work with a teacher who is recognised by very important scholars of Buddhism in Japan and America, as someone who knows more than just what is obvious. I enjoyed this and found that some part of me relaxed because I could relate to people who were also doing the same on their spiritual path, following the quest of "Who am I?", in the real sense, as a group, rather than just an individualistic one. That was my most interesting experience because I was leaving the family, leaving a cultural and social setting behind and creating my own cultural and social setting of inner search with other people. It was also the most difficult time of my life as I went to transitions that were profoundly shaking the core of who I believed I was and what I felt my personality and ego were.

It was not an easy time, but within that, I felt it was one of the best time. My family was a litle concerned about my 'new' interests, but I was quite happy and enjoyed pursuing this. I decided that from that moment on, I would follow this in a real sense with other people, as I found it was important. It is so easy to get lost in the world today if you do not have a group of people or a guide to help you. It is essential in a way not to get lost as most of us do. If we are profoundly lost in the depth of who we are and there is no bridge to take us to something more meaningful, it is difficult because we stay in that space of not knowing. In that sense, the Zen master was really the first person to guide me.

I would say that after some time I decided it would be better to leave the monastery and explore the world, finding groups of people to see and work with how things are in practice because in the monastery of course, it is a very easy life, on one level. I still worked very much with the Zen master afterwards but in a different way.

So you left Scandinavia at around seventeen-eighteen to go for two years in a monastery in California. What was the name of the Zen Master you worked with? Who was he? How did he inspire you? What did you really like in his teachings and doings?

The name of the teacher was Kyozan Joshu Sazaki Roshi. What I liked was that I felt he was real. There were many other Zen masters in Japan. I felt they were interesting but not straight to the point, not as direct as Roshi Sazaki was, from what I read and what I saw. There were Zen masters in other places, which were more interesting and beautiful to me than northern Europe, like Hawaii of course. Nice tropical places were very tempting, but that was not the important thing for me. It was finding the right person. This person was living outside of Los Angeles and I decided that realness was important so I went there.

What I found to be interesting was that the Zen Master was not just teaching Zen Buddhism. There was no compromise in his teaching and although it came out of a Japanese culture, he did not do things according to that Japanese culture. He was really a free spirit, in the sense that he was totally Japanese – he was born in Japan and grew up in Japan and did not speak English properly, just a few words – but he left behind that cultural moulding and was a Zen master in the real sense.

I found it very important that the work of being free was actualised not just in the dogma of Zen Buddhism of attaining freedom but also in the practice, in the personality, in the whole way of doing things. He adapted Zen Buddhism to the western mind, which influences a lot of how I teach today, rather than escaping into a cultural context of: "This is Zen Buddhism and we have to do this that way". He was quite flexible. His *koans*, the parables used in Zen Buddhism, would be seen as wild by a specialist because they had nothing to do with traditional *koans*. He would use *koans* that were totally practical and relating to a Western mind's experience.

"What is the sound of one hand clapping?", for example, is a traditional *koan* that was made famous by many people in the West. The sound of one hand clapping is much more than just the sound of one hand clapping. It has a whole history in Japanese philosophy, and you need to understand a little bit about it. It is a parable to find the answer without thinking because of course if you think logically then there is no sound in one hand clapping and it is ridiculous because you do not use one hand to clap. These koans are just a way of testing the student to see if their meditation has brought them to a point of letting go of certain concepts. This is probably what I enjoyed most. The other thing was that he seemed very humble and childlike. He was not very young. When I was there he was in his seventies, yet he maintained a childlike innocence.

Has he been a model for you?

Yes of course. Being in the presence of someone for whom you feel such respect, you take on certain aspects, which you feel very useful and inspiring, and drop other aspects of who you are, which you feel were survival mechanisms or personality aspects that are not useful, at least in the spiritual work. What I dropped were many things and many belief systems, rather than taking on a new belief system such as Japanese ideas.

I understood that freedom was the most important aspect in the teaching. It inspired me to be free of all things, especially the fear of being free. I could let go of what my parents thought, what other people thought, or what I thought, and just follow the inspiration and creativity that came out directly. Of course at that point, many people, such as my family – with whom I communicated through phone calls once a month or so – and old friends who went to school with me, were worried because my actions seemed to be very different than before. The way I saw things and spoke about them had changed so much. The previous person that they knew was difficult to find again because the transformation was not just about ideas, it was total.

Were you like a monk with shaved hair?

No. You could be a monk or a lay monk. A lay monk means that you are a monk in all the senses and initiated as such, but you do not have to wear the robes and shave. Of course you wear the robe while you are in the monastery but if you go outside you do not have to wear it. Monks have to wear the robes and in California it looks a little bit strange when you are going shopping in a supermarket dressed in Japanese robes. I dressed in normal clothes because I considered dressing as a monk interesting but not necessary. Yet, I could understand the purpose of it in the monastery.

Did you have a personal relationship with the Zen Master? Like questions-answers and so on?

Yes, definitely. I would say that I was seen as a very interesting character there and the Zen Master really had a deep relation to me. He had one with everyone of course, but a little bit more with me because he considered it important to do more than just be a Zen master and he was more like a personal friend. I think that in one sense he was quite unapproachable, yet approachable in another. There were hundreds and hundreds of people, but on one level, I was able to communicate deeply with him.

Perhaps in the beginning, he was more like a father figure for me, but after a while he was not a father figure anymore, rather it was so nice to see someone with whom I was able to feel connected to in a deeper sense than just friendship. So yes, I would say I had a lot of personal time with the Zen master but it is a monastery, not like a community where people just sit around chatting to their friends. There is not that much socialisation or talking about mundane things, it is all meditation oriented and directed towards spiritual growth.

Did you have any nickname?

"The laughing Buddha", or "The smiling Buddha", I cannot really remember. People loved me because I was very young. There were two young people and the other person was maybe three or six months older than me. Since I was very young in such an environment, the people looked after me as this environment was pretty much a traumatic and intense meditation experience and it was not very common for young people. Maybe it is in Japan but not in Europe or America, so they did have nicknames and love names.

When you decided to leave the monastery, did you have an exchange with the Zen Master to explain your point to him before you left? Was it common for people to go to spend some time in the monastery, spending the time that is good for them, and leaving it after a while?

No. Most people enter in two ways, at least in this monastery. The first one is called a *zazen* retreat, which is meditation for one week where you come in to do the course and then you go back to your everyday life. It is not like you stop what you are doing in life to do this but more like doing a retreat once, twice, three or four times a year. Some people would do ten *zazen* a year because there will be one session almost every month. Then you have the lay monk, which is what I was doing. You are in the monastery and do not leave it, the monastery life is your life. After the lay monk stage, you can become a monk, which is the same but initiated into taking part in daily monastery life and also looking after the space in specific ways, so you can be the cook for example, or you can be one of the people doing a particular job that helps the monastery to function.

I still worked in the same way of course, but I could not be a cook. As a lay monk, I was assisting the monk who was the cook. So back to your question, is it normal to come and go? Normally when you go to a monastery it is up to you how long you stay, but it is not normal to stay for a short period. The idea is that you would stay at least for six months otherwise you might as well do the courses, but there are no rules that you have to stay for six months.

It was natural for me to leave after two years. I think most people would have stayed longer, because once you go into that space of being in a monastery, it is almost like exploring a whole new world and it takes more than a couple of years to explore that world. It was not that I stopped wanting to explore, I just felt that it was more important to go into the world of everyday life to see if my dramatic experiences during that time were real outside of the monastery context. I was challenging myself to really see and the Zen Master was not worried. Yet, as he knew there would be many pitfalls and distractions, he was not sure that it was the best thing to do but of course, he respected my decision and supported me in every possible way.

The way I chose was of course to go as far away as possible from Los Angeles. I thought that by going further away, my sense of seeing the world as too difficult would not lead me back to the monastery. I was quite hard on myself but I made the decision and felt I needed to explore it for at least six months. I went to Europe and then to Australia. Of course, once I was in Europe a whole new set of dynamics entered into my life and I was not sure anymore that it was the best decision to leave the monastery. As I said, I was still working with the Zen master during this time but from a distance, through energetic work and meditation work, but by myself.

Was it a monastery of only men?

No, it was both men and women.

You did not leave the monastery out of non-satisfaction, as you seem to have found what you were looking for there – harmony and peace – but you left it just to know more about life, to challenge yourself?

To challenge what I felt I had achieved in the monastery and that was, I felt, like an enlightening experience. It was not enlightenment but what they call Satori in Japan, which is like a glimpse of enlightenment. That is at least my understanding. It was almost like the meditation had taken me to the space that I had always been wanting to come. I was wondering if beyond the meditation, that space would still be maintained in life and this was the challenge I was setting for myself in the world. That is why I went to London.

At which point did you go to India?

After the Zen monastery I went to New York, London, and later Australia to study marine biology. I was only in New York and London for a short while and then I decided to go to India on my way to Australia, but I did stay there for a while. This was when I was very interested in Buddhism. I went to a beautiful place with many temples that were very important for Buddhism and Hinduism. Then I travelled around India, a bit like a *sadhu*, although I did not dress as such. I would just survive on what I had.

Was there any special learning for you in India?

I think what shocked me most was the poverty and the suffering. It is one thing to read about it and to comprehend it with your feelings but another thing is to see it. It grounds you to the diversity of human experience. India taught me things that cannot really be explained in words. I saw people dying on the road and this touched me because it was eye contact. Not only were people suffering but animals too. India was the learning that suffering is so real that we have to deal with it.

India was for you more this kind of heavy learning than meetings with sages and yogis...

Historically there are many wise teachers, especially the ones espousing non-dualism and a direct connection to the sacred, or God, however, I met very few people who I considered wise and able to teach me something profound. Yet, at the same time what I learnt from the culture was the diversity of experience, which in India is amazing, you can have the best and the worst. India is a contradiction for me because with all this poverty, pain and suffering, people were somehow still embracing my world and helping me to do things. I met wonderful people but, from what I saw, I cannot say that people in the general society were thriving in India. The pollution, the rubbish and the suffering coexist with everything else and seemed to be accepted because of the culture. The Hindu belief of *dharma*, and the idea of salvation being progressive rather than direct, seemed to hold the political system together, but for me that is not spirituality in action. There are so many gems within the Hindu tradition that could be very transformative for the world today, and when I listen to words from some teachers, I feel very connected to their depth.

Spiritual Experiences in The Amazon & Peru

Back to your personal spiritual history, you mentioned having deep experiences at seven-eight, fifteen and twenty-seven. Would you say more about what happened at fifteen and the deeper experience you had later?

At fifteen the experience was more a spiritual crisis. My question was not just an intellectual question but one that affected my emotions, my sense of being, everything deep inside of me, so it shook me up. The questions were: "What I am?", "Who Am I?", "Why Am I here?", "What is the meaning?", "What is the purpose?". It was not just as philosophical questions, it was very much internal and needed a reply. There was no possibility of not addressing these issues because if I ignored them, they would come up in every aspect of my life. That is why it was a spiritual crisis in the sense that, at fifteen, the normal thing around me, at least when I grew up, was to focus on other things and not such a concern.

Often, people would say: "Are you OK? Don't be so serious!", but it did bring up the earnest question inside of me: "What is the purpose of life?". I could not just 'go out' and ignore this part of myself, pretending to do what my friends were doing, like going to night-clubs, drinking and thus ignoring something else. In the end, I became what seemed to some, as very quiet, profoundly serious, thus internalising the energy rather than what was normal for a fifteen year-old, such as exploring interactions with friends and girlfriends, living and growing out of a family unit. It is not that I did not have friends or girlfriends but my attention was very far away from that. The enlightening experience happened when I recognised for the first time that the questions could not be answered from the outside, they could only be answered from where they were was rising. That is, very briefly put, what happened at fifteen.

At twenty-seven, the questions were no longer as dramatic, at least emotionally, nor were they internalised in that way anymore. There was no doubt in my mind or in my life experience that the answers could not be found by reading one page in a book. It became obvious for me that it was my lifestyle that clarified the whole scenario. I say this because of course, at twenty-seven, spirituality, the inner and the outer search, and the questions no longer had that same quality. I had been practising meditation for many years and many things opened up various levels of understanding that, at fifteen at least, were not obvious to my intellect and to my feeling.

At twenty-seven, the whole experience was quite different. To put that experience in words is almost impossible because if I give it a word, all of a sudden it creates a picture. Trying to find something that gives it more meaning than just a word, I would say that at twenty-seven some part of me breathed out and was able to relax. People who met me then would think I was very relaxed and still, but it was a different type of relaxation. It was somehow being able to let go of something that had occupied my internal mechanism for a long time. Some would consider this as an experience of awareness or attention focused very much on a deeper sense. Others use the word "enlightenment", which I do not like because it categorises things in a way that I do not believe. Yet, of course, if you read literature, people would probably say it was a very enlightening experience.

It was a "special moment" …

Well, again, I am only measuring it in the time frame that we understand, to be able to communicate as a human being to people because otherwise we sit in silence, which does not produce a book! Still, if we want to look at it in a time frame, yes, there was an obvious time frame that could be measured in that situation.

Was it after having spent a few years in the Amazon and Peru?

Yes, it was after.

You already told a little bit about your thus monastery experience but would you say more about the Amazonian and Andes experiences? You went there with the idea to work for the protection of the rainforest and many significant things happened to you. Who did you meet? Where was it exactly? Did you stay in a specific tribe and if so which one?

When I left the monastery, my idea was to be in the world and practice what I learnt in the monastery in daily activities, so when I went to the Amazon, my intention was not really to work but to do something worthy of my time. I felt that conserving and preserving the rainforest was very important for me. It still is but at the time it was very dramatically in people's awareness. This was my intention to go there, but again, I remain vague for many reasons, one of them being that I do not wish people to go and find that experience outside of themselves. People often ask me: "Where were you in Peru? Can you tell me the exact location and the person that I can meet?" I keep it secret, not because it is esoteric and needs to be kept secret but because I believe people do not need to attach such importance to it. At the same time, since we are writing a book, I have to be a bit more specific, so in the Amazon of Brazil, the area where I was, was on the border of Bolivia on one side, and Peru on the other side, where three countries meet, and I was working on all sides of the borders.

Who did I meet? I met *ayahuasqueros*, people who work with *ayahuasca*. None of the people there that I was working with could be termed as "pure natives", like some of the people in Brazil. It is the group of people who are not in that part of the Amazon but more on the land side of the rainforest and they have mixtures of Europeans who came a long time ago in the region. In Acre, the mixture was much more what could be called a *mestizo* culture. The blood and the lifestyle was Indian but the European culture had been introduced by people like rubber tappers who went to the Amazon to collect rubber and intermarried with the native people for survival. I suppose it is the same for the Maoris today where almost none are one hundred percent native because they intermarried with Europeans who came a long time ago. Although there are very few Maoris that are "pure blood", the Maori culture is still there in the same way that the mestizo culture of that area is still there. The culture that I worked with was a shamanic culture, but I had no interest in the shamanic culture itself because when I left for the Amazon, my whole work was still very much focused on the Zen Buddhist tradition. It was not as if I had left it behind and started looking for something else but I was introduced to shamanism in essence. If you look at all spiritual traditions, there is a similarity, so I recognised many things. It was not very new or exotic.

You found the same human quest...

Yes. I found that even though some of the rituals I slowly got introduced to were culturally different, they had the same drive, the same focus and I felt very comfortable. It is not like I was feeling alienated to what was around me. I felt at home, which is not obvious for a Westerner. I actually felt the rainforest and was very comfortable in the space. In the beginning the rainforest was external to myself because it is so powerful. For any person who has been to a rainforest, it is not just a forest, it is so overwhelmingly present that you cannot but experience it. Unlike the forest here in the German northern European climate, which is much more approachable, travelling through the rainforest, with its noise and its smells creates a very strong impression.

In the beginning I was not afraid of the rainforest but also not really recognising some aspects of it, yet during one period of the time I was there, I made friends with it. It was through a situation where I simply recognised the trees. It sounds very silly and New Agey but for me it was not so. It was a very profound experience. By the way and just to get a complete picture, the trees in the Amazon are very big, grand and massive. One of these trees was extremely big and old and its trunk was very present. It was not just a tree that went up to the sky, it somehow extended to the ground. You could actually be around the tree and feel its presence. I communicated to the tree in a way that was not possible for me to do with the whole rainforest and so, by interacting with one aspect of the rainforest, this introduced me to the whole rainforest. People could say that it was the native culture that did this, but it was not. It was my coming home to being comfortable to the whole situation that opened the space for me to interact with the tree.

This interaction with the tree was to recognise what some people call a spirit. I personally do not use the word "spirit". For me, it was recognising the essence of the tree as much more than just a tree; recognising that it was a part of myself and that I could communicate to it, like one can communicate to the emotions, to the mind or to the body. It is not so tangible but I could communicate to this part of myself. The love that I felt for the tree at that moment was so deep and overwhelming that I did not want to leave that space. It is like when you fall in love with someone. You do not want that space to ever be disturbed, finish or change.

The native people got worried about me because this space was not in the area I was living in. It was outside and closer to the border of wilderness, as the native people lived in an environment that was somewhat safe and the Amazon approached at the edge of that living space. I had gone outside of that living space to the wild side of the Amazon. They knew that I was not from there and that I had not grown up there, so my senses of knowing what was dangerous or not were not as developed as children of the Amazon. Yet, I did not feel that. In that moment, I felt completely and totally at home. I felt there was no danger, no problem. I just wanted to stay there. I even wanted to leave the shamans and the community and walk to the middle of the forest to be at one with nature. That experience was very profound.

I also met very wise people. Within that culture, the *ayahuasqueros* were very wise. Of course, these healers were very different from the Zen Master, and were perhaps not the masters of spirituality in the same way as Roshi, but they were deeply working on the spiritual level, with the focus being more on creating balance for themselves and for the native people around in the process of living there. The people that I met were shamans, categorised as shamans or more precisely *ayahuasqueros*. Their whole focus was to work with healing, using herbal remedies of the forest and certain rituals, based on imbibing *ayahuasca*. This is basically what I slowly got introduced to. The healing, of course, started with healing aspects of myself. This is what interested me because I felt that in the monastery many things got clarified but many other things remained untouched…

Like nature?

Like nature, exactly. Buddhism is very much sitting and internalised. Somehow the activity of shamanism is much more external and ritualistic and even though *ayahuasqueros* were not ritualistic in the same way as some other shamanic cultures can be, it was still externally ritualistic. There were certain sounds, certain movements and certain things that happened that did not really happen in the Zen monastery. Emotions were very much part of the work, working with fear, working with limitations that are in the body, working with organs that are holding on to that fear. It is a whole chapter in itself and I will only briefly go into that. The people that I met were mostly men, because in that particular culture, men were the healers but there was also one woman. She was the mother of the main local shaman but I do not really remember her very much. There were many shamans, many *ayahuasqueros* but he was the shaman that people respected and went to when things got difficult. His mother was also very respected and often, people would go to her because actually, on some level, it seemed to me like she was the one pulling the thread of what was going on in the community, rather than her son. So yes, I met several people and I worked in many areas of the Amazon. This was in the Brazilian area, and then I worked very much in the Bolivian area. I worked with many people…

At this point you had left the association of the rainforest work?

Yes. I had left it a long time ago. The association I worked with in Brazil was exploring a new concept of preserving the rainforest. It was not only preserving an area that excludes human beings, like previous conservation ideas that see human beings as the evil forces that destroy nature. The idea there was to create a National Park and this concept was quite new as it was about encouraging the native people or people who lived in harmony with the rainforest to preserve that lifestyle and to stop the intrusion of western influences from civilising and building houses, hospitals and all these things that bring the problems of civilisation to that area. It was preserving what was believed to be an integral part of that ecosystem. I was very fascinated by that concept which seemed very logical to me.

On paper Brazil was slightly ahead, at least in that way, if compared to Bolivia, but in action it was not really, because of the gap between what was said and what was done. All of South America is really like this, but in Bolivia, they did not even speak about it. Instead, if they thought it was good to cut down the rainforest to build a city because this was the best for the country, they would just do it. In Brazil, at the time, people were at least very interested in conserving their nature. I do not know how trustworthy it was then, or how things are now, because they would say one thing, and then they built the roads or built a dam regardless, but at least the beginning of such an approach happened in Brazil. I mention this because you asked about specific things, from when I was living in the Amazon. I also remember there was a very famous person in the area who got assassinated. He was a rubber tapper, more of a European than a *mestizo*, living in the towns of that area. This shows you a little bit that it was not easy. One thing is to say "This is what we are doing", but there is the stark reality of what really happens in that untamed and poverty stricken area of Brazil. I think he was assassinated because he was too radical. He was really trying to improve things for people by saying: "Everyone has the right to do certain things", but whoever had the power did not want this to happen. I did not really follow what was going on because I was not involved in politics.

I also remember thinking at one point if I should stay and live in the Amazon as I felt so comfortable and so at home. I still remember the faces, I remember the songs. I remember emotions and particular situations but the names have faded away. I also wondered if I should get married to one of the young women there. I was young and had the feeling that it was important to get married, or to have a relationship, and build a wooden shack by the river that the people there lived in, with a piece of land to grow beans and rice, bananas and other fruits, and have lots of children running around.

I really had to put everything into perspective because for me, a relationship is always a very serious affair. It isn't just a part-time experience where relationship is just to meet someone and if it doesn't work out you can go away. I put a lot of myself into a relationship, so I was always very hesitant and I pulled back rather than putting myself in that situation. As I observed my thoughts, I realised that this venture – a relationship – meant that I would stay there forever. For me, this was going really too far and it was at this moment I decided to leave the Amazon.

This is also when I started putting more energy into ceremony participation, rather than into the distractions of physical attraction. It was a special period in my life, participating in the whole ritual that was happening where the *ayahuasca* is collected and prepared with people involved all the time on this matter, from morning to evening. You get very little sleep, as it is very intense work for weeks, with the ceremonies providing me with many visions.

What happened?

I did not know what was happening really, because from drinking the *ayahuasca* I could not find a reference point. Sometimes when people drink *ayahuasca*, they have a sense of who they are, even if it is in the background, but during a ceremony that sense of who I was disappeared, and I got lost. I did not know what was going on and I relied on the ceremony to guide me. The music, the sound and the whole situation made sure I was all right, which was good because I was totally disoriented. When you drink *ayahuasca*, the identity of what is going on becomes very vague, so I do not know if there was a storm, or if the storm was myself, but the storm seemed vicious and intense to a point I had never experienced in the Amazon where the trees protect everything from the wind and the forest is usually very still. On this night I observed that the storm seemed very physical to me and I started to feel very cold.

This was a death and rebirth experience but I did not realise that yet. I thought it was coming from the outside. I started shivering and got closer to the people around me so that my body would absorb their warmth. Yet in the tropics it is always very hot, so in hindsight, my body must have been cold in the physical sense, because of the storm coming down from the mountains. Interestingly, there were no mountains around but it seemed like the wind was chilly and blowing down from the top of a mountain. It seemed to be coming into my body and I was trying to protect myself. The ceremony then intensified and it seemed like everything was blowing. I would look at the trees and they looked like they were very solid yet moving. They were moving not just as energy, as it was actually the physical aspect of the tree moving. I got very frightened and I thought it would reach a point where the world would be destroyed. I was somehow thinking, because I do not know if you could call it "normal thinking" – that it was a good thing I was there because it was a very good place to be if the world was ending.

The ceremony lasted all night and was an experience that was so powerful that in the end it seemed as if my whole body was exploding into little beads. It was going to different points of the forest, different points of the universe. No longer could I hold a sense of who I was. As a physical being I really thought I was dying and it was the end of the world. At one point I remember praying everything that I could think of to protect my journey, Christian prayers, Buddhist prayers, Hindu prayers, all the songs that were being sung to me. I was trying to use everything because I was just so afraid of this sense of disappearing. This was the death of the ego experience, which of course, was followed by a rebirth experience afterwards that slowly integrated my whole sense of being. It was as if I was connected to the forest, connected to nature, and connected to the power of nature. In the end, the death experience was not that dramatic. It was very peaceful because even though my eyes had always been open, when I opened them in the morning and looked around me, everything was very still. There was no storm. It was very beautiful and very harmonious.

I had let go of something important, and felt I had reached a point that meant that I was ready to leave, because I now understood why I was in the Amazon forest.

You once said that you also had an initiation experience with a snake during an *ayahuasca* ceremony. Would you explain what happened?

Just for you to have a bigger picture, the snake is not just a physical aspect of initiation, the snake represents the *kundalini* energy as it is called in India, the life force energy. My profound encounter with the snake was during an *ayahuasca* ceremony. Although this snake had the same quality as a snake, I knew that the image, the sensation and the reality that I experienced during this initiation was not a real snake, like for example when you see a snake in the Amazon forest where there are many. I do not want to go too deeply into it but I can say that I felt that the snake was more than just a snake in nature. It was more like a cosmic snake, as if the snake appeared out of nowhere. Looking back, what I feel is that it came from the universe to devour my whole being. I suppose it is the same with dreams, where the energy of dreams becomes symbolic. In this sense, the snake was symbolic and the symbolism was the life energy, the *kundalini* energy changing everything in me. The snake was changing the life force in my physical body.

I had pain in certain parts of my body but I do not remember where because they rapidly changed from one point to another, however, I do remember having a lot of pain in the lower part of my back and in the spine. Sitting down was painful and I felt – as the mind does this – that it was because I was sitting uncomfortably. I had to keep moving so that my spine would not have so much pressure. I felt like there were points inside of the spine that were internally exploding. It was very strange and very strong. There was so much happening that I did not have time to focus on this. It would change from one thing to another. It was not like, "Oh the spine is hurting", and then you just stay in the spine. I simply had no time to focus because when the spine was hurting, then all of a sudden something else was happening, inside or outside the body, and demanded my attention. I would start feeling uncomfortable or I would feel threatened by the fear that my body would disintegrate. That would be the word I would use afterwards, as I would feel that some part of my body would disappear. I would think, "Ah, it is still here. My leg is still here, it must just be asleep". The logic was still working in the background but, slowly, that logic was being eaten up by the whole experience that was going on. I felt the snake was gobbling me up.

Slowly, all these aspects of me were disappearing, even the pain became something more. In the end the pain was not just physical, it became energetic. The physical changed before it was very uncomfortable. I would feel almost like standing up and running away because I just wanted to go somewhere, but then someone would put his hand on me and say, "You need to stay with that". I remember this very interesting moment where the physical pain was still there but became less acute, it was above all energetic. I felt like my body had become flames. I was changed from being cold to being hot and sweating. The sweat seemed like the fire and I had the feeling that I was burning. I looked at one point and I was sure that my body was on fire. This is the *kundalini* energy expanding dramatically. What I was seeing was not an illusion. It was real but it got translated into a picture of fire. I was so terrified that I was burning that all of a sudden, I made the decision to run down to the river to sit in it to put the fire out of my body.

When I look back and see the whole picture I think it is very funny because I can understand what was really going on, but at that moment I could not. I started running. I do not remember exactly, as I do not know what people around me did, but something happened and there was an *ayahuasquero* near the river. I do not know how he got there. All of a sudden he was there, by magic, and he said, "You must not go into the river. You must stay here. You must stay within this circle of fire. You must experience the fire". As I was really focused and wanting to get to the river, I was wondering how to trick this person. I could not understand what the problem was. Why not go to the river? There was obviously some point to it that I could not comprehend. So I just stood there. Time stood still also. It seemed like this was happening in one second but it was happening in hours and maybe it was an eternity.

Then other things began to happen. All of a sudden, without knowing it, I was back sitting down. Then I began to ask myself, "Did I ever go to that point? Was I ever running to the river physically?". I began to be very afraid because I thought I was going crazy. There was no reference point. When I looked around me I saw people with their eyes closed as if nothing had happened, so I knew this could not have happened. It had just happened on another dimension. I was getting totally confused, totally disorientated because I was having many experiences all at the same time, one of them being what was going on now. I recognised that there were a thousand experiences happening at the same time and that all I was doing was getting lost in one experience and then coming back to another. I realised that I was no longer in my body: I was floating in the universe.

When I looked at the person next to me, what I could see in my body was just another experience that my sense of reference was no longer grounded in me. Then I understood that my ego was dying and I let go of the process of what was going on. There was not much confusion or resistance, nor holding on or trying to make sense of everything. And, as soon as I said to myself, "Stay here please. I do not want for those parts to disintegrate!", the whole situation changed and I woke up with a different reference point. I felt that it was all related to the snake that came to devour me in the beginning. This cosmic snake was guiding me not as a totem or as an animal separate from the experience, it was rather my experience of the *kundalini* life-force, actualised in a picture that I could relate to, the snake.

I was grateful for the guidance from the *ayahuasceros*, especially when I was 'on fire', but having done this in this way, I now know that it is not advisable to connect to consciousness in this way.

In shamanism, people often refer to the spirit of a plant and it seems that visions of snakes are recurrent when taking *ayahuasca*. Do you consider the snake as the spirit of the plant or do you see the plant as having a special chemical property allowing people to connect with that symbol?

In the Amazon, people say that *ayahuasca* has a spirit and that its spirit will protect you and help you to fight negative spirits. This is where my disagreement with that culture began. The *ayahuasca* for me has no spirit. The snake is not a spirit but an aspect of the mind. What the mind is doing is simplifying an experience so that it can comprehend it by symbolising it, creating an archetype or a picture that we can relate to, in the same way that we can relate to fairy tales.

Why are there all these visions of snakes? Could it be because the stories of people having experienced these visions simply have an impact on people's imagination?

No. It is an archetypal picture. It is a symbol of the *kundalini* life force and of this aspect of yourself that opens up. Although the snake is the most common picture with *ayahuasca*, it is not necessary to have that picture, or consider it the only picture.

Then why does almost everybody almost systematically experience being swallowed by a snake?

Why? Because we are all the same.

Do you think this plant releases a special chemical producing these visions? An anthropologist, Jeremy Narby, wrote a book called *The Cosmic Snake* a few years ago that became very popular, in which he explains that there is a connection between the shamanic snake visions during *ayahuasca* sessions and the DNA, that may be seen as representing two intertwined snakes.

The DNA is not the life force but this is an interesting idea. One thing that is clear is that what *ayahuasca* does for you is not exclusive to the plant. Other plants and also other specific techniques that do not use plants can do the same. I am sure that at certain spiritual crises and developments this is possible. Is there a chemical? Maybe there is a chemical that stimulates certain points and that arouses the energy. I do not know for sure, as I am not a chemist. You are asking me that question and I am thinking that one thing I know about what *ayahuasca* does, that is generally different from *San Pedro*, is that it stimulates the base *chakra*. This is one hundred percent equal in everybody that has been part of the experiences that I have observed over time.

Ayahuasqueros say that you have to be very careful with sexuality because the *kundalini* life force and sexuality are quite connected as they come from a very similar space. In a ceremony the *ayahuasqueros* would always say, "Be very careful not to use sexual energy to connect to a person during the *ayahuasca* ceremony because it can then connect to archetypal energies that are not personal to that person". This is why ceremonies are often with men and women segregated and practicing in different ways. Actually it is not very common for women to even take *ayahuasca*, as the societies are very male dominated, at least in the part of the Amazon I was in.

Is the status of women different with *San Pedro*?

With *San Pedro* it is the Peruvian and the *mestizo* culture which are also very male dominated, yet women are very present in the background so the shaman's wife is as important as the shaman. It is a whole unit that is working with the community. I remember that I really enjoyed being with the wife of the shaman with whom I worked the most, because she was so motherly and so welcoming. She actually would say to the shaman: "No ceremony today, not possible. Go and tend the plants!". It was not like she had no purpose or no space in that healing. He related very much to her to see what was possible.

During a retreat you also mentioned being bitten by a dangerous snake in the rainforest. That experience apparently helped you to realise it was time to leave the Amazon to pursue your spiritual quest further. You also said that you were not quite satisfied with the philosophical dualism, opposing the good and bad, that was underlying the local understanding of things.

Yes. My major disagreement with the culture was the importance of the spirit world, a dualistic world of invisible dimensions where good and scary life forms are independent from our experience as who we are. When you have major philosophical disagreement with someone, it becomes almost impossible to practice in the same space. It is not that there is anger or conflict in a negative way leading to affirm that the other is wrong and I am right, but just that it seems irrelevant to be in that same space. My love of the place, the people and the culture never diminished. I just realised something that is similar in all cultures, people try to create a safety net and an explanation to everything that is there.

Since their experiences and explanations of the world were not mine, I thought that maybe it was not useful to stay there anymore, but when you are used to being in a place, it is not so easy to leave. I did not know where to go. It is a bit like being in a relationship. You know that the relationship is beautiful but that there is no real relationship, that somehow the relationship is very different from relationship in its essence. What we then hold on to is the idea of relationship rather than living a real relationship.

I was also becoming less interested in what was going on in the life of the community I was in, and that feeling became actualised in an experience I had. I was wandering off to explore, finding out what it was like around me because there was not much to do. Cutting the story a bit short, I was walking for hours and then come across a place where there were beautiful fruits and I felt it would be very nice to eat some of these fruits. This is very biblical in a way – even though they were bananas and not apples – but I did not think of that at the time because my attention was focused on getting where I wanted to get. I do not remember if I stepped on it or if I just was very close to stepping on it, but a very poisonous snake bit me in the leg.

The snake only attacked once, which is very interesting because sometimes snakes in the Amazon attack many times. This one only attacked once and then stood back. Then of course I immediately stood back and put my hand where it bit, it was just instinct. I do not know why I put my hand there and in that moment I thought, "Well that's an interesting way to go", as I realised the venom of this snake was deadly and I would have no time to even walk back – at least I felt so – to the village and see if someone could help me, since I had been walking for many hours. My logical mind was saying: "OK, now the venom will go all over my body. So what to do?"

I saw the river down there and I thought maybe if I just lie still and I float down the river, there might be a hamlet – hamlets are always by the river – and someone will realise a body is floating downstream. Many things were going through my mind and then I looked at my leg and there was no wound nor puncture from the snake. I then realised that the message was not to stop life but to invite my life to go further. I looked at the snake and we stood looking at each other, which was a very interesting experience. I do not know if it is easy to understand a wild animal just looking at you and really not moving, not doing anything. There is a sort of interesting energy that happens. It was almost like a meditation, as if I totally accepted the situation with the snake. I was not angry at the snake nor grateful to it. I simply realised this was what needed to happen and I walked back.

The next day, I packed my things and left the area I had been living in for months. I remember sitting in the canoe leading me back to civilisation to the next town and looking back at the village, seeing this image of myself reflecting on all that had happened in my life from the moment I arrived there and how I was now leaving all this behind. It is a very long journey in a canoe so you have time to reflect. The hamlet and the community got smaller and smaller and the children were waving "good-bye, good-bye, good-bye" … I did not leave in anger or disappointment or unhappiness. I left with a sense of completion. What an amazing human experience it was to be there.

Then you decided to go to the Andes…

Slowly I left to a different part of Bolivia and worked with a few people there, but maybe from that *ayahuasca* experience, I felt a calling for the mountains, a calling to go to the Andes. As you know, Bolivia is at the beginning of the Andes and the forest follows on. I travelled towards the Andes and then, from a certain point you could not travel anymore because the jungle was too difficult. I got a plane, a very small and tiny aeroplane to La Paz, the capital of Bolivia and it was a very interesting journey, but this is a long story. In La Paz, unlike Brazil it is a much more multiethnic society, where the integration of natives and Europeans is not so clear.

As I did not have much money and I also felt more easily integrated with native people, I went to the indigenous quarter. It was a totally different atmosphere from the jungle and of course I felt very interested in what was going on. There were many more people, hustle and bustle and a lot of pollution, incredible pollution. It was a very different type of environment from the pureness that I had left but I enjoyed it. I met some Aymara and Quechua healers, called *curanderos*.

Usually, a *curandero* is not much like an *ayahuasquero*, he is almost doctor-like, dispensing herbs. I would not really call *curanderos* "shamanic" because there are not so many rituals, which are very based on belief systems. They mostly use black magic with dolls and such things but it is interesting to observe. From there I learnt that the most powerful *curanderos* did not live in La Paz but near Lake Titicaca, which is a big lake north of La Paz on the border of Peru, so I went there.

Lake Titicaca was of course a very nice environment, very beautiful, and much more interesting for me than La Paz, despite the Quechua and the Aymara people being a little wary of foreigners, making it not very easy to enter their culture. They find it very strange that a European comes into this culture and they are not as open to people as the *ayahuasqueros* were, so I was somewhat on the periphery. This is not to say that people were nasty or did not include me, as they included me in the most beautiful and amazing ways – right into the middle of their home, looking after me and giving me the best care. Yet, I always felt like I did not belong there, so I spent very little time. I don't mean that I only stayed a few days, as really my journey there was for many months.

Something I learnt was that a sacred plant that was used a long time ago was the coca leaf. The coca leaves are seen as a representation of the divine aspect of Pachamama and every Aymara and Quechua uses it, not the cocaine of course, but the coca leaf is what they chew. They do many things in which I did not really have interest, as it seemed very culturally connected to that group of people.

I later got introduced to *San Pedro*, which was not very much used in the area of Lake Titicaca where I was, but rather on the Peruvian side and, although it grows everywhere in Bolivia, it was not seen as medicine. So I went to Peru. In Peru, I then worked with people who were also called *curanderos* whose ceremonies were based on something very ancient that did not seem so culturally connected to the situations that they were living now, like the Aymara.

I think that before the Europeans came, the Aymara and the Quechua practised things very differently but their cultures adapted to the new situations they found themselves in, and in the middle, some things were forgotten. I think that the Quechua are related to the Incas, who did things very differently from what they do today. Of course, compared to the way the *ayahuasqueros* did things, the *curanderos* that I met in Peru did things very differently, but there was an element that was the same. This element I recognised was very ancient but they could not explain it themselves. They had just received the practices, handed down from generation to generation.

I got very interested in the *San Pedro* because I felt deeply connected to this way of working, so I started using the *San Pedro* with the *curanderos*. Unlike the *ayahuasca*, I felt it to be more gentle on the body, in fact overall, much more easy-going and I still have this idea today. I did not feel it was very dramatic and in the beginning, I actually thought, "This is nothing!", because I was comparing it with my experiences of *ayahuasca*. Nothing was apparently happening. The visual and the feeling impacts were just very mild. Yet, there was something else that touched me. I felt the medicine was working on many other levels. I call it a "medicine" because that is what it was for the *curanderos*: a medicine that they used when the situations were too difficult to heal using the normal herbs that people used in Peru.

I stayed and worked for some time with one person. This *curandero* that I worked with a lot practised with many native people who called him Maestro. Every *curandero* was respectfully called "Don" or "Maestro" before the first name. People would go to these *curanderos* and, depending on which group of people they came from, would have different terminologies to call them. The one I worked with lived in the northern part of Peru, not so far from Trujillo, but the journey was rather circuitous so the location is really a place I cannot remember. As even once there, it is an amazing two-day journey high up into the mountains to get to the hamlet. It is not a village because it does not really have anything. It is just a little hamlet with a few people but it is well known for hosting many *curanderos*, and notably those who have a reputation for very strong healing.

I was very interested and I spent some time working with that person there, drinking *San Pedro* and learning how it was used in their rituals. Then, after a little while, I left and I worked by myself in Peru. It was not that I was formally initiated into their whole system, in the same way that I was formerly initiated into utilising *ayahuasca*, but I slowly developed a process by myself, as I continued my wanderings throughout Peru. The way I did this was to work with people for free. I never charged. I would go from one village to another and if there were sick people, they would come for a healing.

I do not know how but people knew I was there so I would be working with the local people, like a nomadic healer, travelling from one place to another. Sometimes I used *San Pedro*, but traditionally in Peru *San Pedro* is not given all the time to everyone, which is different from *ayahuasca*. It is mostly the *curandero* who takes the *San Pedro* to be able to see what is really going on in this 'other world'.

Did these healing sessions happen at night?

Yes they did. What I enjoyed, was that people had no money but they would feel so grateful for the healing, that they would want to give more than what they received. Everything from the garden, such as food, was given to me as gift, so I always had more food than I could eat. I travelled and I loved Peru, feeling totally connected to the country. I was guided intuitively to go to certain places in Peru and became quite well known in the many out-of-the-way places where there was no tourism. It was not like Machu Picchu, Cuzco, the Inca Trail, with hostels and vegetarian restaurants, and everything organised to make sure that your pathway to heaven is all laid out. In fact, all the time I was in Peru I didn't ever go to Cuzco or even to Machu Picchu. I had no interest in these sites, even though I knew they were special.

I went to wonderful places, where my first impression would be of seeing a lot of children rushing towards me, asking me questions, as they were very surprised to see someone new and exotic coming to their village in the jungle. It was very nice because through the children I was able to connect with the people more deeply. It was a whole journey and I enjoyed it.

I discovered also that according to the Peruvian government, it was a very dangerous area and a no-go zone had been created due to acts of terrorism. Often I would meet military barricades and they would check my passport and ask "Why are you going here? Are you crazy?", but I still went, as the *San Pedro* was guiding me. I reached a town that was amazing because the architecture was totally different than that of Machu Picchu, totally different from Cuzco. It was unique to this area, which was the first thing I noticed as I was interested in architectures and ruins. That was an important point to go to because for me it meant I could pick up the knowledge that was present in that area. I would often lie on what was the temple floor, which is now just rocks, a little spring and nothing obvious, and I would do ceremonies in that space, as I saw it as a power place or what is known as *wahaca*, which means a "point of power" in Quechua. That place was not considered a *wahaca* by the Peruvians, but for me as it was a totally tourist-free place that had only being explored by some archaeologists. And, for me that area was a place that I found very mystically and energetically relevant but that was forgotten. I had some very profound experiences and inner revelations there.

I then slowly moved from this powerful point to what is now folkloric and modern *curanderismo* in Peru. I was very interested and I looked at the people because their facial expressions and even their genetics were very different from other Peruvians I had met. I do not see natives as isolated from the world, like the common theory states and my idea is actually that in some historical periods, human beings travelled from one point to another and were interacting with each other much more than we give them credit for. I believe that this area was a passage for many different groups and for some reason, just like Rome was a civilisation point of reference for many people during the Roman Empire, this also was a great point of knowledge of that time. I stayed there for a while, and really loved the place and the people. The people were now Christians and Catholics of course, and so had forgotten almost everything from their ancestral past, but they were a little bit open to their history and proud that they had these amazing ruins in their little area. There was a sense of pride but the knowledge was not there, at least from what I could find by asking them questions, so I spent time doing solitary rituals.

When you say "doing rituals" what do you mean exactly?

I mean, I made *San Pedro* ceremonies for myself, healing myself and the world from this ruin that I found to be a place of power. Prior to that, all I knew was what I saw being done by the *curanderos* of Peru. Up until then it was very much, not imitating, but following in the steps of that tradition.

Did it implicate people?

Yes, and it implicated using certain objects. I kept using them for a while afterwards but I finally decided to auction them and raise money to pay to preserve the rainforest. They are interesting in a folkloric sense, as they have no other interest to me and I am not attached to them.

What were these objects and why did you stop using them?

They were what is known as staffs of light and in the shamanic world-view they represent different worlds that you enter and you travel through. Each staff is like a sword, but it is not a real sword as it is made out of wood. You put it into the earth, like accupuncture needles that move the earth energies, because it is believed that the earth gives that staff power and energises it so that it becomes alive and represents that energy in the real sense. I had these as well as a rattle and many objects that are wonderfully Peruvian, but I dropped all of them. In the end, what was important for me was just the ritual, without any objects or artifacts. For me, the initiation was internal rather than external, through the ritual. It was an internal understanding of *San Pedro*. When I understood *San Pedro*, *San Pedro* became me – if that makes any sense. I got in touch with the plant frequencies and was then able to heal people without the need to actually take the *San Pedro*.

... a part of you or an expression of you?

I did not need to do all these rituals, or use the objects to activate the spirit of the plant. It was simply activated through everything that was done naturally in a ritual. It is difficult to put into words. For example, to make it more practical, the traditional way of activating the spirit of *San Pedro* is to blow tobacco smoke onto the *San Pedro* that you drink. The *curandero* blows tobacco smoke to make the *San Pedro* stronger and in Northern Peru for example, the way to imbibe tobacco is not by smoking but by drinking it, not through the mouth but through the nose. The idea behind this technique is that it allows the spirit of *San Pedro* to come into the breath so that every breath you take when you are drinking *San Pedro* is breathing in its the spirit.

You drink the *San Pedro* not just once but many times. Once you have drunk it and it becomes infused in the body, the shaman believes that it is the right time for certain rituals to happen, among which is imbibing the preparation of the tobacco through the nose. I am not judging this as good or bad, rather I understood this to be more within that culture. For me, it was unnecessary, because I felt I was so attuned to the *San Pedro* frequencies that I did not need to do anything to activate its spirit. I felt the *San Pedro* was like a medicine so close to everything that there was no need to do anything more.

What happened to me is that I moved away from the shamanic culture of healing to a point of utilising *San Pedro* in a way that goes beyond cultural and social healing, or even beyond physical healing, to go onto the path that I originally grew up with the events that happened when I was fifteen, twenty and twenty-seven. This later led onto a whole understanding of many things, among which I find the cumulative experiences that happened to me at the age of twenty-seven, where I stopped using *San Pedro* for myself. I stopped not because I did not want to use *San Pedro* but because I was so in alignment with it that it was no longer necessary.

Did you also stop using it in ceremonies to heal people?

Yes. I stopped drinking it and using it in ceremonies to heal people. From that time, all I needed to do was close my eyes and feel that the space of knowledge was there, without needing to drink or do anything specific. This is still what I do today.

So your experiences in South America were more the prolongation of a quest you started earlier in life than really being initiated into specific traditions by specific people?

I met many people and many were quite special people, but none so specific enough to say that that one person was the driving force, or was related to the work that I found helpful in my multi-dimensional self. Nobody impacted me to the point of changing me in a complete sense, as did the Zen master for example. It is not a judgement. In the end all those changes happened by themselves. The people that I met along the way, the *ayahuasquero*s and *curanderos*, only were there because the change was unfolding. Some people say, "You got initiated into something and so something must have happened at that point". The focus is then one point, one person, or one situation. I do not see it like that but rather as starting from pre-birth to now. Nothing happened really at one specific point as such, so to focus on a *curandero*, an *ayahuasquero*, or any specific person, or culture, or even one's family, misses the point.

Sacred Plants

It seems that in some part of Peru, some sacred plants are consumed under the supervision of people who already have been initiated to them, in three steps: first in liquid form, like a tea or decoction, then in a solid form, and only after in an airy form. The same with tobacco: first it is drunk, then it is chewed and then smoked. This is so because taking the plant through the breath at an early stage is supposed to bring the person too much into an airy state without that person being grounded first. On the other side, what happens in our society is that people take the tobacco straight to the third step – by smoking. From a shamanic perspective, the result is that the spirit of the plant takes the spirit of the person away. Obviously tobacco, whether it is psychoactive or not, creates a big dependency among people, especially the young ones. What was your experience of the native usage of tobacco?

This is very much connected to Peruvian culture and the philosophy of shamanism. It is interesting but it is where I walked away from that situation. I totally understand the principle you explained, and I am not saying it is right or wrong but if you ask my opinion, I would never say that there is a plant that is sacred and another one that is not. The humble lavender bush is as sacred to me as tobacco or *ayahuasca*. To somehow quantify that one plant is closer to the Spirit – whatever that means – or to something more divine, is a projection of that culture, in this case of the Peruvian culture, which I believe is influenced in a way that is not totally clear. It is not what shamanism was originally, thousands and thousands years ago.

To think that by doing certain things with a plant, like to drink the tea, is necessary as a first step and to smoke another plant is somehow the ultimate, is not what matters to me. The way I see it, the plant never communicates to you in a physical way. It is just that your perceptions are catching on to certain things that are going on in your body or in your emotions, and the plant only helps you to relate to these parts of yourself more easily.

As I see things, a plant will touch your essence in the same way as anything in life because it is a part of you. That part of you is not separate from you. It is not that you have to do certain things or certain rituals for that part of you to be understood. For example with tobacco, the energy of the plant relates to you before you even get close to it, before you even are aware that it is there, because it is beyond what we realise as an interaction in the physical sense. Of course, the *ayahuasqueros* in Peru see *ayahuasca*, tobacco and certain other plants as very sacred, as they act like a gateway for them to see a world that is invisible. Yet, it is not invisible. It is only invisible because you cannot see it. It is there. You do not need any of those things, even if they are sacred, to make the invisible world more sacred. It is what it is already. We are just unable to see it because we are just human beings on one level, but that limitation is not real. In the end, tobacco is not good and not bad. Its interaction with you is what is good or what is bad. This is what affects you.

Like all plants, tobacco has certain chemicals that will interact with your physical body and to a certain degree with your emotional, and perhaps your energetic body. I do not mean energetic in the sense of etheric energy but more in the sense of the energy related to the physical body, its organs and to the whole physical aspect of the body. In my opinion, tobacco in itself is not useful for human beings. I am not saying it is not good. It is just not useful because all you have to do is communicate to the tobacco plant, learn its song and attune your body to that same song. Even by simply touching the tobacco, the song will communicate its magic to you. Therefore, you do not need to cut the tobacco plant, you do not need to smoke, to drink, or to chew it. It is not necessary because, in the end, that is just one aspect of the sacred, and focusing too much on it actually distorts the picture.

Can sacred plants create an addiction for humans?

Addiction is not created by the plant. It is created by the human being.

Does this have a connection to the energy of the plant?

No. I mean nicotine is addictive. It is a chemical. It is a drug so it is addictive just like cocaine and heroine are addictive. To feel attracted to that chemical and to want to utilise that chemical to make it addictive by smoking or drinking is the human trait. If you have no interest in the plant and do not want to smoke it, there is no reason why you will be addicted. It is the same with alcohol and with any addiction. It is not that there is a spirit to alcohol that is negative and that captures your soul and then, all of a sudden, you are there and addicted to the plant without knowing why. It is just another aspect of the sacred. The plant has certain chemicals and, just like arsenic, it can kill you. We do not go and feel attracted to the spirit of arsenic and drink it. The problem is the human being, not the plant, and the human being is you. To focus on the plants as being problematic, or having the power over you to do certain things, is to forget that it all starts from yourself. In the end, I would advise people to not smoke cigarettes at all. Why? It is not useful. It is not like eating an apple, which is useful for maintaining health.

Ayahuasca is a little bit different. I would not say it is a useful plant to take in our culture, but it definitely has been and is culturally useful for some people in the Amazon forest. It is also useful physically, but Americans, Europeans, Japanese and other people nowadays go down to the Amazon forest because they want to utilise *ayahuasca* as a sacred plant to open up a perception that seems impossible to do otherwise. I think this is very cheap tourism. It is very interesting that a person does not realise that he or she can do all this work without having to drink *ayahuasca* or without having to go all the way to the Amazon forest. A person that is not of that culture does not need to go there to drink *ayahuasca*. If you do, what happens is that you see things from your own culture and you forget so many other subtleties.

It is almost like moving to Germany and pretending you are German without speaking the language, without knowing the dynamics of what it means to be German and saying, "Well, I am in Germany, so I am German". It is the same when people go to the Amazon forest and drink *ayahuasca*. Of course you see a little bit, just like when you go to Germany, you explore and you sense something, but things are much more complex. It requires years and years of work to understand and those years could just as easily be spent doing something else, like meditation and certain spiritual practices. I am saying this, because to believe that certain plants have a power that needs to be explored is only true on one level.

I do not know if I have answered your question. Addiction is a very interesting thing because I have worked a lot with addiction in the past. The one thing I recognised in people who have addiction is that they are not different from anyone else. We all have addictions to certain behavioural patterns, to certain mental thoughts, to emotional traits. It is just that addicts are more obviously addicted than normal human beings. They have got so caught up in one of those traits inside of themselves that it has become externalised into a whole situation such as addiction to drugs or alcohol. When I work with people I find out all these secrets.

People have human traits, such as locking the door and wondering, "Did I lock the door?" They know they have locked the door, but they have to go back and check the door to make sure that it was locked. I think that is a very interesting behaviour because they are somewhat aware of what they did. It is just that some mechanism made them forget that they locked the door. They believe that they do not remember but actually they do. It has just gone to a part that is unconscious. Then they had to check. First you think, "OK, it is only once. It is forgetful", but when you find that trait many times, it is like a habit. It is interesting to consider how that habit with the door would be in other circumstances, in other situations, maybe not with the door but with something else. It is all right for two, even maybe three times, but if you do it twenty times then of course it is a psychological problem. Drug addicts have not set that boundary. They are not in a position where they can resolve it. They feel that the door is not locked, and they need to take something to lock that door and make sure it is locked. For me the plants have no power over human beings, it is just that your internal dynamics take over.

Still, some mushrooms and plants such as *ayahuasca*, *San Pedro*, *peyote*, *amanita muscaria* and others are known to help enhance the perception. Do you not consider them useful for this purpose?

For me they are not useful at all.

71

Have not they been helpful at some point in your spiritual process?

No, not at all! (laughs). I am joking but I am serious, because the process I went through was pre-determined, or destined, rather than dependent on the plants. In reality, the plant is doing nothing. It is you who does what needs to be done, but because we are so unaware of the subtleties of these dynamics, it is sometimes useful to utilise something strong. Now this strong thing can be anything. It can be meditation. It can be chanting. It can be vigorous exercise. It can be confronting your fear climbing a mountain and really seeing what it is like when you are there looking down and it is a long way down. It can also be taking something such as *ayahuasca*, or *San Pedro*, or *peyote*, as you mentioned, which puts us in that situation – whether we like it or not – (but obviously this is not advisable for most people), where we have to analyse much more than the visible world. Our fears, our limitations and our perceptions then expand to points that are invisible or seem to be invisible to people. When we take *peyote* or *ayahuasca* for example, we see worlds that we normally do not see. Those worlds are hidden, or just kept away. If we were to fall into them with all the neuroses and negative thoughts and limitations that we have, and had to deal with all that at the same time, it would be too much. It would be overwhelming for the mind. The mind has to filter certain experiences, even daily experiences. If something is traumatic, it has to be filtered so that we have a capacity to cope with it in a way where survival is guaranteed.

To say that *peyote* or *ayahuasca* is useful is, in some way, actually right because sometimes we simply need to shake our old habits. We need to shake the ghosts that are hidden behind or inside cupboards and under carpets and look at things a little bit more deeply. Basically we need be more real. I certainly believe that all natural mind altering plants have created deep changes in the evolution of humans and of cultures throughout history, not just today. I also believe they have been a gateway to jumping to points that were not accessible, helping evolution to continue and move forward to see things in a certain way. However, to rely on the plants as the saviour, or as the power that brings that to you, is to forget that the essence is not the plant.

The plant is the key that opens something and the rest is your path. Once something is open, it is not necessary to open anything more than that. This is probably where western cultures abuse the sacred plants as they use them out of context and for the wrong reasons. They get used from a selfish and also a narcissistic perspective of wanting more rather than opening to the beauty of being connected and in union with the earth and with the profoundness of what it means to be alive. When that cultural thinking is part of a ceremony that uses natural plants which stimulate altered states of consciousness, unfortunately what happens is we get the same problem as with any strong religion or any strong technique: we can fall into the trap of dogmatism and forget the bigger picture.

Some people say, "I have to go to Peru to do the *ayahuasca* journey for six days and cleanse my body", giving power to *ayahuasca*. The plant does not want to give or to take away any power. It just wants to be what nature is for every human being: part of our existence. That is a completely different philosophy than what we can see today in using these plants. I feel to some degree that even native people have fallen down a trap with certain plants. With *peyote* for example, what matters is not to just take the cactus but to acknowledge the whole interaction of it with the world. It needs to culturally be part of a whole existence in the form of paintings, songs, a relationship to where the plant grows, children, families, elders, etc. There is so much more than just a plant that you take and drink. That is lost even in *ayahuasca*, which is most of the time today sold and consumed as a drug.

In the end, any drug is just what it is. It is to take you away from your reality. It shows you another reality that then becomes a form of entertainment rather than an invitation to go deeper into the mystery of the universe. This is why, although I was formally initiated as an *ayahuasquero*, I stopped using *ayahuasca*. I just felt it is of no use. It is the same with *San Pedro*. Many people will drink *San Pedro* and it will continue to be the same experience over and over, because they are not learning. In the end, it is only helpful if we relate to the *San Pedro* on a much more profound level, which means relating to ourselves and to nature. The plant will not do anything. It is you who will do something.

Yet, having an introspective spiritual intention when taking the plant is crucial but not enough. It seems that a guiding person is critical in the process leading to a deep experience...

Some people say that they will take *ayahuasca* by themselves but in my opinion, it is necessary to have someone guiding. It is very dangerous to take any mind-altering substance. I do not say this to create fear but just to somehow make people aware of things. Taking mind-altering natural substances by yourself is very hazardous because when we go to the spaces that the plants open up for us, our reference points are not often as strong as they need to be and we can get lost. That means that if we had an experience of trauma for example, we open up to the trauma that has happened in the past and that has been affecting our whole outlook on life. We are afraid. We are afraid of doing anything because we just want to do what is safe. Then the plant says, "You need to look at this. Rather than being afraid for the rest of your life, let's explore", but because that fear is strong and has affected your whole life, it becomes your reference point. You can get lost in that reference point of fear and to be in that space by yourself is not good.

This is why, in most cultures that I know, natural plants were always used in conjunction with a shaman or someone initiated in this work. Of course, the shaman was hoped to be a person who could act as a bridge through this transition period, working with the fear that may be coming up at that point. What you experience is not necessarily fear, sometimes it is something very nice but plants always take you where you need to go to. It is not like, "Please plant take me somewhere nice. Show me angels and beautiful things". Sacred plants will take you where you need to go. If you need to go to beautiful things, it will take you to beautiful things, and if you need to go somewhere else, it will take you there.

This is why experiences with sacred plants are different for everybody...

Every experience is different. From time to time it is even different for the same person because every experience is unique for that moment. This is why it may be dangerous for people to take plants, especially because our culture is not holistic. I am therefore very hesitant for most Western people to take any of these because their culture requires a different way of work.

Yet the psychoactive plant somewhat obliges the person to let go, and this may be interesting in western cultures too...

Of course, I have seen people transformed so rapidly and so dramatically in a way that was not possible otherwise. The opening was so profoundly insightful that these people changed their whole reference point of how they are to the world, to other people, and to themselves. This is why, if done in the right context, ceremonies with plants are useful.

Once someone has experienced something deep during a ceremony with these sacred plants, it seems to truly change his or her perception of life. Then, there is often a desire to repeat the experience. Is this essential? Is willing to have more profound experiences facing oneself really useful or is it just another trap in the spiritual path?

It is complicated to answer that question and some people would perhaps disagree with what I say, but there are certain plants that are good in the sense that they are useful for the body. They act as a medicine, just like Ginseng, and are useful for certain people. There are also other plants like tobacco that deplete energy out of the body.

Alcohol, which is a common drug, is more accepted and I do not know why because actually it is very dangerous. It is not risky if you drink one or two glasses of wine, but I am talking about people drinking a lot to the point of getting drunk. It is more dangerous as it really kills the cells of the body, affecting the brain cells, the liver, and depressing the energy level. Alcohol is a depressive so it takes energy out of the body, which has to be repaid in a different way later. It lowers the immune system and does many other things. I am not sure of all the physical effects that happen when you drink alcohol but there are many.

Then you have plants like marijuana. Marijuana is seen as something soft, which is sometimes useful to cure certain diseases, but I believe it is not a good plant for general consumption for most people. It can actually cause mental problems as it destabilises certain parts of the brain, blocking certain functions and creating the possibility of mental dysfunction and, in extreme cases, even mental sickness. This is of course extreme and not the reality for most people but what happens for most people is that the THC substance which is in marijuana stays in the brain for many years, affecting a lot of the spiritual work. It actually blocks certain energies from flowing, and affects reproduction. I actually believe that it changes something in our DNA structure that is passed down to the children, if you have children, and will affect them. I am not saying this to scare people but just to show another side and to suggest that you evaluate plants if you can do so.

Then you have *ayahuasca* which, in my understanding, is less dangerous than marijuana. *Ayahuasca*, of course, is very strong and some people see it as very hard, traumatic and dangerous. That is true, it is dangerous! If you are mentally unstable or have a history of mental problems in the family, like the mother, the father, or the grandfather, it can trigger these problems. This is where it is important that the shaman decides if it is useful or not. How can you decide for yourself if you have never tried *ayahuasca*? I do not know how you can make such a decision. The same with alcohol until you try it. Sometimes it is so strong, but it is too late: you have created a problem.

If the *ayahuasca* experience is outside of the cultural context, it tends to relate more strongly to the ego. It is like a warrior plant that wants to kill the ego because it relates to aspects of the ego more strongly. If we have not done any preparation work to be ready for the journey, it can create very strange attitudes in people. On the physical level, the plant *ayahuasca* itself is unhealthy. Still, some people would say, "But *ayahuasqueros* are healthy and strong…". Well, I worked with a lot of them and I actually saw what *ayahuasca* does to their physical body. They are healthy firstly because they have more nutrients. They are also healthy because they live in the Amazon forest in a very beautiful pure environment, they eat fresh food, and they do many physical activities that strengthen the body. If they are healthy, it is not because of *ayahuasca*.

Is *ayahuasca* a medicine?

It is a medicine but like anything, it is a medicine within a context. If used as a medicine for all ills and problems, I think it loses its validity. The Santo Daime religion uses it in this way today, assuming that the plant is like a sacrament and the way to the divine. In my opinion, the plant is not the way to the divine. You are! Your centre, your heart, is the only way to the divine. The plant is useless. It does nothing.

The *San Pedro* is different. This cactus was traditionally used to heal mental disease and it is always important to look at how plants were used traditionally. The shamans used *San Pedro* when someone was unstable, but of course, they have a much more understanding culture. Sometimes that sense of not being stable became even stronger under a ceremony. If you are trying to get better you may get worse, but many people who suffered from paranoia or even some types of what might be labelled as schizophrenia – I do not know if it could medically call it schizophrenia as I am not a doctor but this was my observation – and taking *San Pedro* changed this and they got better.

We then see that mentally, something in *San Pedro* works slightly different than *ayahuasca*. It is also much softer, in the sense that *ayahuasca* really shakes. For some people it shakes everything traumatically and that is very useful. *San Pedro* does not do so and some people even say that it is softer than getting drunk with a lot of alcohol. That is because the point of working with *San Pedro* is not so much the visual experience, it is more the changing of certain chemical structures in the brain that limit our perception. *San Pedro* is for example very useful for mental illness and neurosis. Some scientists have told me that there are chemicals in *San*

Pedro that are anti-cancerous. I think that it is the only mind-altering plant that is a very strong cure for certain cancers. It is actually a medicine that heals physical elements in the body such as pain, emotional disturbances and schizophrenia. It is also good for cleansing the body when one has cancer. To believe that *San Pedro* is the way to enlightenment, or wherever, is perhaps misguided, yet for me it is the most useful plant outside of its cultural context even though it is of course better to use it in a pure environment. However, it can be used in a place that is not as pure as the mountains of the Andes where it originally grows.

This is just a little bit about plants. Would I suggest that *San Pedro* is the remedy for all ills, and create a Santo Daime type religion, where the sacrament is *San Pedro*? If that happened, it would be against everything I believe and teach. It would be creating another dogma of being caught with the necessity of taking a mind-altering substance to make you see things a little bit differently. For me the only true sacrament is your heart. That is where the divine is. There is nothing outside that is the same. There are things we can do that bring us closer to our heart such as being in a relationship with a partner, or exploring love to a child but this is not the divine. To believe that your partner or your baby is your saviour or what has opened the divine for you, misses the point. You would then start projecting onto elements outside – your partner, your child, your family, your religion, the *San Pedro*. *San Pedro* is just the gate to the divine that is beyond it. The divine is there and always there. Nowhere else. It is not in the *San Pedro*.

What would be for you the best state of mind for a person when absorbing *San Pedro* in a ceremony?

The best state of mind is to come back to your heart. It is not to stay in your mind or in your thinking because if you have a thought when you are drinking *San Pedro*, then that thought invites another thought and so on, like expectations. The best is just to come back to the heart, which is a work in itself but a wonderful work. If you are not in the heart, remind yourself, "'I am present here, watching the breath and doing whatever brings me closer to that space". Then just trust.

And what to do when a sudden rise of energy happens? Is just watching it already a healing and spiritual process?

Watching it is a good thing to do. The rise of energy is like when you fall in love with someone, which is also a rise of energy. Your emotions get expanded and you feel wonderful. If you identify with that and you try to hold on to it, it kills it. If you just honour that space, then it has the freedom to grow, to mature and to be beautiful.

Zen Buddhism & Shamanism

As you know these two traditions from inside, would you say that Zen Buddhism emphasises the idea of controlling the body and the mind while in shamanic spirituality it is more expressing the wisdom of the body, being present, observing what happens and learning from this? It seems that both have the same finality but through different ways.

Zen Buddhism is certainly part of the Japanese culture, which is quite martial, strong, rigid, and controlled. I would not say that this is the essence of Zen Buddhism but controlling the mind and the body through the mind definitely is a very important perception in Japan and in the West of what it means to be a Zen Buddhist.

Is it different in shamanism, which appears to put the body more in the centre of the practice?

In the shamanism that I explored, the body is the instrument of change to a much greater extent and the focus is on releasing many things. The body is important in the whole process just as it is in Zen Buddhism but it becomes a focus in the sense of being something that the person has to work with. For example, if there is fear, in Zen Buddhism people would probably sit and quieten down the fear through the mind and the stillness of the body. In Shamanism, it is much more active so the way that I understand how people would work with this would be to let go through herbal remedies or through points that have contracted in the organs, for instance in the kidneys, or liver if the fear is stocked there. Shamans would prescribe certain remedies and certain movements to cleanse the body out, so that it is easier.

The body is clearly a much more active tool in shamanic culture, but of course I am not saying that shamanic culture is better than Zen because in a way it has also become corrupted. A lot of the remedies are given today because of a cultural rather than an individual understanding. *Ayahuasca* for example is a remedy given to many people because it is seen as a remedy for everything in some places in the Amazon. It is considered a strong remedy not only for spiritual things or inner dynamics but also for cleansing the body. There are lots of dangerous parasites in the rainforest that people can pick up through food and so on, and if your intestines are full of parasites you can die. *Ayahuasca* is then given to totally clear that system out of the parasites.

Today there are fewer parasites because people live a different lifestyle, but *ayahuasca* is still given for many things that I see as unnecessary. For example, if the belief systems says that people have got a negative vibration or "black magic", as they call it, and has been exposed to this, then they need to drink *ayahuasca* to get rid of the negative from their body. This is misleading. I do not believe there is any negative, and there is definitely no "black magic", except in the mind of the person who refers to it.

Rather than using *ayahuasca* to try to clear the negative in the cultural sense, it is important for the people to understand why they are creating this space where they are exposing themselves to these silly ideas and *ayahuasca* can be used for this important purpose instead. Yet, mostly because of the cultural limitations of the people using it, the plant has become very much associated with "black magic", "negative spirits", spirits that harm you and certain things that are not so good for your well being. All that, in my opinion, is imagination gone wild. By taking *ayahuasca*, we just allow that imagination to become stronger because it goes much deeper into those thoughts.

In that sense, shamanism and Zen Buddhism have gone down different paths and got corrupted in different ways. I do not consider shamanism better than Zen Buddhism. In actual fact, my disappointment, or rather disillusion, with shamanism after a while was to see that so many of human traits became fixated in the shamanic cultures and it was difficult to go beyond them, and actually, trying to go beyond these traits was seen as lacking respect for the cultures. This is why many people today in modern shamanism think that if you do not do this or that, or do not believe in the established beliefs, then you are not practising shamanism. It is the same in Buddhism where it is believed that if you do not do this, then it is not Zen Buddhism, it is not Tibetan Buddhism, or whatever. This, in my opinion, misses the point.

In shamanism, at least if it is approached with a spiritual attitude, there is this idea of letting go instead of controlling, like in Zen Buddhism. People who take shamanic plants say they learn things about themselves through this letting go. They learn just because they cannot do otherwise, as the plant takes them away ... or deep inside, which may be the same thing.

Yes. You can let go. This is what is very interesting about shamanism. Letting go is the opposite of what we do in Western cultures. Once we explore that, we can let go more than just on the mind level, we can do it in the body and on the energetic level. We realise that letting go is not just letting go of an idea. It is a whole experience in itself. From what I know, shamanism is one of the paths that is using that aspect the most actively and this is positive. However, it sometimes gets caught up because letting go does not prevent you from being initiated or from initiating others into belief systems that immediately take over what you have let go of. It is complicated.

By "belief system" you mean for instance ideas of spirits, stolen and retrieved souls, witchcraft, etc., which seems to be unavoidable in the shamanic world-views?

Exactly.

If letting go is interesting in a given cultural frame, your point is that it could be of better use without the specific associated cultural frame of reference?

It could be better without the need to fill that space with other things, to find answers and so on, because once you let go, the answers will come whether you like it or not. It is just about trusting and giving it enough time to create that space. Once you let go of anger, whether you like it or not, love will take its space. That is the essential human trait: to love, to be caring and to be compassionate. Whatever people may say or think, it is so. When you let go of what stops it, love comes through. You do not need to put something else or to do anything to bring that force. You just have to allow the process, even if the process takes time and is not an easy one since there is a lack of cultural concepts to grasp it.

New Beginnings in the Pacific

What made you leave Peru?

As I explained a little bit before, I had a vision and there was also a very strong feeling that I needed to go, but unlike in the Amazon where there was a specific event that made me think "OK, now I need to live", in Peru there was really nothing to make me leave. I loved Peru and I could speak Spanish very well. I was a healer working with people but I always have been a little bit restless. I was reminded this by my mother when I visited her a few weeks ago. She said, "When you were young, the restlessness made you want to go to different places". I do not remember being restless but I do remember feeling that life is an adventure so why be in one place and just do nothing? Why not explore? Even in South America I did not live in one place. I travelled from one village to another and did not want to settle down, wanting to be on the move but differently than just travelling. I was always exploring and going deep into something.

I decided to leave Peru simply because it was time to go. There was a strong feeling to leave South America and deep inside, there was this pull to go to Australia. Australia is an interesting country because of the nature and the Aboriginal people, but it was not like Polynesia, where I felt attracted by the deep beauty of the place.

What were you searching for in the Pacific and what did you find?

I stopped in Polynesia on my way to Australia. What was I searching there? I do not really remember my initial drive to go to Polynesia but I have always had a fascination for islands, tropical islands far away from civilisation, so when it was possible to stop in Polynesia I took this opportunity. I was somehow drawn to the Polynesian culture without really knowing what it was and, although these Islands were beautiful, I did not find Tahiti particularly interesting except for the fact that it is far away from civilisation and in the middle of nowhere. Coming from South America, what struck me was that the people in Tahiti were very modern as if they wanted to be French, living like the French and watching television. I have nothing against the French, but it was not what I expected of a Polynesian island so I was a little bit disillusioned and this is why I left the main Island. I wanted to go even further into more natural original settings.

A week later, I met a very interesting man who was Polynesian and introduced me to the deeper culture of Polynesia. I ended up in the nearby Island of Moorea with some people who knew about the healing methods of Polynesian massage and worked with stones, and with their spirit. As soon as I got off the boat that I had taken in Tahiti and set foot on Moorea, I had a feeling that I needed to be here for some time. The feeling in Moorea was totally different than from Tahiti because it was not modern with cars and traffic and all this sort of rubbish. It was much smaller and people were much more connected to each other with something beyond the obvious. It was an intense island and I liked it.

I was living with a group of Polynesian people who invited me to their traditional meetings where people ritually stand up and speak. They were talking about certain traditional aspects that they were loosing and it was quite a big discussion. They were actually trying to preserve their culture in a way that Tahiti could not. There were many dimensions entering into their lives and they really had to establish what was important and what was not. I did not understand the language but we managed to communicate and I could understand what they were saying. I found it very fascinating because people were very real. They were able to express themselves strongly and it was very powerful.

In South America the stones and the earth have a very important role to play. I was telling this to the man I got close to and he explained that for them, stones are magical. I cannot exactly remember why they were magical, but people could connect to the stones and certain things happened. I was introduced to the native healers and I met people doing Polynesian massages, very physical, like the massage in Hawaii called *lomilomi*.

In someway, as Polynesians embrace you once you are part of something, I got involved in the whole culture of Moorea and I stayed there for many months. Living in French Polynesia is very expensive and I did not have much money so I was very lucky that some people let me stay for free in their house. I was then introduced to a French lady who had horses and I was able to help looking after the horses by cleaning and feeding them, and taking them out for walks. I made some money in this way even though it was actually very minimal money but I was able to survive for several months. It was beautiful. I loved Polynesia and I felt I could live there forever, unlike the Amazon forest, which was beautiful but where the environment was much more harsh on my body and where I felt I could not stay there for very long. This is also why I went to the Andes that I loved very much and where I stayed for a long time. Polynesia has a mystical quality with the sea and the mountains. It has always been my dream to be in a tropical island away from everything, with simple people who love nature, who live a very simple life. I was very happy to be there.

Where did you go after Polynesia?

From Polynesia I went to Vanuatu, which I also found very interesting. In the main island I asked, "Where are the healers?". I explained what I was doing in Polynesia and people directed me to a specific island where most of the healers apparently lived. They were known to be the best magicians and witches. I got a very small aeroplane to get there and it landed on a grass field. I remember seeing this Island in a totally different way than from the Polynesian ones where people are much more related to the sea than the land. I met a priest who drove me to the village and introduced me to the elder or the person in charge of the community, but I stayed there for 5 or 6 days only.

I worked with these people and I found it very interesting because it was a totally different atmosphere than anything I had experienced. It seemed to me that these people lived as primitively as one can get. They were very much into magic and they were showing me all these interesting tricks that did not interest me much. I was more interested in plants and remedies that they worked with so they introduced me to the ritual that they see as the most important one with plants, which is a *Kava* ceremony. To me, *kavakava* tasted awful, like water with cigarette ash. They sat, took it and gave me more and more. My belly was so full of this water and I wondered why they were drinking all this. Then I remember trying to move my face and I just felt it was totally numb. I realised I could not speak because my tong was also numb. I looked around and everyone seemed to relax and be in a pleasant mood. It was interesting. I did this two or three times because they enjoyed doing this *kavakava* ceremony with me and then they showed me some hot springs that were on the Island.

I was fascinated with these hot springs right on the beach. Some were very hot and you could not sit in them. I remember sitting for two hours in one that was slightly cooler, looking around and entering into a deep meditation. I felt very connected with the people and they took me to a village that was important for them. I remember looking at the people and thinking, "This is amazing". I had a very interesting feeling for this place. I do not believe in reincarnation as people normally understand it but it was almost like coming back to a place that I knew. Yet, again I did not stay... Probably my restless or adventurous spirit...

It was paradisiacal but in a very pure sense. I enjoyed being there and speaking to the people who were very simple, very down to earth and not pretentious. In Vanuatu, they were very direct, not ashamed of their ancient way, unlike many Australian Aboriginals who can be quite ashamed and try to hide their original nature behind. They were quite proud of their culture and of themselves. From there I went to New Caledonia because the plane was stopping there but I did not like it at all. It just seemed like the worst of the colonial French. At least in Polynesia, the French people that I met in Moorea were very open to the culture and wanted to understand it. So I continued on my journey to Australia.

What did you do in Australia?

I think the most significant thing was that I had to readapt to the modern world. I did not realise how difficult that would be. It took me some time to adapt to doing things in a way where people could understand what I was saying because in the beginning I did not know how to speak to people. This is a long story in itself but basically, I met someone who had a bookshop and who was very interested in what I was doing. She wanted me to come to her monthly meeting to introduce people to my work and from this meeting I met someone else, and then someone else, and I went further and further.

So you started your teaching there?

It started itself, really. I was just doing what I normally do and more and more people were coming and I had to travel by aeroplane to various locations throughout Australia, which then led to me also visiting New Zealand.

New Zealand is one of the best countries in the world for me. It is where I would go and live if I did not have any responsibilities working with people here in Europe. I had a very deep and close relationship to the Maoris, and how they have blended their lives with the Europeans that settled their shores, when some of the first settlers in New Zealand needed to marry because there were not that many women. Then of course, Maori women were part of the beginning of the interaction between the Europeans and the Polynesians. I am fairly sure that most New Zealanders have some Maori heritage. If they are from the original settlers that came 200 years ago, they have a lot of Maori blood.

In New Zealand I met some amazing Maori people and elders and one of my very wonderful friends was a lady who was pure Maori. She was related to the Maori queen or the Maori royal family. She introduced me to many things and decided to come to Hawaii with me along with a friend of hers. She was in contact with many of the Hawaiian people and I also knew some people I had previously met in Hawaii. We met many kahunas – local shamans – on Big Island and on Kauai. The people we met seemed to know a lot about their heritage and really wanted, even in a militant way, to preserve it. On the Big Island we did a ceremony with a *kahuna* near the volcano that is like the heart of Hawaii. The *kahuna* was singing in Hawaiian and doing his rituals. At some point he asked if I could do rituals from South America to bring the South American spirit in relationship to Hawaii and then something happened. The volcano slightly erupted, a cloud appeared, and four white birds flew to the centre, one from each of the four directions, and he said: "The goddess of the volcano welcomes you. You are now part of Hawaii…" Beautiful words, not just to me but also for the Maori lady who did a ceremony for the Maori people. It was a wonderful connection. In Kauai we also met very interesting people and it was a wonderful time travelling and meeting with lots of people.

Then my fellow Maori people left back to New Zealand and I carried on to Europe to teach in Spain and Portugal.

Teachers & Students

Most people see you as a "Teacher". Do you consider yourself as so and do you consider those working with you to be "disciples", "students" or simply "persons"?

This is a big question. I personally do not like the word "Teacher" because, in English at least, this word means that there is something to learn. The teacher has "students" and the students need to learn the teaching. That is not exactly how I see the picture. For me, the knowledge is inside. Nobody has to learn anything. On the contrary, we have to unlearn. Unlearn all of our socialisation, our mad thinking processes, our habits, our identification with certain situations, with ourselves, with other people, with family dynamics leading us to try to fulfil our father's wish because he wants you to be in a certain way, although deep inside we have another dream. We have to unlearn all the madness.

How can you be a teacher when you are helping to unlearn that process? In English that word does not really fit. The word *guru*, would be better, as in Sanskrit it means, "Someone who helps you to take the darkness away", but there is no English word for this. I do not like the word *guru* either because in the West it has a whole picture of dependency associated with it, even though the meaning of the word is the closest to what I do: removing the veil. Some people call me "Master". In English the word "Master" almost makes it sound like you are the best, highly developed, and the people around you are less developed, less masterful. I feel uncomfortable and do not identify with this word but I allow people to use it.

Some people call me "Master", that is fine, others call me "Spiritual Teacher", that is fine and others call me "*guru*", that is fine. Many people just call me "Friend" and that is also fine. For me, they are just labels. The West needs a label because people say, "What is he?", then of course, everyone is trying to define the person, "Ah, he is a Shaman", or "Ah, he is a Teacher", "he is a Spiritual Teacher", "he is a Spiritual Master". Who knows? In the end, does it really matter?

Would the word "Philosopher" suit you?

A philosopher? It would be difficult because I am not so intellectual…

A Philosopher of unlearning…

I do not know. There is no English word for what I do.

You do not want any title and you let people decide how to see you without attaching to what they project on you?

Exactly. I let people decide. It does not influence the work I do because this work is beyond a teacher/disciple relationship. There is no "disciple" for me. There is only a disciple when you decide to be a disciple, meaning that you are a disciple to the knowledge that is within yourself. If you are not a disciple to the knowledge within yourself, then you are not. If you are a disciple of the knowledge inside, then you are a disciple to the knowledge that is everywhere. That knowledge is then just recognised not just inside of yourself but also in art, in music, in people, in sculpture, in the beauty of creation. So where is the disciple?

In your teaching you do not seem to consider yourself at the centre of the relationship between the person and his or her inner wisdom but rather somewhere at the periphery of the work, between the person and his or her self...

Totally.

Is it also a work for the teacher to see the funny sage-like behaviours of people who are really involved on the spiritual path but, although they do their best, are very distant from the humility the teacher may express as a person?

It is a big work for the teacher too. My whole life is dedicated to people, so it is not like I am doing a course, like some people go and do yoga, learning certain postures, learning Tai Chi, or learning herbal remedies. The work that I do with a person is as deep as with your own children. When they are totally helpless in that space of ignorance and unconsciousness, you are doing everything to sustain the environment where they have the space to grow and to communicate their consciousness. It is a very difficult thing because, on one level, you can do too much.

Everyone wants you to do everything because the more you do and the more deeply people go to that part of them, the more they realise they need more. In the beginning it may be that people think they are just learning meditation, but in the end, it is going to a space where there is no other reference than the person you are working with as it is unknown territory. It is uncharted. You do not know where you go.

Even in books it is confusing as one book says this and another says that. So where do you go? Of course I say, "To the heart", but in the practical sense people then want to know more.

This work requires a lot of time and I give that time in different ways, physically, through initiations, but also energetically. It is the biggest job ever! Really. It is like looking after hundreds and hundreds of babies. It is complete work. I am just using the analogy "babies" as of course it is guiding someone through this unknown territory. In a way, it is like when a baby walks out of this sacred space of possibility of growing and decides for example to jump off a veranda because he or she thinks that what is down there is exciting. Many babies will try to do this and their mother then worries. She wants to pull the child back and say, "Do not do this. If you fall, you will hit your head, you will hurt yourself and you can die".

I personally do not say this but I discretely suggest it, to make it obvious that if you do this it is not very healthy. In the end, I will let the person go, even though it is painful to see what the person is actually going through. It is almost like I see everything in that moment from that decision, like the mother knowing that if the child climbs on the table he is going to fall and hit his head because he has done it before and because the legs of that table are wobbly. What to do?

Your way as a teacher is not to tell people what to do or to judge their acts...

Of course. You cannot tell people what to do because by telling them you take the power away from them. With a child, of course you know it is a physical thing, so what I do is I let the child climb on the table but I am very prepared to be there just in case he or she falls. With an adult, it is different, they do not want you there because they want to fall. They want to experience life and want to jump into this territory that they discovered, these detours we just talked about. Therefore, you cannot say, "No. You should not to do this. Stop doing this. It is a mistake". If you do, you build a conflict. In the beginning, I would make my point very strong as I really wanted people to understand, but now, when someone writes to me and says something, I just say, "It is wonderful. I will support you in every way. Go for it".

So you observe people's detours. You may wish they are fewer of them but you do not intervene in people's choices, as if they were fully part of their own process?

If I intervened, then I would be doing something that I promised myself not to do. My way is to allow the divine to choose the path that is best for everybody.

This appears to be an unequivocal part of your teaching.

Yes. In my opinion, a spiritual teacher can never know the whole picture as to why this needs to happen. I can see that these things will happen because it is obvious to me, but in the end, maybe the suffering, the pain and the whole emotional turmoil for that person is part of what is needed, so why try to change it? I do create limits though when people start to hurt others, just as if you have two children and one child starts banging the other with a metal spoon on his head. You do not just say, "Well, what is going on is terrible", while the other child is still banging on... You have to say, "Look, you can follow your path but when you start creating this, it is too much and you really have to stop!" This is why I can be very strong by really drawing a line. I do not leave the person completely. If I see someone going to a space of total damage for her and others, then I will intervene.

You often denounce dogmatism as a limiting conceptual frame in people's lives. How is it preventing people from raising their spiritual consciousness?

Words can be understood, depending of the person, on so many levels. They reveal many things because there is much more than just words that are happening now, but when they are written, they do not have these other dimensions that speech and presence have. I was just reading last night about dogmatism because this is my biggest concern in my teaching. Dogmatism has created so much pain; it has caused so many people to move away from spirituality because they see strong, charismatic, dogmatic people portraying their ways as the only spiritual path. When spirituality is transformed into dogma or into a very rigid belief system, it is amazing to see how it can create a lot of crazy situations, much more than normal everyday society can. It becomes extreme.

This is why when working with people, in every step of the spiritual journey, I always emphasise that extremism or fundamentalism is not something to be valued at all. This is even the case for vegetarianism, which I consider crucial and vital for everyone, not just for a healthy body or for the spiritual work but also for the environment, and many other reasons. I find it very negative when people judge others who are not vegetarians as not having reached a certain point of spiritual development. There is a sort of fundamentalism in this attitude and some things may become extreme such as proclaiming that vegetarianism is a good thing for the world.

On the website of the Samara Foundation, many people have asked me to put links, but I am very cautious because on some level, that means I am endorsing whatever I am linking to. There are organisations such as Greenpeace, which in essence I believe are doing a very good work, but I do not agree with their methods nor their actions sometimes, even though they can be very useful. I think it is a form of extremism that, if not done with consciousness, can cause alienation from the masses.

What I am trying to do is to reach everyone without having to change people's belief systems, religions, cultures, or ideas into something else. It is not adding another cultish group but rather opening up to the beauty of who you are, in what you are doing. If you are Christian, Muslim, Buddhist, Hindu or atheist, it does not really matter because I am not trying to change that. I am trying to open up the experience of what that beauty means within that context in a bigger sense. It is not me or my words that do it, but more coming back to the space where people do it for themselves. This is why, when looking at some cults, I am amazed to think that the people who originally exposed their presence, their belief systems and their words, before the cult was formed around them, did not really mean for it to become that way.

Words are necessary to understand things but you are aware of the difficulty of using them as the ideas they carry may involve belief systems. How do you deal with wanting to say things without saying

too much to the point of being dogmatic? It does not seem an easy in-between space to be for a teacher.

Yes. This is why I always make it clear that what I say is not general but quite specific to a person or to a situation. It addresses unique points in development. Therefore it cannot be taken out of that reference and generalised for everything. If I value vegetarianism, for instance, I do not wish people to say, "Ah, Tony is saying that vegetarianism is necessary", as it is not for everyone. For some people, there are other points that are more important to address than vegetarianism, and getting stuck in that aspect is just a waste of time. Things are very subtle.

Some people on the spiritual path are willing to change their name to a spiritual one. It also happens around you. What is the relevance of this?

I do not change names to let go of your background, of your culture, of the family or of the love that the family put into giving a name to you, but often a name carries with it the limitations of that name. If you look at children as they develop from babyhood, the ego becomes the name. If, for example, your little boy is an individual, separated from other things and yet he does not feel that, know that he is preparing the ground work for that "I" aspect to become an aspect that the mind will use further towards his individual experience to become a self, a mature individual, a personality within society. Often that experience is laden within pain and suffering because it is letting go of our core, the home that we came from, the centre that we are, to become an individual fighting and wanting to become better or a more beautiful person. The name identifies with the process of individualisation. This is for me an interesting process but it becomes neurotic when that individualisation is connected to the ego and the self rather than the bigger picture.

This is the problem we have today in the world, individuals become limited to the concept of "me", "you", "this", "that" and the world. They become limited to the concept of time changes, of responsibility and of humility towards life changes, because they are self-centred. If the name, I mean the first name, carries any of those things, which is the case for most people, then it is important to make that conscious in a different way. That means either changing the name or working with it so that its associations are more holistic, more profound, and more beautiful.

What is important is your relationship to that name, using the ego and the sense of self in the whole process. It is so much beyond what we sometimes understand, because the name is one of the first things that we make conscious about ourselves. As people say "Hello John", "How are you John?", John is uttered thousands of times as a reference point to you.

But you never changed your name...

No, because it is not necessary. It is only necessary if you feel it is necessary.

Is it only interesting for the persons who feel it is necessary?

Yes, but even if you do not feel it is necessary, it can be. It can be important to work on the name and disassociate it with any points where that name becomes selfish, egotistical, full of the past, not part of the bigger picture, letting go of all this.

So we carry with our own name things we may not want...

Yes. We can change the name by keeping it and just changing what we want it to carry, so instead of separation, we have love, union, and holism. If we look at the meaning of our names, it is interesting to find the essence and the meaning behind them.

Why change the name if we comprehend the name from that perspective? Original names in Europe usually came from Hebrew, Aramaic or Arabic and then became English, French, or so on, with different variations, but the core is the same: full of meaning.

Initiation, Projections & Expectations

You spoke about initiating people. Can this important phase on the spiritual path also have some negative counter effect such as creating a kind of dependency from the person involved to you? A close work with a teacher implies certain kind of projections and expectations from students on him or her. People often speak about having their life changed since they started working with you. Therefore, you may become a reference point to them. How do you deal with this?

Initiation is complicated as it happens on many levels. One of the basic initiations, very subtle and brief, is when people decide to come and work with me. It is so subtle that it may even not seem like initiation because there is no ritual around it and it is not dramatic as in some cultures or spiritual traditions. Often, when people come to a retreat, a seminar or a course, they feel that the initiation happens afterwards. The reason they have come to work with me is because the path has been opened for that possibility, so often the work is not that you read a little announcement in some magazine and you realise that you come and work. It is more. It is rather that once the interest is activated, the work begins. That interest may for instance be activated on the dream level. It is a very subtle process and in the beginning, most people will not recognise this, as it is just a dream and beyond the everyday experience. Yet, that is an initiation. It is a way of saying, "Thank you for embracing your knowledge and wisdom, and for coming and exploring that with me".

Then that space is created in a formalised way in the retreat or the workshop where people sit, meditate, move, or do whatever the activity is in that moment to experience this in connection to themselves but also in connection to the whole space they are in. It is not just individual but in the work of the space that is being created and initiated at that moment.

When people come and work with me it is not as simple as listening to words. There is a whole change of atmosphere because I energise this atmosphere to create a space of possibilities. The person walks into that space having accepted that this space is also a space inside of themselves that they want to explore more deeply. This space inside of themselves then interacts with the space that is everywhere, with other people, me, the atmosphere. It creates a whole path. A path that is obvious. It becomes clear that it is not an esoteric path and most people, at some point feel, "This is so simple, so easy. I know this. It doesn't seem new. I recognise it". That is perhaps the most noticeable thing that people comment on. And then I say, "Of course. Did you think you were coming to learn things that you did not know already?". It is knowledge. That is the first initiation.

Then of course the initiation goes further. Because once that space is opened, it activates many aspects of who we are but we do not know. The initiation carries on from there to other aspects, one of which being the opening of the third eye. Most people do not know that we can use it in the spiritual work. By opening the third eye, we allow the possibility to be more perceptive of what is going on in us, around us and in the world. You can say "It is me", or you can say "It is another aspect of the earth", or "It is you". It does not really matter because it is not personal to one thing. That initiation is the first step that a person has taken into the space of possibilities. As you have started the process, the third eye opens, whether you want it or not. It is like music. If you start practising piano, whether you want it or not, in the end the music is there. The music will get more profound, it will touch a deeper aspect of you, like the third eye. The spiritual activation will begin to develop and communicate with the world in the same way that music begins once you become more adapted with communicating with the piano. Then there are many other initiations.

There is the activation of the *kundalini*, the life force, so that it is not depleted or stuck. That life force is everywhere in the body to make you more healthy physically. It is not an overwhelming life force, it is a life force that is there but is being stopped by limitations like fear, contracted organs, or simply breathing in the wrong way. When we release the life force, what normally happens is that people become more alive energetically. They usually need to sleep less. Their diet changes naturally because certain tastes are not longer valid. Many things happen physically, energetically, mentally, and emotionally during this life force release, and that is very good. It is not like in India where people believe the *kundalini* is dangerous, or can move too quickly and shake you to produce unbalance in you. It is totally different. It is a life force that is natural and that needs to be there. This other initiation is activating the whole body in a way that it was when we were a baby, free, alive and full of life force.

Then, among the other initiations, one is working with sound, which is similar to one of the Andes' initiations. This is introducing the sound of the essence of the universe, so to speak, to vibrate everywhere, including in the essence of every thought we have. Then, when we have a thought such as "My bank manager is going to meet me tomorrow so then it is really important that I have to get my paper ready but I do not have this ready so what am I going to say?", that thought still happens, yet with the initiation of that sound, the whole picture changes as the vibration of those thoughts changes and becomes transcendent. You still think of the bank manager but rather than focusing on the mundane aspect of what the bank manager might do and on the fear connected to him, you see the divine essence of the whole theatre that is taking place and you detach from it, although you are still part of it, because the sound is in the background. The sound is the heart singing in tune with the primordial sound that was creation, that is creation, and that is creating you now. Your heart sings in tune with what is sustaining that thought process but you bring it to its essence. I am using poetic language so it can make sense but the thought does not become mundane. It has another quality to it.

When you have this other quality, you see things in a mystical way. Everything touches you, your heart and your essence, in a way that brings joy. You no longer spiral down but are part of the ever-expanding beautiful sound that is creating the universe, which is the divine creating itself, that is expanding endlessly without limitation. As you create that form in your mind or in your thinking, your thoughts expand beyond any limitations and access many things. Then what you find is that you are able to access other people's thoughts, which is called telepathy. You do so not by intruding upon them but because you have let go of that ego aspect. The connection is natural because it is embracing what is common and equal in all human beings.

The thought and the sound that were initiated into that thought process then carry on in many ways. It changes your life, not just by chanting one of the sounds that people are initiated into for example, but by going into the mystical dimension of who we are. If we were quiet enough to listen to the sounds that we are in this moment, most of them would be very negative sounds. There will be worry, thinking about the future, how to prepare for it so that we do not get hurt, how to do things in a certain way so that we do not suffer, experience pain or create pain and suffering for other people.

All that has a dimension of sound to it. It has chemistry, an essence to it, which is far removed from the sound that is in tune with our heart, which is our essence. It is so far removed that both the pain and the essence do not manage to even touch each other. When we are in that space of pain, we do not even realise that the other space of bliss exists. It is almost like the mind and the created space take over everything. We forget the joy because the mind, having already created its sense of joy of controlling everything to make sure that it cannot suffer, has simply lost itself in that process.

The sound is what I think the Bible spoke about as the essence of everything. That is an initiation that happened to me in South America. I was twenty-seven and I remember listening to all these amazing universal sounds. Even during *ayahuasca* ceremonies, I remember that in one of the initiations, the first thing I thought and did was to ask shamans around me "What is this sound?", as I thought it was coming from outside. I did not I realise it was coming from inside. They said, "There is no outside sound". I thought "How come? That sound is from me?" and this amazing sound was going on. I thought, "What is it?" because it was very strange. Now, in hindsight, I can understand that it was my movement from one dimension to another, from the personal mundane to the essence, to the deep and profound. This journey was so quick that this is why shamans call it "a flight". It was like flying, but inside. The sound that I could hear was the sound of that journey. The moving through those dimensions in split seconds created a sound and when I listened to the sound, which was amazing, I moved even quicker.

Then I found a way of travelling through different dimensions or to connect to those dimensions just by listening to that sound. It was startling because there was no suffering anymore. I did not have to stop at points of pain or limitations and, before I knew it, I was at a point that was total bliss, ecstasy or opening. For most people, it would be many things and suffering, and they would cry, but for

93

some reason this did not happen to me. I realised the importance of sound there, and of course in Zen Buddhism through some of the *mantras*, but these sounds were much more intense than anywhere else prior to that time. Afterwards, the sound that came to me when I was twenty-seven was the sound "*hu*", which I use very much as the focal point of meditation to stimulate the mind to come back to something that it has forgotten. This is the initiation or one of the initiations with the sound.

You mentioned doing several initiations but you also mentioned that people might not be fully aware that they take place. Is the initiation time and process a one to one teacher/student relationship in a specific place? Does it happen in a retreat or it is without the person you work with being physically present?

It is everything. For some people, it is quite important to be physically close at some point but it is not essential. Still, I would say that ninety nine per cent of the time it is important as there are certain things that happen which are part of the initiation. The initiation is not like a ritual that is predetermined in a formal, special moment. For some people it happens when they are speaking to me walking down the beach for example, like in Egypt where we did one of the retreats, talking about something totally unrelated to anything important. Yet, in that moment, the initiation happens.

Is it because you chose that moment or it is just "their" moment?

Who chose the moment? If you have no ego and no desire to control anything, is the moment already destined and chosen? Do you choose the moment? Does the person choose the moment? That is a question too difficult to answer but it is interesting because then you come to other points that are destiny, willpower and intention. For me, the moment is just that it is right. The person knows the moment is right. I know the person knows and I know that the person knows that I know this. The universe knows this. All the aspects that help through with this initiation know this, so it is just the right moment. There is not a determined date such as, "When you are twenty-five, or when you have worked with me for twelve months and three days, this initiation happens".

People can work with me for ten years and nothing happens. Others may have been working just one month and wonder why so much happens to them. It is not that one is better than the other or that one person is more or less advanced. It has nothing to do with any of that. It is just the way things are meant to be. There is no reasoning behind it although people may think, "When I am initiated, then I reach a certain level that is better than where I was before". It is not so because you have not reached any level, you have not gone anywhere different, you have always been where you needed to be.

So a person can be initiated with your help to a better understanding of who he or she is without realising the moment of initiation but just by feeling better later on in life?

Of course the initiation can happen at any time and it is totally irrelevant to every experience that you have had. It makes no "reasonable" sense and it may not even be visible or obvious. It may simply be that the person gets upset with me...

Without knowing why?

Yes, thinking and reacting in a certain way without knowing why. I have had one person I worked with who said, "It was very nice but I am not coming to anymore work. It is not for me. I have learnt all I needed to do". She was expecting me to answer, "Oh, I am so sorry. I hope that you can stay and learn a little bit more", but I said, "It is exactly the way it is meant to be". She got very confused, wondering what I was talking about. In a way, it is like meaning, "I need to go somewhere else to learn what I am needing to learn". Five years later, that person realised that that moment was a very strong initiation but she could not comprehend it through her normal perception at that point. She could only react in an emotional way.

Seeing these processes, people around me sometimes wonder how the person cannot see the work done. They get upset and think, "How ungrateful that person is after all the work Tony has done for her!". I just tell them to be quiet because it has nothing to do with that. I am not looking for appreciation, for gifts or presents. I like them and I do not say I do not need them, but I do not need them to show that you understand or you do not understand the initiation. The initiation can even happen during sleep. This is when I work most – the initiation work – because I find that at night the mind is not as strong at preventing what is going on or trying to intellectualise the process.

So you are working discretely with the person although she may not be aware of it. Do you also concretely and in an obvious way work with the person?

Of course. Part of the work is removing certain things that would be removed anyway but doing it quicker. It is not overwhelming the senses with anything that is not possible to understand but just saying, "All right. This is not necessary. Let us play around with it". For example, if there is something stuck in an energy point, why not just press that point and see what happens when the energy moves from another point so that it flows in a totally different way? Then the person sees that there is another world. He or she understands that this limited world is not everything. It is just a perception. Sometimes that act of unblocking energy is necessary because if not, things are slow. We reach impasses and it is difficult to get beyond them. It is like music. Sometimes it is necessary for the teacher to say, "Look, this is where the hand goes. Press like this and see what it feels like. What you are doing is actually just an automatic reflex and it is not right. Press harder, do that, relax the body, breath in like this". Sometimes that is required.

During an evident initiation, the release of the energy opens something in the person that may strongly shake his or her life and

create a strong feeling of gratitude towards you, which in the worst case can become a feeling of spiritual dependency. How do you deal this possible process?

I was speaking about an obvious initiation. This is why such should be done little by little because of course it may produce the possible side effects of gratitude. I am trying to remember a poem by a very interesting mystical poet called Rumi. It is just three sentences and I do not really remember how he put them but he said something like, "Where should my gratitude go? Should it go to the divine that I have experienced or should it go to the person who showed me the divine and opened the gate to the divine? My gratitude goes to the person who opened the door to the divine". This poetry explains what you are asking me. Rumi was of course very aware, but if you are not, then the gratitude can become personalised and it can induce projections that are dangerous. Gratitude in itself is not bad, rather it is very valuable, as it is an aspect of the heart.

A feminine aspect?…

Yes, gratitude is very feminine, so long as it does not become too dogmatic. You see this in the Hindu religions often with gurus who become the focus of me such adoration is not really the point. I saw a very interesting documentary of an American yet very Hindu guru whose name I cannot remember – who was worshipped in his whole process of work. People around him were obviously showing gratitude, kissing his feet and looking at him in the same holy way that Jesus has been pictured. They were doing things and acting out in a way that would seem totally extreme from the outside. Although the man called himself a God and was said to be an avatar, meaning a manifestation of God, wasn't he really just a human being?

Seeing this, I thought it incongruous because the gratitude has almost become a ritualistic worship rather than gratitude in the feminine sense, in the real sense of appreciation like Rumi is speaking about. Rumi's gratitude is because the heart has opened so much, that it is no longer stuck at that point of opening, rather it has opened to the divine that is beyond. This is where a lot of gurus in Hinduism take themselves very seriously and feel they are very wonderful, and are comfortable beings adored by their disciples. This happened a lot for example with Osho, and I do not understand why he did this, really. I mean I do of course, because on one level he was playing a game, but I feel he took it a little too far with his people and at a certain point he should have stopped what was going on.

Could you be more specific? What should he have stopped?

He should have stopped his people from their God-like adoration. Whenever I see this happening too much towards me, I quickly do things to dispel the idea and make my point. People sometimes think I am really strange and their perception of me is quickly shaken because I say something or I do something very un-spiritual. Their idea of me that they had built up is broken. I do that to help them. I have no personal interest because it is uninteresting to be adored like a God. What is the purpose? I would much rather be active and working.

So the teacher has to be patient and never enter into a relationship of authority/dependency with grateful people...

Of course. This is the biggest thing and this is why I have not found anyone who can take over the work I am doing, even though I have been initiating people to work in this way. This is not that there are not enlightened people, but most get trapped into the adoration of the ego, the inflation of the ego. What I am saying is that people working with me, who perhaps are able to teach these things like me, may get caught at that point of feeling important. That feeling arises when the ego senses that this adoration towards them is possible, wants more, and gets dependant on it. Often people who have worked with me feel that they have reached "teacher level". This is all in their mind because I have not said any of that. To stop this ego inflation, I just break any idea that spirituality is about being adored, being a God, being better, being bigger or more masterful than anyone else.

When I break it, I usually do it in public, in front of everybody. If someone acts very strongly like a spiritual teacher, trying to say "I am this, listen to me. I know what Tony is speaking about, so just listen", then I will make them feel as silly as possible so that at least in their mind, they feel they have been dropped from "teacher level" to "bottom level". Humility is important. Making them feel silly is not to punish them, although some may think this way, but it is rather coming back to the basics of compassion and humility to yourself. If you can find that in yourself in that moment, then you are a spiritual teacher, but if you feel punished or humiliated by me, if you look around and say "Oh, my gosh, look at everyone now, what will they think of me?", then it is a mirror to work with that ego that has no place in the spiritual awareness.

I am speaking about this because it is all part of adoration or admiration. Overcoming this is so difficult and probably the biggest trap of all spiritual work. Spiritual ego is narcissism, and when you start falling into the narcissistic trait, it is the most hazardous trap.

Too much self-esteem is one trap and dependency, which may be understood as not enough sense of self-worth, is another. Some people working with you say they are missing being more in your presence. It seems that the middle way would be to assume one's responsibility in life and avoid entering a kind of addiction towards a teacher who has become a central significant other. Dependency is a psychological state of mind that is pervasive in people's lives but it may be even more on the spiritual path, when people are looking for answers in life and, sometimes, have huge experiences transforming their mindset.

People who have that feeling of dependency towards me are usually sent away, so it is not a very good feeling to have. I know people that would say, "I cannot work and do any of this without your presence". On one level, there is some truth to it because to have a reference point of love makes it easier to discover the love of oneself. It is very useful to have a reference point of going beyond aspects that you do not know, but to have that reference point as a dogma, as a dependency, as you say, is in itself moving away from the real teaching and from the real self. It is renouncing the real work and it becomes a projection. Projections, like when people project me as being a father or as being the person that is more this or that, is often a sense of smallness about oneself.

But in doing so they think that they express the best of themselves...

Yes, but it is not good if that is not seen for what it is. For instance, if the person is projecting me as a father, that father figure is expected to act out back in certain ways. Then I am expected to be nice, kind or loving and if I am not, the father figure illusion is somehow broken and the person is hurt. He or she believes I have been personally bad to him or her. I am not working on a personal level because I do not even see that as an important point. The over dependency can be good if it is a specific process in itself that is being transcended but it is not good if it lasts for a very long time. Sometimes we clearly need to transfer our feelings from something painful – for example, our father who was traumatic because he never loved us in the way that our heart desired – to find that love present and to express that projection onto the person. We thought we gave up, that our heart closed, and suddenly we discover that love does exist. We open our heart. Of course, this opening is not negative. It is evidently positive but it needs to move, so that it is not just me as a teacher but it is yourself, the world and everyone.

Projection can be good in the beginning but in the end it needs to grow beyond that. Growing beyond that is not just saying, "I need to be self sufficient". Often people would react from being so called "dependent" to moving away and thinking that they can do and need to do everything by themselves, which is actually the opposite problem and a problem that can be very disturbing for the whole spiritual growth. People saying that they need to do everything by themselves are not affirming that love is union, that love is oneness and that there is no individual self in love. They do not acknowledge that there is a union of all selves merging to create a transcendent self, to experience the divine.

Without that union there is no love. Being selfish and say, "I can do this by myself", sends us back to a cultural dysfunction of me, you, I, this, that. Many people who work with me do not understand it and fall into this trap. They declare, "Tony said we should not be dependent so I need to be self sufficient and move away from this sense of love that I have for you and find it elsewhere", but it is not about stopping that love or finding it elsewhere. It is about expanding it and embracing it.

The challenge is to find a humble space in between fragile dependency and overconfident self-reliance?

Exactly. Dependency sounds so negative, but in the end, we all depend on each other. That is the law of nature. Without the trees we cannot breath. Without the soil, the tree does not grow. Without the sun, there is no photosynthesis. It is a cycle of union. To say that dependency is an aspect of the mind, to judge things as good and bad or as separate, individualistic and dualistic, is a sign of a sickness of the mind, not of healing.

Back to the teaching and to the teacher/student relationship. A student might have projections – temporary and unavoidable – on the teacher but expectations seem to be much more problematic. How do you deal with that other process?

Well, projections are not just on the teacher, they are on everything. This is actually part of our whole personal development, of how we sense ourselves as an ego person within a very egocentric culture. For example, we can project onto our relationship, onto our partner in the relationship, onto our children and onto parts of ourselves, creating certain expectations of how we need to be or what we need to do. We can also think about what is expected of ourselves from within, from ourself as a person, rather than from the outside and from other people expecting certain things from us. Projections are a natural consequence of the ego being out of balance with a more harmonious reference point. They express unbalance and a lack of connection with ourself. They are a link to connect to everything that we perceive as outside of us. This is why projections are not just on the teacher, for most human beings they are in every aspects of life. The teacher having become part of the personal relationship of that person, projections are just a natural consequence of that relationship.

Expectations on the teacher are, as you say, more problematic because with those expectations comes a certain judgement built into them. Expectations vary from person to person but most often they are that the teacher needs to be kind, to morally follow certain rules, to do things in a certain way, to smile at the right time and other such things. When those expectations are not fulfilled, then it is problematic because many things can happen. It is difficult to generalise because every person has such a different experience but usually what happens is that our judgement and our expectations are not being fulfilled.

The judgement that goes with this becomes, "The teacher is not real", "The teacher does not love me", "The teacher does not fulfil my expectations so maybe I need to find another teacher", "The teacher is not giving me advice, he is remaining silent, so maybe he does not know anything", "The teacher is acting in a way that is not really teacher-like", etc. These judgements do not come from the essence of the work but from a subjective perspective about what is going on. A teacher can remain quiet because it is not necessary to say anything but that could be perceived as a rejection or as a lack of love. Then that becomes very problematic because it builds a whole set of predetermined dynamics.

These dynamics are a problem not for the teacher but for the relationship. The fact is that as soon as there is judgement, a moralistic judgement or any judgement from other perspectives, you bring other aspects of yourself into the relationship. You can bring emotional aspects of yourself into the relationship that overtake the sense of work that needs to happen. When emotions get in the way, it is just like in a relationship, you get angry all of a sudden and that takes over the space, controlling and filling it. That anger puts everything out of perspective.

If someone gets angry in the relationship with a teacher because his or her expectations are not met, or are not completed in some sort of way – which is usually the case when the teacher is really working deeply with the person – it can be problematic if it is not seen for what it is. I personally do my best not to encourage people working with me to have expectations, as this is not the way I work. Usually expectations are more at stake in other traditions because there is a whole in depth philosophy to have this idea of a teacher/student relationship, which I talked about previously.

You often mention during retreats that you are working energetically with people. Knowing that someone does something for you, cares for you, and is continuously helping you, definitely creates a good feeling because whatever people do or don't do, they think the work is still going on for their personal benefit. Couldn't it also induce people to have at least slight expectations making them fall back into a world of ideas rather than experiencing the present moment?

Of course. This is very true. However, in that sense, everything can create an expectation. The essence of working energetically with a person means that the veil, the darkness or the mask that stops them from directly experiencing what is there – the depth and the essence – is being worked on energetically. The energetic work happens on many levels, not just by the teacher – and I am only using the word "teacher" because you are using it – but the teacher might do things. It is a bit like a masseuse for example who rubs certain points in the body that are blocking the energy from flowing to the head such as tense shoulders. It is not so much that there is an expectation that the masseuse or the teacher is doing anything. They are undoing and removing what does not need to be there. They are removing something or emptying a cup that is full.

Actually, all the work is uniquely done by the person individually rather than someone doing something from the outside. Yet it is difficult to understand because if our whole process of thinking and understanding the world is in a certain way, then of course we will have an expectation. We will have that expectation no matter what. It will be an expectation that we put on ourselves. It is not just coming from the outside. This may be, "I need to do things in a certain way. I expect that if I do this in a certain way, then my expectations are fulfilled".

That logic of the teacher doing this work for someone can be extended to many dimensions. In the end, maybe it is good to have an expectation because then we see that this expectation in itself is a hindrance to coming back to the present. That hindrance becomes more obvious because the teacher will work with that expectation if it is internalised and not conscious. If the expectations are just projected within oneself and not seen as mirrored from the inside, then it is more subtle and more vague, therefore not so easy to sense.

Human beings are human beings. We are obviously not perfect in our actions in everyday life. We have our faults and it is not that we need to be angelic or perfect in the spiritual work. What matters is to see that imperfection for what it is and then to drop it because it is of no use anymore. That can be in the relationship with the teacher, in relationship with yourself, with the world, with your partner or with your child.

If we think about Krishnamurti, when people where looking for answers he would systematically question this attitude as submissive, trying to express with words what is beyond words, and always inviting the person to be his or her own mentor. He was very critical and, somewhat like Socrates, always interrogating people's intentions and expectations. On the other hand, other teachers may be doing too much for their students, which invites them to be a little bit passive. As for you, it seems that as a teacher you keep saying things – providing words – and inviting people to work on their spiritual awareness, but you also clearly state that you work on – and maybe for – them. This seems a very special aspect of your teaching.

Yes. Words are not enough. Krishnamurti has used the mind to make the person conscious of the situation. He worked very much with words. Ramana Maharshi also did that, but not only. I think this is a very good and interesting way but from my experience, I have found that people's minds are too clever. If you delve deeply into the mind, you will find that, at some point, the mind circles around insanity. In fact, what seems logical is rarely what drives people. There is much more. Human beings are much more complex than just logic, than emotions, or even than what they think drives them. In certain situations, people will act in ways that they do not even recognise.

There is so much to a human being and many spiritual teachers who use words are aware of this. I personally have found that what is essential is not to go from the outside, for example the mind, and trying to convince the mind that its insanity or craziness needs to be transformed. What is essential is rather to go directly to the essence of the person, to go to the divine aspect of the person, to transcend that madness from within that space of transcendence.

To reach that point, we need to engage in the energy work that I refer to in the retreats. It is like playing music. I am not a musician so I am talking from my limited understanding of music but it is like playing one tone, or even chanting a sound in a certain way. That tone creates an ambience that harmonises everything around. That sound reverberates everywhere including into the person who becomes in tune with it without even being aware because somehow that tune is natural to their body. Therefore their body recognises that tune and expresses it in the same way. It is playing some of these musical instruments that have a very pure tone. It is recognised musically in many things, even in the body. This brings us to a certain awareness that is very difficult without that bridge. If we were to explain to the person, "Well, there is a tone and you need to do this", it would be understandable, but it is much easier to go directly to that source and to work with the person. That is energetic work. This is why when people say, "What do you mean by energetic work?", it is almost impossible to put it into words because it is so beyond words. Even if you use words, it would just distort what I am doing so I normally say, "It can only be understood through the experience".

This is one of the things that probably makes a big difference in the work that I do. The energetic work is tuning the body to recognise itself again, to mirror its transcendence in the external word, in action. The mind and the emotions that are the external world then tune into this whole situation and the space expands into a space where there is not even a logical understanding, where transcendence happens. Just like music, there is simply knowing, "This is fantastic!".

As a teacher you are not supposed to have projections on people working with you but you may have your own expectations about the work they could do. If so, what are they?

I do not really have projections on people. I am not saying "I do not because I am better", I say it because my reference point is so much in the moment, that in the moment I am really addressing the situation. For one moment I might be seeing a certain situation but it does not hold for the next moment. The projection means that projection has a continuous reference. It goes from this moment to the future because you think about the future and sometimes even about the past. If you do not have that sense of future/past, and you just see the person in that moment, it is totally different, although it does not mean that you do not see the situation in a way that could be understood. On the other hand, expectations means that you are not seeing the person as they are because you are expecting something different from what they are. You expect the person to be something or perhaps to change something.

If you want people to do something for themselves, is it not an expectation?

I do not have expectations because in the end, I trust that the person and his or her journey has no beginning and no end. There is no place to reach. There is no place that is not good to be and no place that is better to be in. This is philosophical of course. The major thing is actually the expectations that people have of other people around me when they are working with me on other people. For example, if within the context of a group around me, a person is seen as very highly developed, or simply because she has worked with me for eight years, there is an expectation on that person.

Although the expectation does not come from me but from the group around me, it may seem like it is sometimes coming from me and because I do have ideas of what needs to happen, it could be confused as an expectation. For instance, one of the ideas could be that the person slowly drops her attachment to the ego and to what the ego selfishly wants for itself, and rather embrace much more a sense of service to humanity. It is not so much an expectation but for me that is where we all are heading, so I deeply hope for people to reach that point more quickly than slowly.

If, however, I see selfish behaviour, I can react quite strongly and, some people say, quite strangely, because I do not believe that a teacher needs to sit back and do nothing, being like an impersonal object in the background. I believe a teacher needs to be interactive and relating to people on the level where the experience is. He or she needs to be reflecting and mirroring what is happening at that point, rather than appearing to be higher or more divine than the situation is. If there are certain things going on, I will interact on a human level because this is why I am here, to interact not just on the transcendent level, or on the energetic level, but to be a human being in relationship with that person as a human being. This is why people say I am very much a trickster. It is not that I am a trickster consciously thinking that I need to trick this person. It is more that my reference points are so difficult to understand that it seems like I am changing my mind from one moment to another, or saying one thing and the next moment what I am saying contradicts what I said ten minutes ago.

People like to have something that is more linear and more able to fit into the normal logical way of thinking. That is not how I function, so then of course certain people think that I am tricking or interacting in a way that is confusing, but it is never confusing if you really go deeply into it. There is always a picture that reveals itself where one sees very clearly that there is a whole situation behind that. Yet our normal reactions are immediate and normally colour the deeper connections we have to the person.

Often I will say something and it will create a whole way of thinking and a whole process but it will only be clear later. It is not that I am doing this deliberately. It is just the situation because I believe one needs to be available on a fundamental level for that person, unlike in some Hindu traditions where *gurus* or spiritual teachers seem to be totally out of reach, almost intangible. I can speak about very mundane and silly things to people and continue to speak about it while turning it around on some level so that it has another dimension. This is so subtle that it is not obviously clear or does not appear spiritually profound in that moment for that person.

Learning & Experiencing Knowledge

Some people involved in spirituality think it is related to esotericism. This is the case for Gnostics for example who consider that there is a special secret knowledge, not open to everybody unless you are initiated. What is your position on this approach?

Of course there is knowledge that is hidden. Everything is hidden on one level. If you speak about meditation, it is just a word until you practice. The practice makes that knowledge available to you so that you can evaluate it and see if it makes sense to you, but prior to the practice, which is a form of initiation, it was hidden. Meditation is a type of initiation into realising aspects of yourself that are not commonly or easily understood. Yet, to say that it is hidden, in the sense that it is a secret and only available for a few, seems very strange to me.

All spirituality, just like anything in life, is hidden on some level, just like our emotions. We get to know our emotions better once we explore them on a different level. If we go into a relationship, we discover parts of ourselves that we did not know we had. So emotions can also be esoteric on one level, but that does not mean that there are hidden secrets that need some special school to unlock them. It is only hidden because our consciousness as a human being is unable to access the information that is available and not hidden, so the key is not a secret. The key is yourself, and that is not hidden. Yourself is who you are, so it is about knowing yourself more. It is the knowledge that has to be open rather than anything else.

As to esoteric knowledge, I have heard of the word "esoteric" but I get confused because I do not really understand it. If it means that knowledge is only available for a privileged few, I would disagree. Knowledge is actually available to everybody because we are all the same, but if it means that certain initiations need to take place, then I would agree on some level. There are certain initiations that need to happen for us to understand things that are too complex to grasp without the right keys, without the right doors being open, but those keys are not secret, those keys are there. We just do not see them. So esoteric knowledge? I do not know if there is an esoteric knowledge. I think all knowledge is available, and actually more available to us than we know.

It is in my opinion totally wrong to think of spirituality as esoteric. All spirituality is available, even if you do not understand it, because it is registered in our psyche, in our essence. People used to tell me that in ancient Egypt there were esoteric initiations. I grew up in Egypt and I had a feeling that I was connected to a lot of its culture, not the mundane culture but the historical culture of Egypt. People say there were initiations in the pyramids. I think they were not so much initiations but rather trials to see if people were ready to understand a certain type of knowledge. If you were not ready to understand then it would make no sense. It is a bit like a parable that would seem like a foreign language.-

An initiation that is part of all spiritual schools is to see how you deal with fear. By creating certain emotional states or mental states, does fear stop you from perceiving knowledge or are you able to overcome fear in a way that it becomes part of your journey to deeper knowledge, rather than stopping you? If so, the fear becomes a gateway to something beyond yourself. In all spiritual schools, fear was not seen as negative but as natural. It was seen as something that once initiated into its power, you would transcend. The mechanisms of fear then gave you strength to continue on the path, beyond what is normally possible for human beings, because we have certain characteristics that take over and stop us from moving far into the depths of the unknown. Perhaps that is what the esoteric knowledge is, just something that is not accessible in everyday life and in the everyday perception that we have as human beings.

The way I teach, nothing is really hidden. It is all there. It is just that people do not want to see what is there because there are other things that take priority. It is natural for instance, that people have desires and attachments to certain characteristics. If that is very strong, then of course what is there becomes not so obvious. If people are attached to their jealousy or sense of wanting to be better, bigger, more powerful or more important, the inflated ego takes over. Then, as the attachment to the ego is strong, knowledge is of course not that easy to see. Most of the knowledge that I work with requires us to go beyond that attachment, beyond the ego, and beyond the sense of importance of the self. It requires going beyond being separate from everything else, from the world and from the union we have with it.

If we forget that union, which is in essence forgetting love, then it is very difficult to understand knowledge. Knowledge can only be understood from that loving space, from that connection. That connection means that we have to drop certain facades and certain aspects of ourselves that our culture, our genetics and even our personal sense of self, create as a survival mechanism. This means that we have to go beyond a lot of what most people do not even think of going beyond, because it is so obvious that everyone else is doing this.

In America for example, the driving force is success, in a general cultural understanding of things. Success, doing well, getting good grades, getting a good job, getting money, surviving in a material sense... That is a cultural expectation that then becomes part of our personality, as we are part of that culture. The driving force often means competition and seeing yourself as better than others, or trying to make yourself better than others, so that you win in what appears to be this competitive world. This of course is very far removed from the spiritual path. We then have to drop a lot of things to be able to go to a space where knowledge is available. But it is available and free for everyone to touch.

I find it a bit humorous when people say that you have to be initiated into different schools of knowledge. In Reiki for example, just to take one of the more popular kind of schools of knowledge, you have to be initiated onto different levels and different methods. In the end, I find that becomes a little bit childish because it is as if the initiation is going to take you there without any work. For me, it is the work, meaning the understanding of how to move beyond egocentric characteristics, that really takes you to the space where initiation happens by itself. Therefore there is no need to be initiated because you initiate your consciousness to a deeper level of understanding.

The fact that some people may speak about "secret initiations", whatever these people have kept hidden from the masses for whatever reasons, is to me coming from an egocentric sort of, "I know more than you" space. That is actually not possible as everyone has the same knowledge. It is just that most people, because they are too busy, do not know they have that knowledge.

Do you consider yourself having been initiated? If yes, how?

In regards to some esoteric schools, initiation practices are not that silly because many people had to hide from the masses and had to hide certain things from these masses just to survive. To take an example, in South America where shamanism was part of everyday life prior to the Europeans' coming, something had to change. Although it did not happen completely, people had to express a change, because expectations were put on them, otherwise they would face a lot of problems. Then you may say that, at least where Western culture was very strong, shamanic cultures got influenced in a way that made them become secret and hidden.

Shamanism is part of everyday life. It is not secret nor special. It is something else. It is like growing crops or building a house. It is just another aspect of that culture, which perhaps became hidden as a way to survive the dominant culture that was happening at that point. In this way, I believe that the shamanic world-view and principles are not hidden because they are something that everyone in these cultures grows up understanding.

That is understandable everywhere where there were stronger religions that felt threatened by other understandings of things, like in Europe where this was the case. We know that during the dark ages and across history, the dogmatic element within the Christian culture physically killed people who believed otherwise than what it dictated. In the Middle East it was also and still is the same in some places. Unlike India, it is a very conformist kind of society where you really have to hide certain things. I grew up in Egypt and my feeling is that the Sufis and Coptic Christians, for example, had to hide a lot of their knowledge and had to become more integrated into the Muslim culture as a way to make their practice acceptable. I believe that a lot of that profound knowledge was there prior to the Muslim culture and was mixed in to become what it is today. Many of the rituals that may have been secret, as Gurjieff and others have explored, were so because if people spoke about them, they would not make sense to the surrounding culture and people could be prosecuted or killed. You had to hide something because if you went around and said, "Everything is divine and beautiful", for a fundamentalist understanding of what God or the Divine is, that might be sacrilegious.

Misunderstandings mean that people become less open, but I do not believe that those aspects are not open to everyone. They were open to me. Some people say that I was initiated into secret knowledge in South America through the rituals with *ayahuasca* and *San Pedro*. I would say that I was not. It is not secret. It is very obvious. The belief that we have to do certain things or certain changes and conform in certain ways to open up to those secrets is one of the reasons why I hesitate to identify myself with anything, because then people wrongly believe that you need to change who you are.

For me the initiation was opening more to the reality of myself, of my feelings, of my body, of my relationship to nature and of my understanding of the world rather than getting to know something that was passed down as secret knowledge. The knowledge actually came from me – "me" meaning the aspect of myself that is transcendent, beyond the ego – rather than from someone else, from a certain ritual, or by doing certain things.

I think that initiation is possible anywhere. You do not have to go to different parts of the world to initiate yourself into deeper spirituality like it is popular for people to do now. Before it was India, doing whatever with yoga and *gurus*, and today it is more in places like Peru and Nepal. People go to different places to get initiated into secrets but I think you can sit at home in the middle of New York, London, Paris or Geneva and find the same knowledge in any way that you would in South America in the middle of the jungle. Was I initiated into anything? I would say no because it implies that initiation has a certain ritual and secrecy. Of course, I underwent certain things that happened in the context of the culture I was in but it demanded more of me than of that culture. It was an invitation for me to *do* certain things rather than to *follow* certain things.

The cultural aspects were not so prevalent in your experiences?

Absolutely not because I have always been a rebel in a way, not wanting to identify with certain things. One of the major problems in Zen Buddhism for me is that I found it to be a little bit limiting. Buddhism is less limiting than any other philosophy but it is still limiting in the sense that you have to chant, or sit, or do certain things in a certain way that I felt was absolutely not part of understanding the world. They were perhaps created for a reason, but not an important enough reason to follow them if you do not feel they are giving you anything deeper than just understanding a different way of doing things.

For instance, in Zen Buddhism, to sit down and meditate is not essential, but it has become what people understand of Zen Buddhism. It is *zazen*, which means sitting down quietly and meditating. In fact, the Roshis or the Zen masters will let you know that the most profound aspect of meditation happens not by doing something but by doing nothing, which is quite impossible to do if you are trying to meditate. The doing nothing can happen simply by walking in a Zen garden and looking at the moon, realising that there is nothing to do because all you have to do is look at the beautiful light of the moon and let that come through deeper than it ever did in your life. That light then opens up the space of knowledge where you understand what "doing nothing" means. Then your mind stops for a moment – which is the essence of Zen Buddhism – and you discover a space that is normally not perceived because you have been too busy in the mind to access that space.

To create a culture around how to do that all of a sudden limits that possibility. I believe it is more important to be unique as a person and to go deeper into that uniqueness rather than to identify with the culture. I do certain things that initiate people – if we use the word "initiate" – and that is of course working with the energy points in the body such as the pituitary and pineal glands. I often mention this aspect in my work. These glands regulate and create the physical mental and energetical space to understand aspects of ourselves that are difficult if our body is overwhelmed by the toxins of the ego or of daily life – I am going around in a circle but there is a thread to it.

Working with the pituitary and the pineal glands, which are located in the brain and connected to the third eye, is aimed at opening up that seeing but it is not an initiation by specific things. It is an initiation by bringing consciousness to that part of the body as a valid part of your perception, as much as the mind is or the senses are, like touching or tasting. Most people have forgotten that because it is not at all part of our daily evolution to grow in this modern world, but of course in shamanism and in Zen Buddhism, opening up the energy points in the body is very much part of what is important.

For me, the key is the third eye because I believe that is the point that helps you to see. By seeing, by personally uniquely seeing something, knowledge becomes trustworthy and more able to be seen as real enough to do the practice, to create the possibility of seeing more in that way. Without seeing, we just remain faithful to what other people have said or what other people expect you to experience by doing certain things they say. That works for a while but a problem with a lot of New Age spiritualities that are practised today, especially in the West, is that we try and then we give up because nothing, or very little of what we expect, really happens.

We try something else and then again something else and it becomes like the supermarket of spirituality where we take a little bit of this, and a little bit of that, and we put it together. It is very interesting, of course, because as a culture, we are bored of the mundane. This way has plenty of interesting thoughts and food for the imagination but it is a waste of time. This is why I move away from what people label as the New Age because I find it quite superficial. It is not a judgement, it is simply what I have noticed as I have of course been exposed to a lot of it.

Looking for another path or learning another philosophy, or doing something else, is just adding more and more information. This endless approach is very different to what happens in traditions where sincerity and humility is your spiritual work, opening up to the knowledge that is within. Libraries of books are useful in the beginning because they help people to extend beyond limited ideas, but to go into them in depth for a very long time becomes like entertainment. I find a lot of people do not even open up by reading these books.

They read and they want to read a little bit more to find a little bit more, and ... they want to read a bit more. Then they feel spiritual, because when they read a book, their mind is somehow on a journey of spiritual development. They read about Buddha and then they become Buddha for a few days but the actual practice is lost because it is not real enough. I feel the practice is more real in South America for example where people, although they do not have access to books, have access to daily experiences that invite them to express themselves in the deeper sense. Ultimately, what is provoked is your depth. For example, if your neighbour has a problem that he cannot resolve without your help but you do not have any money and do not have enough to give him, it is amazing how it brings out the kindness and connection that people have missed here in the West, where all they want is more.

They have the material, they have the food, they have the house, they have the schooling, and now they want to do the same with spirituality. They want everything for themselves. It is a type of egotistical spirituality, where you are trying to grab everything. This takes you away from spirituality because spirituality is love and love is the practice of humility and opening up to all aspects of life. It is not getting more out of a book, becoming a Buddha for a few days, or dressing up in Indian clothes because you somehow have developed into a more spiritual person...

I am going further away now from the third eye but for me, what I was saying before, the pituitary and pineal glands and the third eye are important because they help you to see yourself. That is spirituality, when you see yourself on all layers, as an emotional person, as a physical person, as a spiritual person, and as an energetic person. As an emotional person, opening up is part of the work that happens when the third eye and the pituitary gland is activated. This is done through love. If you feel it, your heart becomes softer, gentler, and drops what is hard around it. Then that whole space creates an opening up in the emotional body. That in itself changes the dynamics in the pituitary and pineal glands, which then open up the energy centres that were blocked before because emotions did not allow that movement.

Once the energy starts moving, we realise that we are much more spiritually able to sense things than we were normally able to do before. We have sensations of people. We can sense them without even emotionally attaching to their programs. We sit in a room and, all of a sudden, we know that the person there is upset or angry or unhappy. Sometimes we can even perceive things from far away, from not even being in the same room. We can all of a sudden know that something is wrong with a person, although she lives in America and you are in Europe. The energetic perception moves to the spiritual world that is close to that point. We begin to perceive things that we do not normally see. We see the trees, the earth, the animals and the actions in a different light than just from the egocentric senses of the physical body.

To reach this state of perception by opening the third eye, the Hindu spirituality provides *gurus*, disciples, practices, steps for development, exercises, and work. Yet steps for development imply

that thoughts are involved. Then a process, a projection of oneself in the future takes place and the person is not in a full here and now state of attention. Where do you locate your understanding and teaching regarding this point?

In my opinion, to say that in a philosphy there are steps or techniques for spiritual development is often missing the real point. Let us look at the yoga tradition for example, I would say that to believe that following certain steps in yoga means that certain things will happen is totally misunderstanding the essence of the teaching. If I understand the term "guru" correctly, he/she is someone who moves out of the space of darkness, but perhaps it is now used just as a name, as any person who teaches yoga may term themselves as a guru.

I would think that a guru would only do things that are valid for a person following his or her teaching rather than follow a tradition that provides certain steps. The validity of the achievement will then only depend on the person rather than on the tradition. The actions and the steps suggested for one person may be totally different for another person. If not, I would say the guru is caught up in dogmatism. Without judging, it is obvious that many gurus have become more like priests in the Hindu tradition. They preserve the culture, help with the births, deaths and marriages, and fulfil a role rather than break the cycle of illusion for people. They are just part of the whole institutional structure of Hinduism.

As for me, I follow no steps. The steps are decided totally by the person. I follow the person's deeper sense of what is needed rather than a system. There are certain things that I do that could be classified into a system if you want to classify anything. For instance, I look at the body as very important, the goal being to create a healthy body and one of the ideas I speak about is to become vegetarian. I do not say that you need to do this, but I suggest that it is a very interesting way to become more perceptive. Yet to say that by having a healthy body means one would become more spiritual is totally misunderstanding my work and to imply that being vegetarian is to be more spiritual than those who are not vegetarian is just a game. That in itself is not what creates spirituality because spirituality is beyond that and beyond any obvious steps.

So the teaching, as you conceive it, can only be personal?

Yes. It is totally personal and there are certain things that happen. One of them is the opening of the third eye but there are not any general steps that take you to that point, as that depends on the individual. There is a certain way where that third eye can open more easily for some people but it is not always the case because every person is different. For some people for example, the third eye and the perception will open because of what I call "Grace". I use this word to mean that you are just born that way. This is what happened to me.

I was born with perceptions that were not at all part of what my brothers experienced, even though we were brought up in the same way. I was not treated in a better or a different way, so that perception was not initiated by anyone, it just happened. I call that "Grace" and it happens to many people. It can happen when you are a child or when you are forty or fifty. All of a sudden you see things, your third eye opens, and you become able to work in a way that is unusual. You become more spiritual, your behaviour changes, your focus changes, your sense of what is important changes, and your life changes. This has nothing to do with self-development. It is just a sudden thing that happens.

Certain amazing strong experiences happened to me at various times as I mentioned before, when I was a child, at seven-eight, at fifteen and twenty-seven. Some of those that happened when I was twenty-seven were related to certain factors outside, but not the ones that happened in my childhood. At that early time, they were just things that I would call "points of initiation" happening by Grace. I believe everyone has the possibility of opening these points. For some people it is important not to open them too quickly as it is not healthy. This is a bit of a contradiction because of course, what you are opening up to is love and beauty, but a lot of people have parts of themselves that they need to go through before that can happen. This is why we often have to go through situations in life that teach us, prepare us and open us for an experience later on in life.

With love for example, we often have to fall in love with different people to understand the depth of love and what it really means. Then at one point, hopefully, we will meet someone and there will be no doubt. We will be initiated into a sudden, dramatic and clear understanding of what loves means in that moment. We will open up to the person completely. That may be quite different from our previous experiences where we just explored seduction, attraction, physical aspects, or even emotional aspects of love. This can happen for some people when they are very young. It can also happen when they are much older.

I have read stories of people who have not had a relationship for a long time but at sixty-five they meet someone and they really understand love for the first time, its depth and completeness. I am bringing something more practical so it makes sense but it is the same with the opening of the third eye to see things. It is happening all the time. Every aspect of our life opens us up on some level but with so little manifestation that we do not notice that it is a big thing. Yet, at some point, that big thing becomes a dramatic experience and we open up very quickly. It seems like something is happening, which may be the third eye opening or the heart understanding something completely and wonderfully profound in a way that was not possible before.

Can there be any way back once you open the third eye?

No. There is no way back.

Is the opening gradual?

No. It is not gradual because you are not going through a process. You are coming home to yourself. Once you see a part of yourself, it is like having experienced the taste of love. It may be a distant memory once that love is further away from our experience, but the heart never forgets it. It is never forgotten in the depth of our experience. It may seem to some people that they go further away from that opening of the third eye but it is just because they have drifted back into the mundane. Not all aspects of ourselves have drifted, only a part and that part is our daily survival mechanism. To think that the opening is gradual is forgetting the whole essence of the way I work. In my approach, you are not trying to get anywhere. There is nowhere to go. There is no knowledge to try to find anywhere: the knowledge is here, whether you realise it or not. It has always been here. It is just that you are accessing it slowly up to a point where you realise that it is here.

Your point is that spiritual awareness is not about knowing something better, exercising something through practice, doing this or that, but it is to simply take off some layers?

Precisely. Peeling off the layers. This is where what I do is different from some belief systems because it is not about going somewhere, or slowly becoming better or more spiritual, it is about becoming who you are.

The work is to clean and to unlearn, instead of learning...

That is exactly what it is. This is where people get confused because in the process of unlearning, we let go of a lot of rubbish, a lot of things that take our space and once you let them go consciously, it becomes confusing because sometimes we get distracted by what we are letting go. We are usually dependent on family dynamics for example, meaning that the family we grew up in was dysfunctional, which is normal for people to an extreme or to a minor degree. When I say dysfunctional, I am not blaming the family, I just mean that instead of the family supporting the child to grow spiritually – not only physically or educationally – there was something lacking, like a clear demonstration of gratitude and love towards the child in all aspects. Then the child starts to project that lack into other things.

Normally the projection is into education, when, at least for many people, there are expectations on the child to qualify and become this or that. The world is then supposed to give the person the love that was lost when he or she was growing up. That sense of projection is actually one of the most dangerous things that happen during this cleaning out of rubbish inside of us. When we work on spiritual parts of ourselves, we know that the projections of getting a good degree or a nice house are irrelevant because we realise that does not truly give us what we want.

Often we start to project onto things. We also may project that once we find the right partner we will access the knowledge inside of our heart, that because of the relationship our heart will open. Then we start projecting a lot of expectations onto our partner, in the hope that this is the space that he or she will create for us. Of course, it is like anything else, that space is outside of ourself so we are not feeling or do not open up to the parts that need to be explored more deeply. Therefore we start to project onto the teacher – and this is usually where it becomes a problem for me – and who or what we think the teacher is. Then we have certain expectations and certain things that we want to happen in a certain sequence with the teacher, which again become quite difficult if the teacher is totally beyond those expectations and not wanting to fulfil them.

In Hinduism for example, it is not a problem because you have the *guru*/disciple relationship. The disciple of course is projecting this father figure onto the teacher, expecting somehow that, by fulfilling whatever in the spiritual relationship, the blessing of the *guru* will create an opening leading to the space of bliss, or probably a space of womb-like feelings, where everything is all right and there are no problems. Of course for me, whenever there is a projection, I work on that. It is not that I accept that projection, I actually throw it back very strongly at the person. This complicates things because usually *gurus* like to be *gurus*, they like to have their feet kissed and their egos pampered.

Sometimes I let people do that for a little while and then I turn it around very quickly to help them see that this is what they are doing, but to go beyond this does not mean that they need to stop doing it. If they stop, they will sometimes project onto something else. They simply need to transcend doing it. Some say, "Well, Tony is a terrible teacher. He really is not a teacher at all!", and find another teacher who accepts their projections in a better way. It is sad because once you get to that point, you are really working very deeply. You are working at a point where you can transform the essence of who you are, the core of who you are, so that you no longer project to the external but you start working with the internal. This is very frightening as it means that we go into the space of the unknown, into a place with no boundaries. We start exploring a space that has no maps, no territories or no accepted norms. Then, what I aim to do is to strengthen the heart and the love of the person.

Through love, people can expand their wisdom and understanding to the points that somehow seem totally dark, scary and difficult. They can understand for instance that the parents did not show enough of the love wanted by the child unintentionally and that they are just human beings. Then your love expands to have compassion for humanity. Your compassion becomes your driving force rather than your judgement or sense of lack, which create projections on the outside. It is a wonderful thing when we get to that point, because we then create a sense of real love. We touch upon our essence, our deep profound love for people around us.

When we develop that sense of non-judgement and non-attachment to projection, we can create a space where the atmosphere becomes open to the type of energy that is flowing from everywhere. That is an invisible energy for most people but it is the energy of love, which is beyond personal. It is transpersonal or transcends the personal love. Yet, it is physical. You can sense it. When we are open to it, this comes in the sense of a specific frequency of light, which is quite visible to the eyes but in truth it is to the third eye. It also comes to a specific vibration that is the essence beyond it, a sound behind the light that initiates people into change. This light is changing the whole structure of our being.

It can be revealed when you are sitting and learning from nature or from a spiritual teacher who is working on that level, beyond the teacher/student relationship. He or she is working just because he or she is accessing that light, that sound, the mystical knowledge that is everywhere. That specific frequency of light goes deep into the energy structures of the body. You feel better, you feel lighter, you feel happier and you feel that you are touching the divine aspect of yourself, but it is not the teacher. The teacher is just doing what you are doing and because you are doing this together, you are accessing what is there together. It seems like that space with the teacher is what is creating that reality, yet it is actually you who are doing that. People do not like that responsibility because they think that of course, it cannot be them who are doing that, it must be something or someone else. Therefore once that experience happens, they project again onto other aspects outside of themselves to try to find that connection.

You propose exercises to stimulate the pituitary and pineal glands, to open the third eye but is contemplation an exercise in itself? If exercises are putting us into a space and time process, contemplation supposes that IT is right there...

It is a good question because often after working with me, people go home to their life and then wonder, "How do we carry on this work in a practical sense?". With yoga, there are exercises that you can do and there are specific methods of meditation. What to do? I always emphasise that the physical body needs to be part of everything. It is not just the mind that is contemplation. It is exercise, physical exercise.

The number one meditation or exercise I suggest for people – but they do not know that I am suggesting this to them – is walking, if you can walk of course, because it is the most natural thing for people to do. It is also essential because it activates all the body organs and all the energy centres much better than any physical exercise that have been devised by humans, including yoga.

When we walk in nature, which is the best place to walk, walking by the beach or near the forest, just to pick up the elements that are more harmonious than in a city, we stimulate the pituitary and pineal glands. Indeed, every step that we take moves the coccyx and the bottom part of the spine. As we move, that moves. Anyone who has studied physiology, knows that the spine has to move in a certain way as you move. Not running but walking! That movement then stimulates the cranium, which in turn stimulates and massages these two glands in the brain so every step that you take is like practising different types of yoga. This is why the native people used to walk a lot, whatever they did, as a form of meditation.

They have been considered primitive as they could not afford to be in cars but actually they walked because they felt good doing so. I am sure anyone who walks a lot will also feel the same. You walk and you feel better. To me that is meditation: something that makes you feel better. In the end if meditation does

You propose exercises to stimulate the pituitary and pineal glands, to open the third eye but is contemplation an exercise in itself? If exercises are putting us into a space and time process, contemplation supposes that IT is right there...

It is a good question because often after working with me, people go home to their life and then wonder, "How do we carry on this work in a practical sense?". With yoga, there are exercises that you can do and there are specific methods of meditation. What to do? I always emphasise that the physical body needs to be part of everything. It is not just the mind that is contemplation. It is exercise, physical exercise.

The number one meditation or exercise I suggest for people – but they do not know that I am suggesting this to them – is walking, if you can walk of course, because it is the most natural thing for people to do. It is also essential because it activates all the body organs and all the energy centres much better than any physical exercise that have been devised by humans, including yoga.

When we walk in nature, which is the best place to walk, walking by the beach or near the forest, just to pick up the elements that are more harmonious than in a city, we stimulate the pituitary and pineal glands. Indeed, every step that we take moves the coccyx and the bottom part of the spine. As we move, that moves. Anyone who has studied physiology, knows that the spine has to move in a certain way as you move. Not running but walking! That movement then stimulates the cranium, which in turn stimulates and massages these two glands in the brain so every step that you take is like practising different types of yoga. This is why the native people used to walk a lot, whatever they did, as a form of meditation.

They have been considered primitive as they could not afford to be in cars but actually they walked because they felt good doing so. I am sure anyone who walks a lot will also feel the same. You walk and you feel better. To me that is meditation: something that makes you feel better. In the end if meditation does not make you feel good, or makes you feel worse, then it is not working. When most people walk, they feel very good because it not only opens the pituitary and pineal glands, but the entire spine and all the organs are also being stimulated. As you walk you stimulate your kidneys, your liver, you breathe in more deeply and so you also stimulate the lungs. All this for me is working with the temple that our body is.

That creates the space where we can allow what I was speaking about previously: this sense of light, this mystical sound, to come in. Not just into our ears or eyes, but also into our body. What we are doing when we walk is making the physical structure of the body more conscious. I believe we are changing the DNA structure and the cellular make up of the body and walking is one exercise that is not going to impede upon any belief system that you have.

Of course there are other exercises that I speak about. I call some of the meditations that I do, "active meditation". They are based on movement as I believe that sitting down and doing nothing is not healthy. It is important to move. The Eastern concept of sitting down and meditating has created another sort of problem that we do not have in the West. I do not think that sitting down for a little while is bad, but this is where I disagree a little bit with Zen Buddhism were you sit for twenty hours and meditate – at least that was what I did, and this is another scenario. I believe that for the Western mind, and even for the modern Eastern mind, it is important to practice active meditation.

Active meditation is simply having the attention focused in a special way, actively being aware of how your attention is in that moment, as you are doing the meditation. For example, one of the meditations that I do with people in the beginning is moving the body vigourously. When doing this, if there are any remnants of anger or feelings of contraction, you become aware that those feelings are not just in the mind but also in the body. You feel where the pain and constriction are.

Some of those active meditations are quite dynamic, moving and shaking the body, and they are also quite enjoyable yet I consider them only necessary in the beginning. After a while, they may become another distraction, just like sitting down. Then certain meditations, that use not just the physical part of the body, like the active meditation does, but also the glands of the body and the energy systems of the body in a physical way, are also important.

I often encourage people to do what I call the "Whirling meditation", which is a fairly gentle active meditation. This works on many levels, which I can explain another time and it is something that is wonderful to practice a lot. After people have practised this, there are a few other similar active meditations that I also suggest. Some of them have to do with breathing and others with some postures. Most of them are quite gentle and from them, contemplation can emerge. Contemplation for me is not a formula such as, "You do this and then you do that". It is a moment where you drop everything to produce silence and be able to hear what is beyond what is distracting your mind and your body. This is quite important.

I usually do this more during times when there are important events such as the full moon, the new moon, or the equinox. It is then quite essential for the body to be still. The movement that is already happening around us in the world is so strong that, by being still, our body becomes aware of it. Of course sleeping deeply at night is another way. We can practice meditation at night if we do not have time to sit quietly during the day, simply by taking five extra minutes of our sleeping time. We just need to focus on certain things before we fall asleep, so that the dream in the sleep time becomes more than just recovering from tiredness: it becomes a part of the meditation.

Focusing on the breath is another very good way, as well as focusing on a sound, a specific sound with a picture, which helps us to go deeper into that part of the body which dreams beyond the silly dreams that are only about what has happened during the day. One of the sounds we can listen to is the sound of our own breath, not just focusing on the breath but especially as we breathe out, making the sound "*hu*", not so much as a song but just as a breath. Just "*hu*". Then breathe in and breathe out with "*hu*", and so on. That breath sound releases a lot of the stress of the day because sound works a lot with many aspects of the brain. If our mind has been occupied with many things, then the sound changes the chemistry of the thoughts. We go deeper into a relaxed state, so the body actually dreams profound dreams and goes into a state of contemplation. This is very important.

I am not saying that quiet meditation is not important but it has to be done when the body is capable of doing it rather than forced. So the Eastern idea – or at least the way I understand the way people do this – of sitting until the mind relaxes, until the thoughts stop, or until the body relaxes, is the total opposite of the way

I do things. To sit while your mind is in turmoil or when you are depressed is not good because that just invites more of the same. In that sense, we need to be more active to not invite that depression part of ourselves into the stillness.

It seems that through walking, shaking, the whirling meditation and being aware of the breath, you consider the body as a key to raise our awareness and be present to ourself. Do you mean that, in certain physical states, some specific thoughts and states of mind will arise?

Yes, because it is not so much that we need to get rid of our thoughts or to stop the thinking process. It is more important that we discover the intelligence that goes beyond thinking simply using the mind, the intelligence that uses the body, the intelligence that uses the senses, that goes beyond simple thinking. To do that, we need to activate all those aspects inside ourselves. The most obvious and easy way is through the body. It is more tangible than the mind. It is usually as tangible as the emotions. I do another type of work with emotions, but usually the body is the easiest mirror to see what is really going on beyond what you think is going on.

You may think for example that the body is aching in the back, in the shoulders, just because there is something wrong and you need to take an aspirin to get rid of the pain, but it is a message. If you have stress, which is creating pain in the shoulders, the body is mirroring something to you that you need to look at more deeply. When we listen to that, we communicate to that and of course we are doing something that relaxes and quietens the space, so then instead of signalling pain or communicating suffering, the body begins to communicate its essence, the body as it is.

We can hear how to move beyond the mind not by stopping thoughts but by simply listening to everything else. This is very important because some people believe that meditation means that you have to stop thinking. It is impossible to stop thinking; at least in the way most people think how we need to stop thinking, because the thought process is just like the breathing process. It can change and so its identity can move to different points, but it cannot stop. The thinking only stops when you physically die. To try to stop thinking is an impossible task and in the East, some people realised that it was a silly and useless approach … after sitting for twenty years. Things are much more simple. The fact is that we do not have the time in today's world to sit for twenty years and to go through roads that reach a dead end.

This is why the work that I am doing is to speed up the process, but in speeding up of the process, we speed up all the bumps. The bumps become not bigger but more painful, stronger. This is where we need to also strengthen the body as it is part of the whole process of letting go of whatever feelings that have constricted our joy and our life. We need to really let go of whatever is not important to hold on to and depletes the body's energy. When we do this work, it is important to become strong in the physical sense. It is an essential thing but being stronger in the physical sense does not mean we have to be super human. We just need to be aware that whatever we do to our physical body affects everything, not just the physical body. Once we have that awareness, it is natural to be healthier. Once we see the body as sacred, it is difficult to treat it in a way where we just want our desires to be fulfilled. Having realised there is more to the body than just taste or feelings, we go beyond these aspects.

Inside & Outside

The idea of a spirit world, full of entities constitutes a common theme for explaining the invisible world and dealing with it in many cultures. In traditional shamanic societies, spirits are very often considered as malevolent and they have to be somehow domesticated, or at least controlled, by the shaman to help humans. On the other hand, in western neoshamanism spirits are mostly considered as benevolent and ready to help if contacted. I recently spoke with Michael Harner, the American anthropologist who has created the Foundation for Shamanic Studies near San Francisco twenty-five years ago. Although he acknowledges the necessity of a spiritual life, his way to raise the awareness is not through introspection but rather through searching help somewhere "outside" and establishing contact with spirits. Michael Harner considers that everything we need to know is outside and there is nothing to find inside. Distinctively, it seems that you do not give credit to the existence of spirits. Do you consider them as only symbolic and universal creations of the mind? And if the knowledge has to be found inside, what and where is "inside"?

I am trying to understand this idea of finding everything outside. What people do in this approach is actually connecting to symbolic aspects of themselves that they believe to be on the outside. Although this is not understood, these symbolic aspects are on the inside but they are formalised and externalised on the outside and that can be a spiritual work. In the end people who have this approach rely on a belief system, but that system does not correspond to reality, it just helps them to see reality. It is a bit of a catch twenty-two because I do no want to say that what they are doing is wrong as it is helping them to create an order or sense in their life. This is better than not creating a meaning of life, but the questions then are, "What is the outside? Is the outside real? Is it as mysterious as the inside?".

What is the inside, what is the outside? Neither of them really exists! They are all concepts. Whoever says that there is an outside is focusing on an idea that the mind is creating. Saying that there is an inside is creating the same concept but in a different way. The present moment is not inside nor outside. The present moment does not have the gap or the door that says, "This is outside and this is inside!". It is just here! If you are totally here, you go deeper to the inside that is here, now in this present moment, rather than inside in an introspective way of the past or in a search that is somehow internalised. It is not really the whole world that I am exploring when I do the meditations. Some people do this because on some level they need to go inside, just like Michael Harner goes outside to catch the symbolism that is formed inside just as it is formed outside, to get deeper to this present moment.

Some people will introspect into the pain or suffering they have experienced in the past. For them that is going inside, but not for me! Again the words can be misused and understood in different ways, but to answer your question more deeply about the spirit world and the symbolism, there is no negativity for me. This idea is a totally alien concept. There is no negative in any sense. The game that the shamans play of trying to tame the negative spirits that are said to harm people is interesting because perhaps they are taming their own inner dragons. By "dragons" I mean that, like Michael Harner, they need to tame inside of themselves and they need to externalise those images as negative entities that are harming them. For me there is a very real danger when you see things in that way. That danger is that you can enter a space where schizophrenics, and people who have mental states where psychoses happen, see the outside as controlling their world. This means that you do not have the power to change things, that the power outside is stronger than you are in this experience, in this moment of who you are, and in this manifested dimension of things. Focusing on the outside, you give power to the idea that there are all these dimensions that control your experience. I do not believe that to be the case.

I believe that you are the creator of that experience. Nothing outside, not even the divine is controlling you. In this logic, some people involved in Christianity project it onto ideas such as, "It is God's will" or "It is God who is punishing me". That is another sign that somehow God is so occupied with your little world that God will come down to your level to damage your experience. This is an interesting way of seeing things, and perhaps a little immature, but I think it is better to look at things as beautiful experiences rather than to use concepts such as "negative spirits".

If everything is divine there must be a beautiful aspect that is coming to me so that I learn what that beautiful aspect is trying to enrich my present experience with, rather than push it aside, but that is what we do as individuals. We try to push everything and simplify everything to control it and make it easy for the mind to grasp so that we do not loose our sense of existence in that moment. Actually the best thing to do is precisely to loose that sense of existence in that moment because then you are that moment, which gives you a deeper understanding of everything.

At some point, Michael Harner had the project to collect numerous stories of beings and places encountered by people during what he calls the Shamanic State of Consciousness. On the basis of common experiences and encounters during the journeys in the spirit world, the goal was to cartography this "non-ordinary reality". What do you think of the idea that people from different places and culture may have the same visions?

No one ever sees the same but our cultural understanding creates a brain space where we see things in a certain way. This is why some people see angels. What they see may not be reality yet the essence is reality, but then some other people like shamans see something else. I do not know what they see but it is some other expression of angels, so it is not that we are different. The essence is the same. Only the words, the pictures, the code and the understanding of that are different. That is what creates war and this is why I am not endorsing this sort of belief system.

In the end when we realise that all of humanity has the same experience, how can we feel any negativity towards someone else if that person is not seeing things the way we see them? This is the problem that I felt in shamanism and this is why I did not really identify with that approach. People were really externalising so much, like Michael Harner as you are saying with this cartography project, that they lose the essence, the quality that a baby and a child have in their experience.

This only changes as they become socialised in a certain way. Of course socialisation is important but would it not be wonderful if everyone embraced things rather than feared them, or identified them as something that is good or not good, or categorised them in a map, or in whatever religious or spiritual formula that creates differences? Then we would recognise what is alike and what is similar, the quality that makes us humans, in spite of expressed differences. I would say that it is even dangerous to go a lot into that universe of reality because then you get caught up in ideas of spirits. The more we focus on one thing, the more the mind creates that reality to be true and makes it more real, the more we believe it to be the reality. Why?

The interesting thing is that to find answers through the help of the spirits outside, neoshamans have to close their eyes and beat the drum at a certain rhythm. During the process it is basically going inside first and then thinking to be outside. Actually, it seems that the idea to draw a cartography of the non-ordinary reality has been cancelled by the Foundation for Shamanic Studies because the experiences are so numerous and different. In a way, this cartography idea could be seen as what Carl Jung defined as the "archetype" or the "collective unconscious".

If it helps, it is OK, but there is always a danger in doing anything that is far removed from the pureness of an experience. It is just like love, it can be categorised and scientifically studied but then you have the danger of loosing the quality of that experience.

If you put it in a frame, you prevent the spontaneity. It is not alive, it does not move, it does not grow and change anymore...

Just like the philosophy of yoga in India, which I believe became categorised a little bit too much and lost the dynamic that created it.

You distanced yourself from shamanism because of this unavoidable belief system, but if there is no spirits there is no shamanism,

as they are the core of shamanism. You yourself sometimes used expressions such as "the spirit of a tree" or "the spirit of a plant". What do you mean by it?

We have to use language to explain things and words constitute a shortcut to deeper meanings. When I say "the spirit of the tree", it is not so much that there is a separate being or invisible entity that you have to find through navigating other worlds. It is more the presence, the essence, but maybe the "spirit" of tree is not a good concept. I could say the "substance of the tree", a substance that you can feel. I call it a "spirit" because for me it is like an essence. I use words a little bit differently than from the general understanding of what they mean but that may not always be so obvious...

Wisdom of the Body

There is a growing need for people in the West to have deep sensations and emotions through physical experiences. This is why many people, notably the youngest generation, get more and more involved in physical activities that may sometimes be quite dangerous. Is this drive for intense physical sensations an expression of an underlying and maybe unconscious spiritual quest? Is it also the same logic that leads a growing number of western people to want to experience the sacred plants of shamanic societies?

Yes it is. When people desire such an extreme experience, it is a little bit of a distraction from the work rather than a help for it. Often, people in meditations want to feel something strong. They do certain things like you say, jumping with a parachute or whatever people do today, to feel something. It is almost not acknowledging that on some level, people have died inside. This is in the West as well as in the East. Some parts of them have died and they are desperately searching for a method or a way to push away that death and to bring that aliveness back. Yet, the way that it is done is going back down the same road rather than seeing that this road will end up nowhere. You jump ten metres and then you have to jump a hundred metres and so on. In the end, these experiences have no value.

The value is not coming from pushing the emotions to the surface through danger or through shamanic plants or anything, but rather by allowing that sensation to disappear and finding the space that is more alive. That aliveness cannot be found by strongly pushing the emotions all the time, like young people do today through some concerts that they have where they dance for one week. Some people involve in trance dance, which makes them feel emotions very strongly. Of course the sensation is amazing but it is temporary and not relevant to a deep experience. It is temporary, just like relationships. People jump from one relationship to another, desperately seeking to bring back aliveness to the emotions, which of course works for a while...

It is always better to feel something than to not to feel anything, but it has no permanency. It is the wrong way and I do not say "wrong" to mean "bad", because the further you go down that road the more you need that. In the end, some part of you gets depressed because it recognises that it will not feed you like in the beginning. That is the problem also with plants. Many people take substances, thinking in the beginning, "Ah, it is great to take this plant because I feel so alive and I need to do this to feel alive once in a while because my life is so empty". Several people who worked with me do this also, but this is not the purpose, at least in my opinion.

The purpose is that you open another point that allows you to see why doing this is actually a waste of time and how you can move away. You can move away your energy, your attachment to desire for example, and find a new relationship, going deeper into what it means to love someone from a space that is not desire. What an experiment!

Instead of just falling into that old trap which has been conditioned into your culture and the human mind, take a step somewhere else where you are just different. You do not want to feel the emotions, you want to feel the essence of what it means to be in love with someone. Of course the mind has no concept of what that means, so you cannot find it through intellectualising or through reading a book. It is navigation inside and that navigation sometimes makes it necessary to have those strong experiences to realise that that road is a dead end. I am not criticising and saying that those experiences are not necessary. I am just saying that they will not take you where the depth of your essence is pulling you. This is showing you that this is nothing. It is another *maya*, another illusion.

Is it necessary? I think it is necessary for young people to have some of those experiences, because without them they do not understand something. It is necessary for example for young people to have relationships to recognise what a real relationship means. I am not saying this is a necessity for all people to go through but if it is there, it is necessary to experience. Otherwise you end up like some people who drive a Ferrari at the age of 65 as they were never able to live their childhood doing such things. It may look a bit silly to some, but it might be necessary, because as they did not do it when they were 20 or 30 they have to do it when they are 65 to realise that, actually the Ferrari is interesting but it is not as fast as how it feels when one is totally connected to the present moment. There is a sudden understanding that the faster one goes, the less exciting it is.

When you are 65 it is nothing. I think this is what actually Osho did but people misunderstood when he was saying that free sexuality was important to explore and to go deeper into self-understanding. What he was really saying, along with other spiritual teachers, is that it is important to complete a process rather than negating it and pretend that it does not exist. It is important to push your sense of attachment to desires to the maximum to see that on some level they are empty. It is not my way because I believe if you give that too much energy then you get lost in it and it takes you away from the essence. In any case, this is perhaps important for young people.

Is this search for intense body experiences somehow related to this idea that you often refer to of the "wisdom of the body"? What is learning through the body? Does the body know better than the mind?

The wisdom of the body is not really the same as having extreme sensations in the body but in some way it is the same because sometimes the body can experience its own intelligence through deep pain. This is what is often done through initiation, at least in native societies where a lot of pain is part of the initiation, and the body then has a way of understanding beyond the mind. You are somehow catapulted into a dimension that normally does not exist. I spoke to a mother who gave birth and her delivery was very difficult. She said it was so painful that it was like an initiation for her. She did not want this pain but somehow the body took over. It was necessary that she went through that physical sensation to get to that point where the body wisdom was awoken or at least recognised. On many levels this is a lot of the work that I do. Sometimes I push people who work close to me to the extreme.

How?

It can be physically or it can be emotionally or psychologically. Normally it is emotionally and psychologically because physically of course I have to be careful. The work can be emotionally and psychologically extreme so that the mind just stops and the emotions just say, "I can't go any further". Then the body wisdom, the temple of the essence, recognises something and takes over. I think this can also be a very dangerous thing as it does not give the right for people to be cruel or bad. I am never like this.

I always do whatever I do with love in the sense that I am asking for the person to go deeper by experiencing intensity and adding intensity to the experience. It is not to peacefully go to sleep during a meditation but to go deeper into it and feel its intensity. It is not to reach a status quo and say "everything is OK", but to really push oneself. Yet pushing sometimes does not happen from inside because people are lazy or afraid and do not know how to push. So I push.

How? It depends on each person. When I push, the idea is that the intensity awakens the experience of something that is hidden behind, like the body. Often people find that the body is amazing. They are not tired. They felt they were tired − and for sure they were tired − but the body then has an energy and a level of aliveness that was hidden and became recognised.

It is this level of awareness that is sometimes awoken during a ceremony with sacred plants...

Of course. It is very much awoken during a ceremony and during some of the rituals that were done in the old days through walking. In South America I used to ask people to walk. Part of walking was in the desert for hours and hours and people got tired. I said, "Connect to your body which is the earth" and the body would then slowly recognise another level of aliveness that is, as you say, awoken. It is amazing with children. How can children run around all day? They do it with joy and without feeling any tiredness.

If an adult tries to follow the footsteps of a little six-seven year old for one day, he will collapse and rest for a week because it is so much up and down around. You would know that if you live in a small apartment, it is very tricky keeping up with your child. You may try to follow them around but it is amazing how their body has so much energy. I say this also because it is important when people are sick. Sometimes the mind creates sickness by tricking the body to believe that only the mind occupies the space and not the body. The mind creates the sickness and the body believes that the sickness is real.

From one moment people can feel that they are dying and the next minute the body is totally transformed because there is an intelligence and energy that is amazing. Behind the sickness, the body has a lot of energy and this is why miracles happen. I am so tired sometimes when I do ceremonies because I put so much energy into all the work that I am doing that when someone comes up to me and says, "Tony you must be so exhausted", I answer, "Now that you said this, all I have to do is close my eyes". I recognise the body and I am back working. Everyone can do this. A child can do this. It is very easy. This is where yoga is very important. I think yoga, the physical yoga actually makes the body recognise this aliveness. Dancing, some of the dancing in the temple, can do this too.

People think that spiritual work has to be sitting down. For me movement is great, walking is great, dancing is great, swimming is great… I remember swimming in the ocean once and the movement brought an aliveness to the body that created a wonderful space. Sitting is actually the worst form of meditation! I think it is amazing to do moving things. This happens also in the ceremony, some people like to stand and to move. This is what I used to do more before. There was often a dance I did in the beginning of the ceremony. We danced for four or five hours and it was amazing. People could not believe how they could carry on because the whole body was really exhausted.

Would you say fatigue is felt more often when we think about it, and is somewhat a state of mind?

Fatigue is the brain, for sure.

The Initiation of Sound

You mentioned that the Zen Master was working energetically. This is also a notion you keep referring to in your teaching. Can you say more on this matter and compare what he was doing with what you do?

That is a big and complex thing. The meaning of "energetically" is difficult to put into words as energy is beyond concept. When I was working with the Zen master, words at a certain point became unimportant. Understandings were clear, simply by being in a certain space. As you meditate, you explore many aspects of the space-self within yourself and outside of yourself. This space can be the sense of peace or the sense of connectedness or union. Within it there is energy that connects people to one another.

People who are aware of this process realise that this space is also there in another person. They are able to connect beyond words on that level. They actually do things and actions that are energetic and help the person to move along deeper in the path. I hope this explains it a little bit. That was of course happening when I left the monastery. Leaving the physical space did not mean everything stopped, it was just one aspect of the monastery. Many dimensions of work were going on beyond that physical space and were maintained when I left. That is the energetic work that I speak about when working with the Zen Master.

What is the "connection" during an energetic work?

It is a connection beyond anything as we feel at one with someone. It is almost like if you feel connected to someone that you love. In a relationship, you can say it is a heart connection because of course your heart feels and senses things but it is more like with your child. It is a sense that goes beyond just physical or special aspects of the mind or special aspects of the feelings. It is a sense that you have, yet it is difficult to explain. How can a mother explain her connection to a baby?

When you are in connection with someone is it possible to be in connection and communicate differently with other people at the same time?

Of course. What usually happens when you are connected to someone is that there is a sense of expansion. You move out of the sense of the self, or small self, to encompass other senses of self. In a relationship it is the sense of self of the other person, in a child-mother relationship, it is the sense of the child, but in the mystical sense it is not just one person or one aspect of the self. It is beyond that. It is the many aspects that make humanity what it is today. It is a sense of Great self, the Greater self, and the Universal self that is everywhere. It is the depth of you, yet more than just your personality or ego. It is the depth that connects us to everything, not just to people but also to nature, to the atmosphere and ultimately to the divine. We can work with this because even though it has a terrain and a geography that is unknown and invisible on one level. It becomes quite clear once you open to this communication. This is probably when I realised that spiritual teachers are not just individuals. They are spiritual teachers in this dimension of union, everywhere, real spiritual teachers, in the sense that they are not just people who feel to be important or like to be a guru, a Roshi, or whatever title is given.

These real spiritual teachers have entered this invisible field of union where everything is one. In that space of mystical connection, everything is registered in the same way. You can connect to spiritual teachers, awakened people and connected people who are there, as everyone else is. Perhaps this is where Christianity for example, in its original sense, says that Jesus never died, because in that space, the union and the love that Jesus had is really there, present. It is just that we do not have a connection to it, we do not see it or feel it.

It is not just Jesus. It is any Saint, any Prophet or being that has let go of the ego, let go of the selfish aspects of their emotions and their mind, and entered the space of deep connection that becomes registered beyond time and beyond space and this presence is approachable. This is where I realised there were many wonderful teachers that can be personified. It is not just a feeling or a sense. You can actually connect consciously to these persons and understand aspects of their lives. This is how it is possible to understand aspects of Jesus beyond history and understand the deeper mystery that the Bible speaks about, rather than just read the concepts therein.

What happened is never forgotten. What anyone does is always registered. Any human being is always written in the framework of that space of energy. The physical aspect of a person might die but the energy never dies. Thinking might die but the core of that being always remains there. I am now approaching another very difficult angle of my work, which I do not normally speak about. Enlightened beings may decide to not reincarnate into another aspect but to be in that space of helping people from a distance. This space is where I connected to the mystical traditions that were beyond dogma. I connected to very wise people who, at a certain point, helped me to go through a process that opened the path to enlightenment and freedom.

The Satori experiences that had happened to me earlier in the Zen monastery became bigger, not just in size, but also bigger in how they approached all aspects of who I was as being. It impacted even more deeply in senses such as my identification with the ego, than ever before, but there was a preparation and an initiation into this. Some people say you need to be initiated through masters or enlightened beings but, actually, we are initiating ourselves when we are ready. Yet we are not initiating ourselves alone because that path is there and has been walked down many thousands of times by thousands of different people. You are just another aspect of the divine that opens up to that point.

That opening happened to me around the age of twenty-seven as a spiritual crisis. I decided not to go back to the Zen monastery or to any personal being but to really connect to what I would call this other dimension. This dimension is mysterious and unknown and could be misunderstood, as a space that is quite different than your everyday mundane space of consciousness, because it has nothing to do with the seen, the obvious. It is an invisible world but I believe it was the initiation into my teaching that takes place today, which goes beyond the dogma of Zen Buddhism. It was at that point that I left Zen Buddhism and shamanism behind and looked much more at the work that I am doing now.

Before twenty-seven there were of course other initiations that happened in South America with people considered masters, spiritual masters, or shamans and many of these happened with *ayahuasca*. I felt that I worked with people who were fairly enlightened, at least in the shamanic culture that is also biased to many things. This opened up many levels, especially the emotional and the *kundalini* levels, that prepared me for what happened at twenty-seven.

The emotional and the *kundalini* levels are of course the heart, how I feel and my relationships to people. When I say *kundalini*, I mean the energetic points in the body that can be blocked since emotions and stress cause blockages throughout the history of mankind. It is not just as a personal thing but also a family one that includes our grandparents, our great grandparents and so on. If we are born into a family that has stressed for whatever reason, it can affect the energy centres. That somehow becomes more obvious through later symptoms with, for example, a block in the heart, in energy points, problems with expressing our feelings. That may not just be our problem, but also a problem that is historical, in the family sense, because on one level that problem was the same for our grandparents and our great grandparents. Perhaps we just do not know because they never communicated that block, as they never had that feeling or that possibility to communicate it.

I worked deeply on releasing this with the shamans and also when I was in the Andes with *San Pedro*. That was one of the most profound changes for me as it really stripped away the last layers of anything I could identify with. It was almost as if the initiation was making everything disappear completely, which is usual in shamanism, losing one's identity and creating a new one. I did this for a while, connecting to the shamanistic culture and identifying very much with all the ideas of what shamanism is, but after a period, I felt that was too limiting. For me shamanism was wonderful because, just like Zen Buddhism, it opens up so much more than is possible in the modern Western culture – at least that I was able to explore at the age of seventeen – but it is regulated and closed in many other ways. As I said before, I had disagreements with people I was working with, not negative or bad disagreements but disagreements in the intention behind the work of shamanism.

My intention was to be a spiritual human being, to grow beyond certain boundaries and to be free. But in shamanism, or at least the ones I explored, that freedom was to go to certain points that help you to be free enough to work to be the healer or the doctor of the community, or the person who is stable enough in the community to create balance where there is unbalance. Because they identified very much with that community, the shamanic knowledge became insular, in the sense that the community was the only setting where that freedom was possible. I then started moving around South America and working with different people. Yet, I did not get so close to *ayahuasqueros* and the way they work, or to the *huachuma* shamanistic culture that I worked with later, because in South America the shamans operate within a limiting cultural context. I identified very much with one person, but after a while, when I was twenty-seven, all that dropped.

Growing up as a child in Egypt, Zen Buddhism and shamanism all became the interesting history of what created the possibility of awareness for me. These were all steps, slow steps, but steps that were preparing me, I feel, to this point where there was a total change, where I could not go back to anything. There was nothing to hold on to, no shamanistic culture, no Zen Buddhist culture but only that experience.

I have never spoken about this publicly before but to answer your question, yes, in that space you can speak to many spiritual teachers and I worked with some of them in that dimension. These teachers are not living but they have lived in ancient cultures, in Egypt, Persia, and India, and were very much influenced by that setting. I found it very interesting that on some level, I was going back to the culture that I grew up in. It was like a circle. I felt that it was interesting because I understood why I chose to be to Egypt. I say I chose because I believe this choice was deeper than just my family's circumstances, so on some level, I chose to grow up in this mystical multicultural Egypt. It was as if I was going back through many layers to that space, remembering more than just what was obvious for a child, to be exposed to Sufi or Coptic Christian ways, remembering what was even beyond that, what started the whole culture.

At the age of twenty-seven I got very interested in the core of what created humanity. What created language? Why do we speak English? Why do we speak Portuguese, Dutch, German, and Chinese? What is the essence of language? This is where I started the path I am working with today, to go to the core that created language. I realised that what created language was not language. It was a mystical sound – which I use in certain initiations with people – that created the possibility for language to be formalised into what it is today. Unlike some people who say they believe that language came because human beings developed and moved to some continent in the world and then had to communicate with each other, I believe language was human beings wanting to communicate this mystical sound that created our consciousness in words.

This is what all babies and children try to do when they say "*ma*". The mother may think, "Oh, that is so nice because my child is now saying *mama* and is recognising my individual", but actually, the first word "*ma*" is an ancient *mantra*, which is also used during initiation. It is the children communicating to their mother the mystical experience that they are having in that moment, communicating how wonderful it is to be conscious of that aspect of themselves, and consciously trying to explore that in language. Of course, like in any culture, language becomes limited by the concepts, so the *ma* becomes *mama*, and then "I love you mama", and, as the mama is out there, "I love you mama that is out there". Language becomes a completion of culture so to speak.

I wanted to go beyond language to the essence of sound, to what Jesus spoke about, the mystical sound that came in Creation and created everything. I see that as a mystical path. The Bible refers to this. It is the mystical path that we all need to go through to recognise that essence, that mystical sound, which is within us. I feel some languages carry that sound more than others. It is not to say that these languages are better but somehow they preserved certain words in a context that is more pure to its form.

Aramaic, which is the ancient language of the Middle East, and Sanskrit are I believe, two of those languages. I feel somehow they held onto words in a specific way. That is why I got interested in Hinduism. Of course I explored Sanskrit not in books, as all this is in the knowledge that is present in the energy field. I did not read books in South America because I was in the middle of nowhere, with no people around, exploring this by myself. For me this was quite a beginning of the path, creating the path within which I work now.

This explains to you how the initiation happened beyond physical beings in the energetic level. Today I use the sound *"hu"* as one of the most important sounds. I was amazed to realise that not only is it in Sanskrit but it is also in the ancient language of Peru. I also realised that not only is it in the language but also in the local built structures. Some aspects that are universal and not just Peruvian could be recognised and connected back to India, to Persia, and to Egypt. For example *huachuma* is a Quechua word, and *hu* probably means something in that language, but in my understanding, *hu* is the word of "the Divine", some people say "God", or the mystical unknown invisible world of what is beyond the self, and *achuma* is "you are full of", or "drunk", or "overwhelmed by" the Divine. The word *huachuma* is also the ancient word for *San Pedro*. It is interesting how that is so connected to the mystical tradition of India, where, soma is also the same, the mystical experience of God.

Then I realised that all these things are found everywhere but if we go beyond culture and we listen to language, which of course is our own divine language, we can connect to what was before all those other things. We connect to our depth as we connect to concepts that are beyond dualism.

Language is a problem because it creates the idea that it is me and you, or me this and that. It reinforces that picture by creating a whole mental concept where the mind is logically trying to understand everything. I believe we cannot understand anything until we go beyond that conceptualisation but to go beyond it is to enter psychosis because we need the mind to function, as a psychologist would say. Of course we need the mind to function but for me it is not about going beyond the mind but rather going to the essence of the mind.

What is the creative driving force in the mind that is creating language and many other things? This is where sound and light become the point of work that happens in the ceremonies and that happens in the retreats that I do today. That is where it comes from. It is not from Zen Buddhism or from shamanism, which people often like to identify me with and say, "Tony works in a shamanic way or in a Buddhist way". Sometimes people even say "the Hindu way". It is not. It is beyond those things but in essence connected to them.

You mentioned working with sound to initiate people. Would you say more about this?

The word "sound" is difficult to use because when I mention it people immediately wait to hear a sound or they say that the sound that I am speaking about is a *mantra* or a type of *mantra*. In Buddhism, they also use *mantras*, a type of sound to be made, but for me, the sound is the essence. It is one of the aspects of creation with which we can have a tangible feeling and connection to. The whole spiritual work is to go beyond our limited self, our limited concepts, but where do we go when we go beyond those limited aspects? It is very difficult to go anywhere because if you go somewhere, if you drop aspects of yourself, what is left?

Some people say that there is nothing, but of course there is something left. And one of the things that is left is sound. I think Pythagoras experienced that on one level and this vitalised the Greek culture in a way that was understood, but not totally. He was partly understood in mathematics of course but the more essential part of his work was music and sound. For me, that is the essence that becomes tangible once you drop a concept that limits you.

Music is one of aspect of this tangible thing that you can fall into that becomes universal and goes beyond limits of culture, limits of races, like black or white, or Hindu, Muslim, Chinese, Japanese. Music speaks to the heart or to the essence of everyone. But what is it in music that is speaking? This is what I feel Pythagoras was exploring. He explored something more universal in music, something that could be quantified and understood in a conscious way so that it became more than just a mystical experience. It became an initiation into something tangible.

Pythagoras spoke about many things and among these, he created some interesting concepts about music. I believe those concepts were used by him and groups of people around him to initiate themselves into this mystical sound, a sound which is then personalised so that our whole being resonates with it. As the resonance changes the chemistry of the body, the DNA structure and even the head, the heart and the lungs expand and become more conscious. The resonance of that allows the resonance of the divine to become more tangible so that it becomes our reference point rather than the mind, so to speak.

It is the understanding that we get in the music, in the sound, something that allows us to hear the more divine aspect of it. Some people have tried to call this overtones but it is not really what I am speaking about, even though the overtones expand you to the space where it seems that you are experiencing that point, that sound and that mystical connection. Sound is what human beings fall into once they drop everything else.

This is why it is important to sing to a baby, and not to shout to a baby, not to use harsh or strong words. Babies are still in that sphere of music. They can still hear it. This is why when someone says something that is strong or negative like "stop saying" or "stop crying", it is not so much the word that affects the child but rather the bringing down of that angelic realm to this more mundane realm. This changing of the vibration of the music in the body of the baby may be traumatic. This is why the initiation of a mother to the child is to sing beautiful songs so that the child remains in that space and makes that space as conscious as possible in the physical realm, in the mental realm, and especially in the language realm. That may be for instance when you read a story for a baby, not just when the baby is two or three month but up to the age of four. It is not just reading the story in a logical sense but reading it with the sense of sound being mystical, so that it carries more of that than the logic of the story. This is something practical that people can do to experience in a relationship with a child or even with someone that you love. Most people speak too much when they love someone. After a while, people talk too much about their feelings, about how they feel, what it means to feel, how it is to feel, and whatever. It is so wonderful to use very little words and to use the sound of what love creates as an experience for you, to convey that. That can be in very simple things which have been forgotten.

It is not forgotten in the romantic aspect of our culture such as when we read about fairy tales or watch old movies where the prince is the person who opens the heart up and falls in love with a princess, sings to the princess, or, if he is not able to sing, displays an action that reminds the princess of that mystical sound. For example, the gift of the rose to someone, which is to me the symbol of the heart, is still practised in our tradition today. You go to the florist and you buy roses. Roses, given as a gift to the person you feel that love towards, are a symbol of that sound, of the divine that you are experiencing through love.

This is a little bit the sound with the spiritual teacher and someone who understands theses sounds. We all understand these sounds because they are there, but for someone who can consciously work with these sounds, the initiation is almost like listening to classical music. It awakens energy points inside of you, including the pituitary and the pineal glands, which are the most important, and the third eye, which is connected to these glands. This is more difficult in the normal sense, where what we hear is just the sound of our mind speaking constantly, non stop, or the sound of our emotions worrying, the sound of pollution, civilisation, the cars, the hum of a fridge, the hum of electric vibration that goes through our house, or the hum of people's negative thoughts.

I find it essential to have a spiritual teacher who understands this because it overrides so many limitations that, all of the sudden, in the same way as listening to Mozart, it touches a point that cannot be explained in words, and cannot be understood in the normal sense. It is direct. It is a point in the pituitary and in the pineal gland that starts to function in a different way. We begin to see that within this sound, there is light, which of course is what all mystical traditions speak about. This light is a manifestation of this sound. It then creates the possibility for us to see what is everywhere but in physical form.

In the beginning we see light and in the end we see forms. The form then becomes related to a concept of what that form is. If we look at the moon, we forget to see the real light that is shining through, that is sustaining the musical orchestra of life. Instead, we see the moon as a physical form. We see it just in the minimum and limited form rather than as a living and giving being that communicates more because it is part of the divine. The initiation of sound, and eventually of light, is moving beyond dualism, moving to what Hinduism calls Union, to The One. When one asks, "Who am I?", the question of course has the answer, "You are the One".

In India as I understand it, because I never studied Hinduism in books, the One means that you are at one, that there is no separation in that sense of oneness. That is actually the same, I believe, that Jesus, the Christian, Muslim and Jewish religion were speaking about, in a different concept. We are all one. That oneness is all there. When you are at one in the orchestra of Mozart, you can hear so much more than you can if you listen just to the sound and intellectualise about listening to the drum, to the piano, to the violin or whatever.

You said that during initiation with people you sometimes work with a sound. Can you be more specific about this? Is it like having people doing the sound together with you in a retreat or is it a more subtle work with the sound?

This work is individual. It is a personal interaction with one person that can take place outside of a retreat, a ceremony or a workshop, or within a group setting, but the work is done directly with the individual, separately from the group setting. It is not really like some other meditations that are group meditations, working together; it is very private. It is not like chanting together but sometimes, like in a ceremony, it does seem that we are working together. I am actually working very specifically with specific individuals who are aware of the work with me, knowing that this situation is very sacred for them. It is not that it is essential to keep it personal, but in the beginning, it is usually important for the initiation and for the whole situation to develop more deeply in a private sphere.

So working with sound is a way to connect to a vibration and an energy field that is beyond what we are?

Yes. But how can we explain this? It is like a fish in the water asking, "What is water? What does the water mean?". It is so difficult because you are in the water, the water is part of you, and you are breathing the water. What is water? How can you have a tangible connection to water when it is so much everything that is you? The water is the sound. It is the music. It is not a vibration that is separate from you but a vibration that makes you think the thought that is asking the question now. It is beyond any recognition, beyond any understanding. It is so much the core that the mind has no possibility of understanding. We have to come back to the core. We have to be the water, so to speak, to recognise that the fish and the water are actually the same.

It reminds me of Ramana Maharshi's teaching...

I work a lot with Ramana Maharshi, but I did not read any books about him so I do not know his concepts.

Even so, as a spiritual teacher and along Sufis such as the poet Rumi, his approach helped me to see things in a way beyond shamanism and beyond Buddhism.

Ramana Maharshi precisely always goes back to the question, "Who am I?" One of his saying basically was, "When you will understand the truth, you will laugh at all your efforts". It seems to fully resonate with what you say.

Yes, very good.

Energy Points

This question is about the energy, the three energetic points you often mention in your teaching: the pituitary gland, the pineal gland and the third eye. In your work you also talked about a fluid called *amrita*. Would you be more explicit about the importance of working with these energies?

Yes. Just to clarify, the pituitary and the pineal glands are energy points. These glands, which are in the brain, are points that act as a bridge from the physical to the energetic realm. I work with all the glands but especially with the pituitary and the pineal ones because they are like master glands that help spiritualise the body and our experience of the material world. Like all the glands in the body, the thymus, the thyroid and the lymphatic glands are also important as bridges. I work much more with those points in the body than for example the physical aspect worked through yoga, which also works with those points but is mostly oriented towards the physical parts of the body through stretching and so on. Those points are worked through different movements and different postures.

These glands connect us. They help us to spiritualise the body and to create a bridge, a sense of awareness between the spiritual and the physical sensations. I believe that these bridges are often lost in our culture within the whole socialisation and growing up. They are more lost in the West than in native society where the material aspects of life are not so far removed from the emotional or the spiritual ones.

I consider that these points are vital to work with. The pituitary and the pineal glands help us to not only recognise the spiritual in the physical realm but also to make the physical realm more spiritual. Their stimulation creates a sense of protection from things that can often impede or make us move back a little bit in our movement forward such as fear for example. When we work on the pituitary gland, the fear becomes reduced, it impregnates our being less because our body is spiritualised to a point where fear does not latch on to the physical body, the muscles or the nervous system.

This is just one example to give you an idea that this is not far removed from the physical sensations. What we are doing when we work with the pituitary and the pineal glands is changing the quality of the physical body, the cells, the nervous system, the bones, the tissues, to make them vibrate at a different level and to have a different reference point than just the mundane. The body then become spiritualised.

When we work with the pituitary and the pineal glands, the brain also produces a fluid, the fluid you were asking about, called *amrita*. It is a special fluid that enhances this spiritualisation of the body so instead of just being located in the pituitary and the pineal glands, it moves to different locations in the body. I believe what happens is that it moves to the thyroid and to the thymus and then slowly into all the other glands of the body. These other glands are the receptors of this fluid and the pituitary and pineal glands are the producers. The thyroid's physical actions are to balance the body weigh and to balance the emotions. As the thyroid and the thymus receive the *amrita*, their physical actions become more spiritualised and it goes deeper than just our material manifestation of emotions. The emotions, the physical body and its balancing becomes spiritualised. This is the reason why I work with the glands.

You almost systematically associate the pineal and pituitary glands in your explanations. Do you yet distinguish their functions in the spiritual development?

Not really. They are different, they both work slightly differently, but they both are important in relation to each other. The pituitary gland is the master gland, which is the core from where the energy is directed, and the pineal gland is connected to it. When we become older, when we become more set in our ways and our connection to this other realm becomes more remote, we lose this touch of mystery and their processes slow down. This slowing down can be reversed through doing certain exercises, through eating certain foods and through allowing certain emotions to expand inside of us and working through other emotions that are not open to the process. Normally, these glands are stimulated by themselves. Yet when we have fear in the body, when we have negative thoughts, when we have pain or suffering, when there is climatic or geographical radiation, pollution, or when we eat certain foods, that inhibits the function of the pituitary and pineal glands, they shrink and work less.

Are the whirling meditation and simply being happy a way to stimulate them?

Definitely the whirling meditation and being in love and free, not worrying, not stressing, breathing, not being angry…

What is specific for the third eye?

The third eye is a wonderful point, different from the pituitary and pineal glands, even though they are all related, that is able to see and comprehend pictures beyond the physical eyes. I call it the intuitive part of us, the part that picks up things without seeing. The third eye works all the time but of course, if we use our physical and the mundane aspects of ourselves, it does not seem to be working. We have to re-orientate ourselves to other senses which are more subtle to understand how they are working. Some people tend to be stronger in the sense that they are more intuitive, more able to see things than others. Why is this? I do not know. It is not always a sign that you are more spiritual, because there are some very intuitive people who are not spiritual. Yet, for some reason it is the case with some people.

Destiny?

It seems to be destiny. Perhaps also they were born with that ability which never went away, or they had an accident or an emotional experience that opened it...

Are the visions that people can have in ceremonies related with the third eye?

The spontaneous visions are very much related to the third eye. This is why during the ceremonies, a lot of the visions that one sees or intuitively comprehends, are coming in through the third eye.

Is it like a glimpse or a window connected with that substance you talked about that connects us with everything?

It is a connection only because you are moving to a different point and that point is closer to that substance. Yet it is not that substance. Actually the vision is another sense that is forgotten. It is a sense like being able to see, to smell or to touch with the eyes, but closer on some level because we are able to relate more with it. A vision, as you say, does not have to be the substance or be close to it.

Some people have visions of something that is the future. Does it mean this is a connection with what is already written?

Yes it is, because the future is in this moment. What happens is that the third eye is capturing a glimpse of that moment and then translating it to a vision. We see something and although that vision sometimes does not happen exactly, it is on some level a revelation of that moment.

... and the work during a ceremony with the sacred plants stimulates the pituitary and pineal glands and open the third eye...

Very much, but not always, depending on how you work with it.

During a retreat you said the pituitary gland brings us light and arises the feminine side by giving us more sensibility. You explained it is important to strengthen it with the whirling meditation and other ways involving love. You also said that we give up because we think that things we want to achieve are not possible, which brings us to depression.

Often I mention the pituitary and pineal together as I do not really make a big difference because, although they are biologically different, they are both part of the same function. The pituitary gland is more related to the feminine, not just the feminine in the sense of being a lady or a woman or a girl, but the emotional and mental qualities that are less active and more giving, more still, more receptive. I was bringing the pituitary gland because it reacts to those aspects very easily compared to other glands. For example the thymus gland, if you want to categorise it, is a much more masculine gland because it is moving rather than receiving. It is very active, as the masculine is, in the sense that it moves things around. The pituitary for me receives more. It receives light so it is more like a receptor rather than active. This is why the stillness is important because it allows the receptor to function much more.

Is this particular to the pituitary gland?

Yes. It very interesting to bring this up because it is related to the other things that we were speaking about. I speak about it every time, but each time I mention something a little bit different. Why I say it is important is because women and men are different. This is not to say women or men are better, but we live in a masculine paternalistic society that is more active or more outside looking than receptive, in the sense that in the western culture, because of their biology and genetics, women have a tendency to understand receptivity more. With childbirth for example, the women's biology generally allows them to be more receptive and more creative, which is also accepted in our culture. This is why women's pituitary glands usually function more than men's. This makes a big difference in the sense that women embrace or need to embrace more things, and men are more trying to get to one place.

If women were more in the military, the military atmosphere would change because they would see different things that men do not see because of the pituitary gland. I am bringing another example just to show that the pituitary gland is not just a gland. It is not in relationship to our personality, to our emotions or to our actions, but it does influence our daily activities. I feel that if there were more equality – in the sense that women and men were more equal, rather than trying to make women becoming men, which is another way of equality that I disagree with – there would be more balance in our culture.

This is why I am always interested when for example a Prime Minister is a woman because even if she has to be very masculine to achieve that position in our society, there are other qualities that women sometimes bring into politics that I feel are lost in the masculine world. When seeing some women you may begin to question what I say because they sometimes express qualities that are even more masculine than some men express themselves.

They have accepted and adhered to masculine models...

And they maybe have pushed their feminine so far away that they have even forgotten more about it than some men.

You suggest that if the pituitary gland is through reinforcement of receptivity more developed for women, the thymus would be more the action gland for men...

Exactly. The thymus gland has to do with the immune system and with other aspects that require a much more active role. It is not so much to receive but to give. I feel that men, and also women, wear out the thymus gland by pushing that too much without actually giving it the space to function in balance. This is why we have for example the burn out syndrome or diseases like chronic fatigue in today's world. The thymus gland is not worked in balance with the whole action that is happening. This happens when you do not run on the natural flow of the thymus gland, which gives you this strength to be active in the world, but you rather run on the energy that is contained in the glands and in the organs. Then you deplete the batteries of the body so there is nothing left but a burn out. This is why the thymus gland is much more masculine because it is actually giving but sometimes we push ourselves more than our flow. Women usually do not do this as much because they have their periods and therefore they have to change the biological forces. Because they have this wonderful thing – or maybe not that "wonderful" according to everybody – that happens every month, they have to accept that they should listen to their bodies more. Then the thymus gland, which is a much more physical gland, is on some level much more able to act out in a different way. The thymus works very much with the energy of the body. It is like the energy that is required to act at any moment.

Is it an energetic point important to stimulate?

Actually it is connected to another point that the Japanese know in martial arts and that is called the *hara*. It is not the same as the solar plexus but it is connected to it. The hara is just below the belly button. If you know martial arts you can activate it. You can put energy into this point and it reinforces the solar plexus and affects the *hara* or you can actually deplete it. There is a move in martial arts that can completely deplete it and of course this was done in the sense of violence, to take out the strength of people so that they had no energy to fight. That very important point is not separated into compartments, everything is related to one another. The hara is the energy that martial arts in the Japanese, Chinese, Taoist and even Thai philosophies, work very much with to bring energy into the body. For me it is the thymus gland because I am working with the spiritual body, not so much with the physical aspects like in the martial arts.

Raising the *Kundalini*

About *kundalini*, you once said that when someone is enlightened or reaches a certain spiritual understanding, the *kundalini* is raised in that person, but that does not mean that one needs to raise the *kundalini* to be enlightened. This suggests that doing exercises to raise the *kundalini* is useful but not a necessity. Is your point that if a person is involved in this raising process, he or she should do it in the present moment, without projecting any results in the future?

The *kundalini* is life force. It is not some separate aspect that moves in our body that we cannot relate to. To be more alive means raising the *kundalini* energy, and we all want to be more alive. We all want to have a more intense intimate experience of life, so we all want to raise the *kundalini* life force. Sometimes we do it actively, sometimes we do it in a way without even knowing that we are doing this. The spiritual discipline that I explain to people is that there are certain activities which can raise the life force. Among these is sexuality of course, certain meditations, certain breathing techniques, and being in certain environments. Initiation can also open up certain points that allows the movement of *kundalini* to go and flow where it did not seem to flow before.

Is it important? It is not really important, but on one level it is, because as human beings we all want to be happy. We want to feel that life has a meaning and it gets more meaning when our experience of life is more intense, deeper, fuller. To take it to a practical point, if we are in a relationship with someone and the *kundalini* life force is blocked in the physical aspects of sexuality, of course there is meaning to raise it so that this aspect of our life has more completeness, more joy and more ecstasy.

Raising the *kundalini* is an important aspect of spiritual life, but to say that this is necessary for spirituality or that it means that you are more spiritual misses the point that life is much more complex than simply raising the life force. The life force can be raised by walking in the forest, working, breathing, focusing on the heart and sensing the gratitude of being alive. There are so many possibilities that you cannot say, "Is it necessary to practice moving the energy from one point to another?". That is just to help to realise the complexity of the whole picture. The life force moving from one point to another is not the way to be happy because happiness creates its life force. As we do more spiritual work, even if it is not obvious, we become happier, freer, more alive, more in tune with what is profoundly important for humanity. The life force is raised to the point where *kundalini* becomes free.

For some people that experience is dramatic but it is not necessarily so. It is only dramatic because it is touching points in the movement that are limitations and those limitations get removed very quickly. For example, if people feel it very strongly in the body in the physical sense, it is not that this is the *kundalini* but more that this is the process of letting go of what is limiting the life force from expressing itself. The life force is peaceful, totally centred in a space of pureness where there is no masculine aspect to it. In my opinion, it is not like the idea where *kundalini* rises dramatically, moves strongly, burns and explodes. Of course it does seem that way because there are many processes that are released during that point. But no, it is not that at all.

The process of moving life force is part of the spiritual development that happens as we let go of certain things that prevent us from seeing the complete picture. The complete picture is not the yoga idea where, once the *kundalini* reaches the top of your head, all blocks have been released because then life force is moved from the base to the top of the head. If the *kundalini* or life force energy were blocked and were not moving to the top of the head, you would not be alive. It is moving. It is just that we can make it stronger and we can expand that sensation. There are certain techniques that help that sensation to move more quickly but sometimes we have to be gentle. It is not good to push ourselves just as it is not good to sit and meditate for twenty-four hours a day, everyday for a year without eating, without sleeping, without doing anything. Everything is in balance so I do not see *kundalini* energy as vital as some people talk about. I just see it as part of the whole of what is happening.

During ceremonies, apparently there is also a raising of *kundalini*, physically, through shaking and uncontrolled body movements, but there is also the expansion of awareness, which you say is related to this raising. This happens without the person doing anything special. It seems enough to let the process happen, to let go, to open, and to be present without accompanying this with any technique. Does it mean that the plant stimulates what needs to be stimulated inside of the person?

We really do not need to do anything. When it comes to *kundalini* life force, it is so naturally part of ourselves that we honour that part of ourselves by doing nothing more than trying to do something. We re-embrace energy much more by acknowledging that it is a part of us rather than by trying to direct it, to control it, to stop it, to move it, to focus it, or to want it to go to some point or to some part of ourselves. This is where for me yoga has lost a little bit of its essence. The dogma of yoga has created a whole system, which I am not criticising but I just do not believe is important.

Life force energy has intelligence and moves by itself without us doing anything. We really do not have to do anything. It is a bit like when you cut yourself, you do not have to do anything for the cut to heal. The energy in the body knows what to do. All you have to do is to create the space for the healing to happen as profoundly and as quickly as possible so you keep it clean, you create a sterile environment, you do not put your fear into the cut. You just say, "I trust that my body knows what to do". It is the same with the life force energy. Once you trust that this part of you is comfortable and is all right, that it is a part of you that is not separate like an alien that is invading your body, it is totally natural.

In a practical sense, people are often not comfortable with themselves and with their body. I see this especially with women because the focus of many of them is to be pretty and so on as society demands, then they become very protective of their body. People may have been in a relationship for many years and still they have that self-defence mechanism that leads them to try not to be seen in their most vulnerable state, meaning in the physical naked state. The mind has created a picture of guilt about the body so people are very often not comfortable with their body. Can you believe this?

If you look at a baby they feel so free, the body is so natural. They do not have any idea or reference point of guilt, protection, or whatever adults do that creates a sense of separation in the physical body. The body is thus conceived as a thing to protect. Not being a part of "Me", it has to be protected from me. I expose it too much, then "Me" will get hurt, because my body will get hurt...

It is the same with life force. If you see it as separate and not naturally part of you, of course you will have to regulate it and make sure that it does not move too quickly, or make sure that it does this or that. In the end, these are just projections and ideas and, in my opinion, have no reference to the actual life energy that is ecstasy. Life energy is just a physical form of ecstasy. When we accept ecstasy in its essence in the physical body, there is no fear but just amazement. There is no physical trauma related to that ecstasy. When we accept our body, we can relax. Our breath relaxes, our mind relaxes, and our emotions relax. We are freer. But that whole process is not as easy in practice and in action as it is to talk about. To say, "OK, I can relax my body but I am not feeling anything", is not really how it happens.

We need to trust in ourselves first...

That is the whole thing of course, because the trust is not just a conscious trust. It is deeper than many layers. That trust takes time. It requires many things...

... and it can come by surprise.

Yes, like many things it can come by surprise. Enlightenment can come by surprise. One minute you are sitting doing things that are absolutely not obviously spiritual and then you are having a profoundly spiritual experience. It is surprising because the context does not seem to be related. This is the same with *kundalini* energy. It can come by surprise, even when washing up dishes. You are not breathing, not focusing, you are not doing anything, and then all of a sudden, the body has an experience of something. It is interesting because in the end, things are apparently not related to what we are doing. There is a whole bigger picture and that bigger picture is not always that easy to put into perspective in our daily understanding of what is happening in that moment. It then seems out of context.

Are there important differences between people's spiritual experiences?

There are much less differences than we think in the beginning of our practice. There are so many paths but what makes us human bypasses cultural, social and even age differences. In the end, humanity is humanity. In a retreat we recognise this much more. People feel that I am speaking directly to them just because I am speaking to their deeper part rather than their individual part.

I hope I answered the *kundalini* life force questions. Some people are afraid of this force I think because some books about yoga and some New Age philosophies have created this idea that *kundalini* can go out of control and can create a spiritual crisis, burning organs and such. For me that is so unrelated to the reality of life force. It is a projection of fear onto those things that change which can be dangerous. Change for me is never dangerous. Physical change, mental change, emotional change, even energetic change are essential to keep all of us alive. If everything stagnates then everything dies, so change is essential.

It is also essential that change is quick and not slow. It has to be quick because if change is slow then on some level we are controlling it to fit into a structure. When it goes beyond those structures and it becomes spontaneous and magical, then on some level we invite the mystery of life into our physical experience. We discover parts of our body that we did not even know we had or we did not know we were aware of. We discover the mystery in our emotions. We discover the mystery in our completeness in relationship to our partner, in relationship to nature, in relationship to our family and in relation to other people.

That change has to be quick. It has to be quicker than the controlling aspect of the ego: the mind. When it is done in a space of harmony, this means from the heart rather than from the ego, there can be no danger. The danger is only when the ego gets over inflated with the power and the idea behind the power of things. It is very difficult for that to happen unless the teacher that you are working with has a sense of wanting to be more powerful, or wanting you to be more powerful, because of the belief that power is somehow better than coming back to the sense of who you are as a human being, to your heart.

It can also happen if you have a sense of being little, the little idea of yourself can disappear because you project into power. This is the case with money. People believe that by having more money they have more power. They therefore do not feel worthy inside of themselves and think that the money will make them worthier. It could also be in relationship, being more powerful than your partner, controlling the relationship, coming from the ego space rather than the heart space because that makes you feel somehow better, on a very superficial level. This sort of power is dangerous not just on an energetic level. It is dangerous on all levels. To say that it is only dangerous because if you do this something can happen, belittles the whole picture of power. It simplifies it too much.

You say we do not have to do anything but you also suggest it is good to do what you call the "whirling meditation" for example. Would you say more about this technique that you consider as your favourite?

The whirling meditation is one of the core meditations for which I say, "Why not practice whirling in the morning and in the evening everyday for three months to see if those experiences lead you to more realisations rather than just listening to me and following the instructions". As I was saying previously, we need to be active in our spiritual work. The activity is not just mental activity. It goes beyond mental. It goes to the physical, the emotional and the energetic but also very importantly to the energy centre of the third eye and to the pituitary and pineal glands that are related to the third eye. The activity is to create the atmosphere for that space to open up naturally as it was before.

There are many techniques that propose to do this but they will never really do this because a technique does not guarantee that it will happen. It is rather an activity that invites the possibility for this to happen. This is why if you do nothing, it can still happen. If you do something, it can also not happen, but it should be something that creates the atmosphere for it to be more possible. The movement and activation of the pituitary and pineal glands creates an atmosphere where that point starts a whole set of dynamics that are important for what needs to happen in order to see things in a different way.

The third eye is open and you can see things but the unveiling of what stops that seeing needs activity. It cannot simply be left there in the hope that someday it will move away because those hopes are not going to do anything. It is your realisation in action that moves that space to go beyond the veil. It is the same with talking. It is not enough to say, "I love you". Saying that is nice and interesting to hear but it is more important to show it in a real active sense. You can say that silently. You can say it and not mean it, but the activity on some level will invite your heart to sense what love means.

This is the same with the whirling meditation. It invites the heart to participate in the activity. The heart will not participate automatically in that activity, in any other meditation, or in fact in any activity that you partake in life. Still, by creating the space where that is possible, it is more likely that the heart will have the possibility to acknowledge what you are doing and to embrace the whole situation in a more complete sense. When you are whirling, the pituitary gland, the pineal gland, and the third eye open up in a way where you see things in a totally different perspective.

It is exactly like when you actively love someone, you see things that are totally different. You do not only see one point anymore, which is the person. You do not just see things, you see beyond things. That beyond cannot be explained until you are in that space, just like the meditation cannot be an experience until you are practising the meditation and it becomes your experience. From that experience it then becomes your practice and knowledge.

You also suggest doing the whirling with the sound *hu*...

We were speaking about sound meditations previously so the sound is very important. For me, "*hu*" is a mystical sound that is part of the initiation. It is also part of the breathing, synchronising the sound of the mind to the sound that is essentially in the mind, which is creating the mind. It is almost like the external "*hu*" touches the internal sound that is creating life, the mystical sound that is the essence of all life, the bridge. "*Hu*" is the bridge.

Dreams & Everyday Life

Mind, thoughts and dreams are three aspects of our consciousness but the frontier between them may not be so rigid. Do you see dreams as just another level of the mind or the thoughts?

This is a very interesting question. The mind, thoughts and dreams are very different even though they are exactly the same. They are very different because the mind comes from a space where it is always active and manifesting itself. The mind works no matter what. It works even if you are unconscious. When people are asleep during an operation in hospital for example, the mind is working but they do not even know because they do not recognise the mind. We recognise the mind when we have conscious thoughts, when we are thinking about something and our mind is aware that we are doing it. These conscious thoughts are in relationship with the world and our experience that we recognise as such. On the other hand, unconscious thoughts are from the mind, working but unrecognised by our logic. We recognise it from another space so it is a deeper aspect of the mind.

Dreams are even deeper than the unconscious, even though they are close to the unconscious. They are closer to the unconscious than the conscious mind but they are beyond the unconscious. It is like another level closer to the mind and it is important to understand that the mind is not bad. It is only bad when we do not see it in its full glory: when we identify with the thoughts, thinking that they are in themselves the complete sense of the mind. The mind – and I mean the divine mind – is actually a part of our essence. We all have a divine mind as part of our mind. This is why when people say to get rid of the mind, I find that it is a very unwise thing to say. You cannot get rid of the mind because it is another aspect of the divine. What we can do is change the way it functions.

When we dream, what we are doing is changing the way the mind functions in the mundane sense. We are going closer to where we need to be: at home. Dreams are therefore very important in the work that I do. For most people, they are so strange, so out of this world, so confusing sometimes, or so remarkable that they say, "It's just a dream". But in no way is a dream just a dream. I say this many times in retreats and I gladly repeat it: a dream is more real than our thinking or than what our thoughts consider to be important in the mundane, for example our worry of a mortgage or our philosophical ideas about life.

The dream is much more real, it is almost like what people call "the soul". I do not believe that there is a separate aspect called the soul, but just to make it comprehensible, it is like the soul travelling to a space and recognising a more divine aspect of itself. During sleep, you could say the soul travels through different dimensions to reach its essence. Without dreaming, the person would lose his or her humanity and would go crazy. We need to dream to recognise the divine, even if we are unable to recognise it in our mundane actions. We need to do this at night or whenever we sleep.

Some dreams, however, are not clearly profound. There are many layers of the dreams, as the soul travels around, up and down to the essence, and sometimes the dreams are apparently very superficial. If we are worrying about something, we are dreaming about the situation that we are worrying about. If someone is worried because a person is dying of cancer, the dream will often be focused on that aspect of that experience in life, but beyond that, there is another level of understanding. If we dream about that person and our worry, it is so that the soul can clear that out of its way to go deeper. It is almost like the soul is removing layers to get to the essence, yet we do not remember the whole journey of the soul. We only remember the part, the beginning part, were we are worrying about a person. The rest is so deep that we forget.

This is why in the retreats I speak about the importance of being conscious in the dreams. As you become conscious in the dream, you can remember more of the journey that the soul takes to its essence. That allows you to let go of the superficial aspects of the dreams, even though they are important, and come to a consciousness of what is deeper beyond having a dream where the car crashes, or where you see the person that you are worrying about suffering. You can get to many deeper levels.

The dream is the most important work in some of the retreats I do. Some people would just say "Well, it is just a dream, it means nothing", while we spend seven-eight or six hours – how many hours do you sleep? – dreaming. That is meditation. It is probably the main meditation most people do everyday. It is the most profound time to unveil the soul's journey to the essence, to coming back to oneself. This is why I talk a lot about dreams in the retreats. So is the dream the same as the mind? Yes and no. Is it the same as the thought? No.

According to Carl Gustav Jung, there are two kinds of dreams: one is about the everyday life, which is somewhat useless, and the other conveys deeper messages, or archetypes. Do you make this distinction?

No. I am sure Jung was very wise but the way I see it is that when we wake up and remember the dream, we remember that aspect where our consciousness is most focused on. This is why practising meditation everyday is important. We then recognise that the dreams which you say are not important are just layers of that journey that happened during the night. Every night, our soul will go to the same profound space but we just do not remember. We will only remember whatever we need to remember from that journey. If our consciousness is occupied with identifying with suffering or a certain problem, then we will remember that layer of information. Sometimes we may think we had a very profound dream but it is not that it was a special night where we had a profound dream. Every single night we have a very profound dream but we just do not remember.

But some dreams seem to impress us much more than others…

It is not that some impress us much more. It is just that at times we need to recognise the divine much more strongly. The dream that I had about the golden chair [cf. *A Shaman's Wisdom*] was a very profound dream for example. For some people dreaming about a golden chair is rubbish and does not mean anything. It was so profound for me because when I woke up the next day, I recognised that in that dream I did not need to go anywhere. I was there. The chair was there and all that was not there was me recognising that the chair was there for me to sit in. Now did that dream just mean that it happened at that point or was that chair always there and I simply never recognised that it had always been there? Was it that in that moment the dream became so important for me to recognise that when I was awake it impressed itself upon my conscious mind so strongly, reminding me of something? No. It was always there.

So even the little silly stories in dreams have depth?

Of course because those little "silly stories" are the layers to more profound stories. By working on those silly layers – I am using your words – you are giving a chance for that soul journey to be more conscious and remember itself next time more consciously.

Do you mean that whether we give or don't give depth to dreams their depth is always there?

Yes.

Where does the method you use to help people understand their dreams, or something that is happening to them, come from? Is it because you are centred that you can connect with what is happening with the person?

Would you mean with the dream or everything?

In general.

Let us take the dreams as a practical example. They are so interesting because they are so clear. In a way, they are more transparent than people because the message speaks louder to me than certain actions people do in life. It is very clear, but for a person who is having the dream the dream is not always so clear. So what do you do?

Is it as if you see things from a distance?

Yes. You know sometimes it is easier to see other people and their situation than ourselves. This is why it is nice to have people around you to mirror what is really going on rather than what you think is going on. The dream is such a deep part of oneself that sometimes we need a reference point that can indicate that there is a meaning to it that is so simple and so clear that we can move towards it rather than away from it. The work with dreams is for the person to recognise what is really going on in that picture of the dream. If the picture is that you are drowning for example and the water is overwhelming you, you cannot swim and the sea is getting rougher, the drowning is not just a picture. It is energy in the body, it is an emotion, it is a physical sensation and it is scary. You do not want to acknowledge it because you feel that if you acknowledge it you will sink into the depth of the see, but that is exactly where we need to go…

My work is to say: "Try going down to the depth of the sea and see what happens, rather than resist. Stop struggling with the wave which gets rougher and with the sea that gets darker…". I do not say what the dream means but rather indicate a way that was not seen but that may be interesting to explore. I have to be a bit cautious because then of course there is a potential dependency of people not being able to see the dream and this is why often I take a long time to work with people's dreams. Sometimes the group gets bored as I go around in a circle saying to one person, "Oh, look at this and at this … and why not this?". It is more difficult for that person to see the pictures for herself than anyone else. Sometimes the whole group can see what is going on and the poor person is still struggling swimming in the water.

That is not only with dreams but also in life. When I am working with a group of people, sometimes it is so obvious for everybody what the situation is but not for the person because they are in the situation, in the depth of what is going on. The work is not to tell that person what to do but rather for him or her to recognise where he or she is at and to see what is really going on. This is so that people are able to make the choice: to keep struggling in the sea trying to overcome the waves that are getting bigger, or to just relax and allow the situation to go where it naturally needs to go. That seems very simple but people do not like simple things. They like complicated things.

It is interesting because the simpler it is, the easier it is for the person. This is why children often understand things much quicker than adults. For them it is simple because they see things differently. They do not have the other complications. When you practice meditation regularly or come to a retreat, the mind is simplified and begins to understand things in a different way than before. When people have never worked with me or are intellectually trying to make sense of something, they just go around in circles because what is really going on cannot be reached from that level. It has to be reached from where you are at – and where you are at is often very different from where your mind is at, or where you think you are at.

Interestingly, your comments about the dream you work on often seem to have nothing to do with the story of the dream itself, but rather focuses on the work the person has to do for his or her spiritual awareness. Things appear very easily to you when you do this, as if you were seeing what happens from outside of the picture. In which state do you put yourself to analyse people and notably their dream?

Often, I will try to make sense of a dream in a way that is totally irrelevant to the dream. People will start working with the dream and say, "Oh yes, it means this, or it means that", but a dream cannot be understood from that level. It has to be understood almost spontaneously. It is not that I can see things, it is obvious for everyone.

If the understanding is spontaneous, with a relaxed mind, it is like an insight?

Yes. With a relaxed mind it is so clear that you see when people skirt around that reality to try to attach to something and make sense of it. This is really the problem because you can make sense of any dream. Some people believe they can work with dreams, but rather than actually explaining what the dreams mean, they are projecting ideas onto the dream to create a picture that is interesting but that really has nothing to do with the dream. It makes intellectual sense for people but it does not make direct sense to the dreams because they are sometimes really silly and their meaning is much less significant than what we think it is. Often people working with me will say, "Ah yes, you know, last night I dreamt about a car, of course my masculine self, and I crashed, and of course, yes, my masculine self is over taking and controlling…". Then I ask, "Is that really what the dream is saying or is that just a mental picture of what you feel the dream is saying?" No dream can be understood directly through fixed symbols or ideas of what means what.

The meaning of a dream for someone is not the same for someone else...

Exactly. Just because the car means something for one person, it does not mean that the car means the same for every person. The car could be a very feminine aspect, not normally but it could be, so by saying, "Of course not. It is masculine!", we do not listen to the dream but we listen to our idea of what the dream means. Then how do we know that what we are seeing is what the dream is saying to us? We do not know because the only way to know is to come back to the space of the dream.

This is why, in the work, I ask people to go back to their breath, to their body, to relax. I do not want them to try to make sense of anything but simply to be in the dream and to expose the reality of the dream to their mind so that the dream makes sense. Instead of thinking, "Ah yes, the car means this", the idea is to actually be the car. When you are the car, what does it mean to you? This is difficult because it is almost too childish. You ask people to be a car and they wonder how they can be the car? Of course you can be a car. After the dream, you still have the impression of the dream in your body and in your energy system. You can honour that impression by going to that space.

When people divert to intellectualism I can be quite sharp. I am not anti-intellectual but the mind wastes too much time and in a retreat we do not have forever. We have many people and it is important to address the situation directly, so I do tend to be assertive and push people on one level. Yet, on another level I am not so assertive because I am always asking the person to reveal to me what they feel and what the dream is saying to them.

That is why people ask me, "How can I recognise anything in a dream? Where do I start? If a car is not masculine, what reference point do I have for a car being anything?", I answer, "The reference point is you. It is not a book or what I am saying. It is yourself". Once you understand the energy behind it then it is like a jigsaw puzzle, or a fairy tale. For instance, if you have the energy of a troll, you know a troll is hiding under a bridge and it is very easy to understand what the troll is. This is something that is quite common in all human experiences. The bridge of course is you, and the desire to see what is on the other side is also of course a part of you. When you understand that you are playing the whole game then the picture becomes very clear.

I think children and some women have more of that imagination than people who are too intellectual. If you are intellectual, then you are desperately holding on to one aspect of something and trying to make sense of it, but you need the whole picture. I suppose that is where you are saying "relaxed". The mind is relaxed so it does not identify with one thing but rather floats around everything and sees that all fits together to create a meaning, like a picture or a painting.

(Ana[1]) **I am very tempted to tell you about the dream I had a few days ago. May I?**

For me no problem. Yes.

(Ana) **I was in a room, lying on the sofa and looking at the window. You were also here. Then I put something in front of me to prevent one eye from seeing. With the open eye, that I tried to keep open with a little stick, I looked outside and I saw the bushes, the trees, and a branch with leaves, as if I were seeing inside a frame. Then I saw the coming of the four seasons on the same leaf that was transforming itself, changing colours and so on. Then the snow came and no more leaf. It was the four seasons but also more than that. Before disappearing, the leaf became almost transparent, like crystal. I was so surprised. In my dream, I talked to Christian about this dream. Then, another frame came again. This time it was the planet. It was like a globe, turning around but in slow motion. I was seeing all the countries and all the cities, thinking: "I do not know this by heart so how can I see it in a dream and even know the names of these tiny towns?". Then if I want to make sense, I would say that maybe the four seasons are all here and now, showing the relativity of the time, and the second part of the dream means that this year I am going to travel a lot around the world...**

---

[1]   Christian's wife, present during this conversation.

No. This is the mind. You can tell this is the mind because you are trying to make sense of something that cannot be made sense of. You are trying to see a picture in the dream but if you go deeper in the dream rather than trying to make sense of the dream, it is the feelings that you had – of course the feelings are deeper than the mind – and the sensation that you had when you were experiencing seeing the four seasons and the globe moving around. So what was the feeling?

(Ana) **With the four seasons, it was a feeling that time can go to the speed I wish. At the same time it was acknowledging the beauty of nature through the four seasons. The picture that stayed longest was the leaf having an orange-autumn colour.**

Wonderful. If we look at dreams as emotions, this is quite symbolic. If you look at the tree, you know the tree that you are looking at is a part of yourself, so you kept your eye open but it wanted to close no?

In some way you had to do something to really keep it open to be able to see this and the tendency is that you do not see this normally. Then you really had your attention very focused to recognise something that is normally invisible in your life or to your mind. The fact is you saw that something got revealed and this was very important. That something is yourself. The self, the tree and the many aspects of the tree were wonderful. It was like one thing was leading to another. It was not so linear but circular.

What you were seeing was on one level the spring, the summer, the autumn, and the winter. You were seeing all the four seasons. If you look at that, then you are honouring all aspects of yourself and they may not have been honoured by you before; all the aspects that you normally do not recognise and do not even see. I am not trying to boost the ego but in a way maybe that dream was showing you that you have more strength and more awareness than you recognise.

When that recognition comes forth, when it becomes obvious, the dream changes a little bit and then you see the globe. You see that globe spinning around and you see different cities. It is almost like that intelligence and that knowledge then moves to different dimensions, not just in a recognising sense but in an actual sense. It is almost like the masculine part of you moves – and this is just one dimension of the dream – and is able to put into action this awareness in many ways. Do you understand? It is almost as if by honouring the tree, its different forms and different pictures, not only have you honoured the tree as this part of you, but you have actually honoured the possibilities of what you can do that seemed impossible before.

Now, maybe not in reality but in the dream at least, that possibility manifests itself because you see that movement going to many places. It is almost like your journey becomes travelling and it is not just observing. The masculine part is the action, the movement throughout the globe that manifests itself. It is almost saying that maybe you can do things that you do not even know that you could do. Maybe things that you think were impossible are possible. This is one level of the dream.

I think it is also interesting that you were speaking to Christian in the dream. It is understandable because Christian is an important part of your life, but in the dream, you were communicating not just who you think you are but you were communicating the magic that is not seen and that you do not see, to him. You were revealing a part of yourself that you were seeing in the tree, the four seasons.

The four seasons are also quite symbolic of many things. Winter is symbolic of a state, summer of another state and the tree is symbolic of another aspect. In shamanism, the tree is very important because it connects us to the earth. It connects us to our roots. Those roots express something that is unique in the earth. They say the trees are points of energy transformation for the earth. This is all mystical talk but you know the tree is not just a tree, it carries much more in a symbolic sense. This is why for example in shamanism the tree was often the gateway to the underworld, to the upper world and to many other worlds.

In stories we often hear about this amazing big tree and of children going and playing around it. Then they find a little cave and look inside and what is really happening is that they are seeing something about themselves. The tree is almost like the picture they are able to mirror about themselves so that they can see this, the journey. You went and saw the beautiful leaves that come from the tree, and you are looking out in the forest. I think it is a wonderful dream because the tree also gives you power and this power is connected to many things. That connection often grounds us when we are going through strong transformations, or when things are happening. Elements of nature help us to ground to this world that we live in, and this is wonderful. This is especially true for trees.

I watched a very interesting cartoon once called *Avatar – The Last Airbender.* It is apparently the current "in" cartoon for young people between eight and eleven. It is very interesting because its message is actually amazingly spiritual. It is all about karma. In a very cartoon form, it has profound messages, and I wonder why people do not create more cartoons like this, instead of those in the old days like Tom & Jerry, simply trying to kill each other, or eating each other, or whatever it is that Tom & Jerry were doing. I am just speaking about this because one of the scenes that I watched was about evil.

Like in any cartoon, the Avatar is of course the good one, trying to defend and protect the world against the evil. Interestingly, there are two wizards, one is a humble wizard and the other gets caught up in his ego and so becomes a wizard that works through darkness, believing that this is the only way to work in the world. One of the first things that this wizard does to control the world, is to chop down all the trees. I found it amazing, wondering where were they were getting this information from. He was cutting down all the trees because that took the energy out of the earth and out of the wizard that did not go to the path of darkness, as the trees were very important for him to get life force.

The cartoon showed that as the cut trees were not harmonising and balancing the ecology of the world anymore, the darkness could come out of the earth. The bad wizard then created soldiers out of this darkness, coming from the space of emptiness. They were almost like robots and had no feeling towards the earth or towards each other. As there were no trees to give life to the earth that these soldiers were being created from, they were totally controlled by this wizard of darkness. Then the cartoon went on and on around this theme.

I am just saying this because of the trees. For me, the main thing that people are doing quite unconsciously and very negatively to the earth is destroying nature, and especially trees. Trees are the pinpoints of energy that create balance in the whole ecosystem. By cutting down the forests, the rainforests and the trees all around, we are disturbing the energy of the atmosphere. That makes it more likely for us to get sick and we introduce aspects to the world that are more difficult to deal with. We are not doing it consciously but unconsciously.

I realised this in the rainforest, as I worked in the Amazon because somewhere close, they were cutting down the forest, which is what some people do a lot in the Amazon. I travelled through both ecosystems, the one where the forest was destroyed and the one where the forest was pure and totally alive so that I could see the people and the whole situation. Sensing the atmosphere in the destroyed part and the pure part of the forest cannot be explained in words. You can only experience it when you are there. Without people knowing, some companies were digging a hole that would make it so difficult for everything around to happen, from simple things such as being happy, to more profound and complicated things, such as the ecosystem creating a whole range of diseases that was killing the native people and the local people. The ecosystem was totally disturbed.

Trees are uniquely bound to our internal experience of joy and happiness. This is why when we walk in a forest we feel the magic and this is why fairy tales and mythology often talk about trees, special trees in forest, green and sometimes dark forests with princesses and princes. There is so much more to nature than we can see, so much more than just the physical form.

Thoughts, Emotions & Health

(A 10-year-old child asks) **I always thought that thoughts were all the same?**

Why do you think all thoughts are the same?

(The child continues) **Because you are talking about thoughts and I was wondering what is the difference between a happy thought and a sad thought?**

That is a very interesting question. What is the difference between a happy thought and a sad thought? Let us find an answer to that one. Is there a difference? I do not think there is a difference between a happy thought and a sad thought, so actually you are right. Every thought is the same but one difference is that one thought makes you happy and another thought makes you sad. If one thought makes you happy, normally you feel that it is a nicer thought, a better thought, to have. If you have a thought that is making you feel sad then you judge that thought as not such a nice thought and may not be a good thought to have or to have again.

When that happens, the whole process that is unfolding is judgement because in it is only our subjective perspective that distinguishes good and bad, happy and sad. What is beyond the thought is always the divine mind, which in essence, is neither happy nor sad, it is just itself. And if the mind is just itself, then really in essence, all thoughts are equal because the energy of the thought is the same. It is just your judgement that is saying, "This is a good thought, and this is not a nice thought". If the wise Sai sees that all thoughts are the same, then there is no need to stop thinking. We just accept that all thoughts are all right. If there is a sense of acceptance of the thinking process, then there are no thoughts. There is just the divine aspect of the mind. You are enlightened.

But some thoughts have the power to change things. Some experiences made with water in Japan show that good thoughts and positive words create beautiful crystal forms, while bad words and thoughts produce ugly shapes. It says something about the energy in a thought or in a word and about the power of our thinking onto matter.

Of course, I totally agree. The crystals externalise what we do to ourselves. It is important to recognise that our thoughts are destructive to our cells because we are made of so much water and so many sensitive energetic points pick up on them. Imagine how many good thoughts and how many worrying thoughts, angry thoughts, sad thoughts, victim thoughts, or unhappy thoughts per day. Now calculate the amount of good thoughts and the amount of not so good thoughts that we have and see what it is doing to us.

To answer your question, all thoughts are the same because the energy that is creating them is neither good nor bad. It is just that the space of subjectivity, which is coming from an aspect that is beyond the thought, changes the thought to be something. When the thought comes up it is neither good nor bad. When the thought comes up, it is pure. It only becomes bad and influences us and the water in us in a negative way when other aspects intervene in this thought and change its form to become a sad or angry one.

That thought then expands even further. Often we think that we keep it for ourselves and nobody recognises it, but as this experiment with the water shows, the thought never stops. It remains in the air, in the ether, forever. It is not as if you have a thought that is private and disappears and no one can penetrate that thinking. Like a camera or a film taking a picture, it is recorded and never goes.

If thoughts have the same essence, their meanings are different. They are the same but they produce different effects...

Yes but it is a little bit like anger. On one level it is bad because the effect of someone angry is not so pleasant for the people around, but if we judge it, we are creating dualism. Everything is part of the divine, even the anger is part of the divine and this is at the core of my teaching. It may be further removed from the essence but then again, we are further removed from the essence in all of our aspects, including in thoughts that may seem to some people as very creative and good.

If we look at it more deeply, if we embrace the anger for example, we realise that it is a communication. It is a level of communication that needs to be transcended from that point where it has reached a limit and cannot go any further. To judge it, to say it is bad and to push it under the carpet, to push it away, or try to be something else than what that space is, is not honouring the divine that is within that space of anger. When we honour that space and embrace the anger, often what we see behind it is the need and desperate call for love. It is actually another face of the divine but expressing itself in a different way.

All thoughts in my opinion are the same because all human experiences, all that is here in this world, is actually the same. They are simply different aspects of the same.

What may seem like a good thought, or judged by outside people as good, actually has many other levels that are not as good as we think they are. It is much more complex than labelling a "good thought" and a "bad thought". The anger, the negative thought or the bad thought that people think that they have, is actually an expression of the divine trying to find itself within that space, trying to fill that space with the best possible potential. That best possible potential is not expressed by removing ourself from that space but by honouring it in the most complete way, embracing it.

Recognising the emotion inside...

Yes, recognising the emotion, whatever it is, like the anger, and say, "Yes. This is part of life". We do not need to push aside our aspects and try to live out to a picture that is seen as more heavenly or more beautiful, like Christianity has done to a certain degree, because that picture is not relevant to that exact moment of what is happening. It is a picture that comes from outside, from cultural, social ideas that being something else than yourself is good. Being yourself is where the divine lives, so wherever that self is, that is the starting point.

If it is anger, you do not need to start outside of that space. You can start in that space, by honouring it. Then you will see that it is a layer that will disappear because there will be a deeper layer to that space, but this is impossible to understand without going to that space of anger. It is impossible to understand the beauty behind anger – which is the call for love, embracing and deeper communication – without going back to that moment where you honour that space. Honouring your emotion is really about pulling yourself away from all the outer pictures and coming to the centre.

In the beginning, it is difficult to get to that space of anger because it is there where your experience is at. This experience takes you deeper and deeper to the point where you will realise your centre and even though anger is not the centre, it is a step towards the centre. There is no need to be pushing the anger away. Trying to be nice and believing that by being nice you get closer to the centre is what sometimes creates, in the New Age environment, this superficial niceness where people are not being what they are – real – but rather talking or acting in a certain way that is accepted as more spiritual. This attitude of trying to be something else is lacking depth. It lacks a quality that is more real, like in people living on the street who do not have time to pretend to be something else than what they are as they have to deal with reality. Even though it is traumatic, their experience is more real.

Emotions have to be recognised for what they are, yet their essence should not be forgotten. We clearly know today that different thoughts can produce illness or sickness. When you speak about spiritual discipline do you imply that a certain morality is necessary to have a healthy life?

If you express your anger and you just stay at that point without embracing the message that is within that anger, you go around in a circle, like buying a car and then getting bored and buying another car, escaping into materialism... I am not saying that screaming and being angry at people is necessary, of course not. I am rather inviting you to honour the space that you are in. By honouring that space within a framework of spiritual practice, you may be conscious of the dynamics in that situation and that consciousness will certainly change the situation.

If, for example, you are aware of physical stress, then it is very difficult to maintain that physical structure because that awareness makes it clear that your shoulders are painful, so you relax your shoulders. It is natural. But if you are not aware, the pain will remain there in a chronic way, destroying you by not expressing who you are.

If who you are in that moment is not so nice, but you are not even aware of that, then what happens? What happens is that we have a society that is totally repressed to a point that diseases such as cancer and AIDS, all the viruses and the new viruses that are coming, feel more comfortable to be in than to be real. It is so because people are not real to themselves nor to other people. That brings the energy to a point where the disharmony is even more powerful than being clear and open. It brings it to a space where it can be dealt with. I am not saying that it is like in Osho groups, or some catharsis type groups, where you need to express any emotion that is floating around inside. It is definitely not that because for me that is not the point. The point is to bring consciousness to your immediate experience.

Consciousness does not come by expression. It comes by honouring the communication that is in that expression. Consciousness does not come by being angry and being unconscious at the same time because then the anger is more harmful and destructive than by being angry. In that split second where you are angry, you are, however, conscious of the dynamics that are partaking outside and inside. You bring consciousness to the expression of your humanity and you acknowledge that you are a human being. By acknowledging your humanity, you acknowledge the deeper aspect of yourself.

Being angry is all right, yet there is a social limit to the expression of what we feel...

You cannot not hurt other people. It is unavoidable because if you have anger and you pretend that you are not angry, you are still hurting people. In our society, it is seen as more polite to hide the expression of anger so that you do not hurt others, but it is hidden anger. What people do not understand is that anger does not only come to the surface and affects people through an emotional outburst or through a physical outburst. Anger actually touches the etheric level. It becomes very clear in the body that you are feeling angry, even if you are smiling at the person and pretending that there is nothing going on. It becomes very clear on this etheric level. It changes the atmosphere and actually touches the anger of the other person.

Then you have this subtler unknown dynamic that is going on that often happens in relationships because people do not communicate so clearly. I see this sometimes when I go to people who are together, supposed to be in love. You walk into the room and you feel "something" in the atmosphere, although there is no obvious tension or difficulty between the two people who are in the relationship. It is just that something is lacking in the expression and the communication.

This is often a problem in groups like communities where the interaction is very important. Everything seems all right on the surface but there are things lurking behind. Maybe better than communities are family Christmas reunions... Everything seems to be going well and has to be fine – "We are here to enjoy

Christmas". People drink, spend more time together, and all of a sudden, things change. Have they changed or have they always been like this? It is just that people have politely hidden the communication or unconsciously been unaware of the communication that is happening and harming in the same way, until the outburst happens during the Christmas dinner.

Western societies are very typical of that. It is like a Christmas dinner, where people have not got together. They have decided to be individuals and have individualised their lives, creating safety barriers around themselves so that they do not have to deal with too much at the same time. They just have themselves to deal with. There are unspoken energies and incomplete interactions with everything around you because you are an individual.

This is creating modern disease, modern stress and modern sickness as people do not have the depth to go and communicate what is really going on, either to themselves, to their families, or to their communities. They are socially bound by norms, regulations and expectations. It is much easier to politely meet once a year when it gets difficult. It is much easier to watch a film together than to really address what is going on. This is the same with children who will often mirror what is going on in the family, but in a real sense, by acting it out. The family will wonder, "Why is my child so strange? Why are they acting out this strange behaviour?", but they will not realise that it is not just a child acting out dynamics.

The child is part of a whole set of dynamics that include the mother, the father, the grand-parents and whoever is part of that family unit. It is just that the child is the most real person and is expressing what is going on. The others have unconsciously got bound by the social expectations of themselves – to be parents, polite parents, nice parents, or pretending to be nice parents, whatever it is – and so do not deal with the situation. In actual fact that causes more suffering and more pain, and children will easily get confused as they do not have anything real to grab on to.

Clarity is very important so that the child understands what they are really relating to. It is better than pretending to be nice and say, "Oh, it is OK, but please do not climb on that table", and then to have another feeling inside of you, a feeling that you are hiding up to a point where the child climbs on the table for the tenth time, and then you cannot stand it anymore and you really snap into what you are. It makes no difference. For me it is better to be real and to honour the situation.

If it is a problem for you, if the anger is disturbing you because it is coming from more than just the interaction with that person, with your child or your family, it has attached itself to other historical aspects. The build up of anger is not just related to one immediate situation but it is related to many other aspects of your development in relation to your child or to your family. That is what makes it confusing because those points have never been made clear. They have never been made conscious but have just remained hidden.

This is why a spiritual teacher, who does not have that relationship to the unfinished energies that are causing this constriction in a flow, can seemingly do magic. It is not that there is any magic, because we all have the same potential to do this, but the intention is much more focused to change something directly. If you are a person that has invested a lot of energy into maintaining an equilibrium with anger and certain feelings of guilt – for example, getting angry and then feeling guilty because you are not a loving person – then this game requires a lot of energy to maintain. It does not do so on an emotional level only but also on an energetic and a physical level.

This is why it is difficult to do magical things – to touch someone on the head for the pain to go away – because eighty per cent of the energy is being used to maintain the safety valves of whatever you have developed as a personality. On the other hand, if a spiritual teacher is free from this attachment, he or she has that eighty per cent of energy that is not being used for those safety valves to invest elsewhere. This is why if a spiritual teacher gets very direct with someone, it can seem like the sword is cutting right through the middle of the most sensitive part of that person because it is direct. There is nothing hidden. It is very forthcoming.

We are still talking about thought. In a sense, "Where does thought begin and where does it end?" may be a more relevant question. Does it begin when you put it outside and you express your anger? Does it begin when it becomes conscious in your mind that you have that thought – "OK, now I am thinking about this"? Has it begun before? If it has begun before, where did it begin and what did it start as? If everything is equal, is the beginning not the same as the end?

That leads us back to intention...

This is the deeper meaning of intention, to go beyond trying to change anything but to go to the essence of where the thinking is. I put up a very interesting cartoon on the website. It is about a *guru* and a disciple. The story is so simplistic and clear in such a funny way and it is about this student going to the *guru* and saying: "I watched this film called *The Secret* and was very inspired with the fact that we can manifest things, but I have been trying for a week and nothing is happening. This law of attraction does not seem to work for me!". Then the *guru* answered in a very wise and comical way, "The problem is not the fact that we need to follow the law of attraction and create anything. The problem is that we do not appreciate what we have".

This is it. We are always trying to manifest all these things and forgetting to appreciate and honour the simplicity of what we have. That is intention. Intention is more the simplicity of what we have in this moment. Willpower on the other hand, is trying to change what we have to something that we believe we need. It is coming out of a space of desire and wanting. It is coming out of a space of ignorance because out of that space of willpower, we do not realise that we do not need anything. In the deepest sense of the word, we do not need anything. If we believe we need something, it comes out of an incomplete space. It is therefore impossible to manifest the simplicity because anything that comes out of incompleteness can never be completed in a real sense, as there is no essence to it.

I thought that story was an interesting one to highlight the difference between intention and willpower. Intention has no desire, no need, and no attachment to achieve anything. If your intention is to love someone, you do not have to will your love to be real. It is rather coming to the space that is there and honouring it more. The intention is an active aspect of that honouring. It is to manifest it so that it becomes clear in your actions.

So to think good or to think bad is not the question. What matters is before the intention. Is this your point?

Exactly. Because in the end there is no bad.

But, again, we can get ill with bad thoughts!

We can get ill by bad thoughts but never by bad thoughts from other people. We only get ill by bad thoughts that we have created in ourselves, which in turn create the space for other bad thoughts to fill up, join in, and celebrate. This was a big thing in shamanism. All the shamans I worked with believed in black magic, in evil spirits, in things supposedly coming and harming you, always from the outside. It was a major part of the culture and the major reason why I do not identify at all with shamanism. I laughed once and I said, "This is impossible". The reason why people are getting sick is not because of black magic. Individuals are getting sick because they have created the sickness in their own mind.

Without the belief in it, black magic cannot hurt...

It is not enough to simply not believe because even if you do not believe consciously, you could believe and fear it unconsciously and then it creates the space. It is more that if you do not have the space for that thought to flourish in, it cannot. This is manipulation, which is something that I also work deeply with in groups of people that are around me. Manipulation often becomes a subtle game behind the scenes with people wanting things to turn out in certain ways, or wanting it to be this way or that way – even trying to manipulate me, without knowing but doing it, can you believe it? I do not say it is a bad thing because it is like anger: it is just a human aspect that needs to be acknowledged and worked with more deeply, but this manipulation can be quite negative, especially when we do not work with it.

It is what a lot of governments, multinational companies and powers are doing to human beings. I am not sure if they are totally aware that they are doing it or if it is just an automatic response to needs and desires, but they are doing this. And people almost want to be manipulated. Once that sort of dynamic begins, it is almost like they do not feel so comfortable anymore if they do not have that, they sort of lose something.

This is where for example most Germans during the Second World War did not really want to know what was going on. The Nazi regime was so manipulative that people even denounced their own children to the government if they were not following the rules. Everyone was insulated and of course, there might have been an awareness of what was going on but it is very difficult for us today to see what that situation was. We are not living in that situation like the masses of German people were during those times, for whom it was not that obvious. The manipulation was so present and everyone was contributing to it in some way that it became a whole societal thing rather than a negative thing that you could identify and move away from or distinguish yourself from it. It was like a disease that overtook the whole country.

This shows the power of an ideology...

The power of an ideology and the power of certain people to manipulate to a degree that it does not even seem like a manipulation. It seems taken for granted and in the case of Germany, people only really understood the whole situation after the war. How could people be so amazingly unconscious of what was going on with millions of people dying? That seemed impossible not to see for the British or the Americans. Now let us look at what is going in America today, the state of emergency, the laws on terrorism and the war... Most people seem to accept it, yet the human aspect of it is forgotten in that crazy thrust to manipulate and control, acting so that only certain things can happen in certain ways.

This touches many aspects, from biology to belief systems that want to safeguard society. I am not saying that this is wrong or right, but just that it is not that far removed from our own experience. We are stepping slowly and slowly closer to a society that uses excuses as to why certain things are necessary and we accept it, watching on television and not wanting what is happening in Iraq to happen in our own country for example. We justify certain things because of others. Manipulation is very dangerous because it is very subtle. It touches the unconscious much more than the conscious mind and sometimes we just accept, as a mass, that this is all right. We forget that we may actually question more deeply what is going on. This passive attitude, which consists in accepting things and being submitted to what is going on, is what politicians rely on to control politics and people.

Politicians and the media are very connected...

Of course, and maybe not consciously. Maybe it is not like some people think that there are some people out there that are simply bad, trying to change and control society. Maybe it is just like any situation: once you are in power, you lose touch with humility.

Until today, the capitalist ideology – buying and selling with profit, etc. – largely contributes to the manipulation and deception of the masses. Do you see the common drive to produce and consume, as an unconscious desire to answer deeper needs? Whether we know why or not, we are always inclined to want more and more...

We want it. Indeed, the drive to fulfil what is empty is more basic and more powerful than survival. When you are able to remove that from the path of spirituality and focus it on materialism or on an ideology, you can create a monster of a human being or a monster of a society, which is what we have today. We have a consumerist society that does not even realise that what we are consuming is being destroyed, even though certain people talk about this.

We have reached a point where we have to really look at this whole situation not just as a country or a political group but as the world. In Third World countries for example, there are people who still consider that they are too poor to look at this now. Before they get to that point of awareness, they want to be like us in the West, to have cars and houses instead of starvation. But the whole situation comes from deeper than that simplistic idea according to which if we all become more "civilised", in the western idea of civilisation, we have the possibility of improvement.

In America and in Western Europe today, everyone has enough. Some people are rich, some people are poor but everyone has more or less what he or she needs to survive. Yet, if you look at people, their goal is still to get more. One only needs to look at Christmas time, a moment where the shops are selling and where everyone is in a buying frenzy. I find it very strange that people forget what is more important – the simplicity – and want a car, a house. That may be necessary, but in that wanting we forget too often that there is something else that we need to honour. Politicians and society make us focus on the want and make us forget what is important to remember. This is totally out of context with reality.

This of course does not mean that if you are spiritual you do not have to want, because of course you need to eat, you need a house, and you need to do all the things that every human being needs to do. It is important however, to keep the needs within a context, within a centre where your reference point is not simply a desire or materialism detached from everything else. It is important to keep the need in connection with everything else so that this connection stimulates our evolution and development as a material society. With that, a new culture of the world may arise, away from wanting in a selfish way and more connected to the depth of our love for the earth, our love for human beings and our connectedness to each other. We could then develop material things in a wonderful way because these material things have a different reference point. They are connected and not destructive.

I believe we cannot go back to being living as we did in ancient times, living in tents, or, like the hippies believed, just dropping civilisation and find a simpler way of living. I think we have to honour where we are at in this moment, in the material and evolutionary sense that humanity as a whole has reached. We need to change the reference point so that technology, science and culture change with that reference point to the extent that the whole concepts of buying and selling, of shops and materialism, are still there but in a totally different perspective. This is happening on a more practical level.

One of the worst aspects of capitalism is banking for example. Anyone who understands the banking system knows that it is a total manipulation and game. The ideas of banks are basically to make a profit and that it is the easiest way to control everyone. If we change the reference point of the bank, so that rather than only looking at profit it actually sees that money can actually be used for cooperation, for building bridges and other community projects, then we have a more idealistic bank.

A bank that refuses to invest in destructive projects or ideas and influences investment towards useful technology becomes of benefit to humanity. It then creates a bridge for the energy and the power of money to go elsewhere than this idea of wanting more, of wanting profits to be higher and forgetting everything else that creates that whole driving system. There are some banks and some companies that are beginning to do this and teach cooperation rather than competition. They are actually quite successful and I believe they could be even more successful if society honoured their efforts rather than just see them as important because their profits are actually quite high.

These banks helping projects coming from people of Third World countries are apparently more and more popular.

Yes, like the cooperative bank I belong to in England. They do not invest in weapons or in pharmaceutical companies that do certain things that are not so useful. It is the fourth or fifth largest bank in the UK and millions of pounds go through their bank everyday, so they do make a difference. This is what I think cultures of the future will need rather than – as some people believe – going back to past social forms. I think that being "primitive" is very useful but impossible at this point.

You said that what matters most is not other's people ideas of us but our own feelings, what we feel of ourselves, and that the diseases we can get through negative thoughts only come from our own. But we constantly listen to depressing news; we are subject to social environments that bring us down, etc. Can we really protect ourselves from what some people call "toxic thoughts" and ideas coming from the outside?

Yes you can but the reason why you normally are in that environment is because some part of you identifies with this. It is the addictive aspect of this part of humanity that loves the dramas of fear, pain and suffering that prolongs the whole situation as an ongoing process. It is doing so because it is so subtle inside that it is difficult to see. It is much easier to quantify and relate to and perhaps to change things from the outside. On some level it is not such a bad thing to be in such an environment. It is only bad if what you are present to is just unconsciously feeding the unconscious part of yourself. To watch the news or to read the paper with consciousness is not a problem in itself but most people do not do this.

I do not watch the news because for me it is a waste of time. Looking at murders and people dying touches and imprints upon the mind and can be quite toxic. We then form the idea that the world is not nice and we are just reaffirming what we believe in already. Yet, if we see this just as a game that needs to be looked at in a deeper sense rather than just the superficial sense of war, murder, or drug addiction, then that consciousness can help us to understand a lot.

In general, however, and because you brought this question up, I do say that it is interesting in the beginning of spiritual work to stop being exposed to the things that can imprint on you. It is especially useful in the beginning because, like a child, your mind is very much like a sponge and as you open up, it will open up to whatever is there, not only the beautiful things but everything else that is there too. It is therefore important to create some spiritual discipline, to move out of these environments that are imbalanced, and expose yourself to things in a balanced way.

Listening to the news is clearly an everyday routine starting in the morning for most of people, and these news are usually quite depressing and somewhat toxic. Yet, not listening to them, and being unaware of what is going on, does not allow us to be a complete social being. I understand that there is a way to listen to them without being touched and imbibed by negative emotions, but to reach that point may take a long time, unless you are almost indifferent to the world around you. What you suggest is to reduce this habit – the everyday news nurture – in the beginning of the spiritual path and understand why we do want to listen to the news?

Yes. It is very complicated so I will take just one point of view to explain.

On one level, being spiritual is not about isolating yourself from what is going on, but on the opposite end of the spectrum, being spiritual is also detaching yourself from the world so that you are not of the world but beyond the world. It is complicated. If I had the time, I would start a whole new TV channel where the news would be positive news rather than focusing on six hundred people dying here or twenty people dying there.

When I speak to Europeans – and even though I am European, I do not identify myself as a European – what I find is that they have belief systems that come from the news, which really have very little to do with the reality of the depicted situations. People believe that Africa is terrible because everyone is dying of starvation, that there is always a political turmoil and something terrible happening there. The news create the illusion that you know what is happening and, on some level, it formats your idea of Africa.

It is very interesting to go and live in Africa because of course, you will see that those things are right, people are dying and life is very cheap, compared to Germany, France, or Portugal. But there are things happening that could never be heard on the news that reveal an African spirit, in spite of the cultural and economical differences, that you can only know by living in Africa. When you live in Africa, you know that it is much more complex than the three minutes that are given to that section of the news.

This is why I find that news can be very one sided because they do not give a real perspective. I know this because my family was working in the diplomatic corps and as they were in the middle of a very explosive society, they really had to be in touch with what was going on. Interestingly, they would get news that was totally different from those they would hear on television and the radio and they would always be quite shocked to see how big the difference was between the news portraying one thing and the information the diplomats need to know to get the whole story, which is a professional necessity to work within that space.

They heard the different sides with many points of view. This is why I thought, "Why not create a new television program which really can go for example to India and speak about some of the wonderful things that happen there and make India a marvellous culture of total magic?". That does not come across when we watch the news and we see these people cycling in the midst of pollution and the rubbish everywhere. I mean that exists, I have been there and I have seen all the dirt, all the flies, and all the suffering. But what about the rest?

In the end, I find most news to be unnecessary. Some people watch the news in the morning, at night and then buy the newspapers on the weekend to read not just one paper but two papers to have the left side and the right side of politics explaining things in different ways. I am not saying it is a bad thing, but I just wonder if it is actually portraying everything? It is nice for me to know the facts because then I communicate other things beyond just the pain and suffering to those people who are watching the news.

Does it affect people? I think it can. I find TVs very obtrusive. Its presence can be so strong and disturbing for those who don't want such a rhythm. I do not say that these concepts are wrong but surely, when you are fed all these so called facts or realities from television, it takes away the creativity and the possibility for you to find out these things for yourself. The idea that because it is on television it must be true, reduces that inquisitive creative mind that looks at things in a beautiful way. This is why I do not have a television. I am not extreme in the sense of saying that all television is bad so if you have to find a compromise then perhaps it is to choose programs that do not have violence or silly ideas inside, or that are not just entertainment, but that in some way are inspiring for you and your family.

For example, there are DVDs, that are beautiful and inspiring. That is what I find is lacking in the news. Is there inspiration in the news? Are you inspired at the end of it to do something that is positive, or does it add to the burden and to the idea that everything is so difficult that there is nothing we can do because the world is so crazy? I do not really know because my family never had television and growing up, I was not introduced to this way of being, so for me it is a bit of a new thing at this point. In the monastery there was no television, and in my life after that there was no television. It is only recently that I had to deal with this situation.

I actually heard from someone in England that a family was refused the adoption of a child because they did not have television in their house. I do not know how the adoption agency put it, but they considered it would create a trauma for the children! It was so strange for them that there was no television in the house and that was the reason given to that family to refuse adoption.

We have become so tied down to this idea of television, media and news as being quite normal, that we never question it. When I was growing up in Egypt they had a different way of portraying the news that I really loved. There were people who went around like theatre people – I do not know how they were called – but they did not go to a theatre: they went to a community and they made jokes. It was more like a comedy about a situation. That comedy could be social and political and it was very interesting because it brought the whole community together to look at the situation and to really see it from a perspective where people could interact, talk to each other and do something about it. It was not a formal theatre with people dressing up in costumes but it was a simple type of play.

Often these moments were hidden, because you could not really openly speak about politics at that time. The climate was very much one-way and you could not say much because it would be politically wrong, but through theatre, poetry and plays, you could imply quite a lot and people would understand what you were implying. People looked at it in a much easier way than seeing it on the news because the news were totally controlled, so whatever was said was very much from a political dominance of that situation.

Would you say there is no contradiction between the idea that some information, some ideas, some thoughts may be toxic, even if they are not ours, and the idea that nothing may really be toxic because everything in us is light? Is it a difference in the state of awareness that a person has reached which protects him or her from bad influences?

Yes, and that is attachment. If you watch the news and your mind attaches to the negative aspect of the news and feels depressed, then, on some level, it is not worth watching the news. It is very different to watch without being attached to it. Often, on the aeroplane there is news on television if it is a long flight, so it is very difficult not to watch it because the TV screens are everywhere. The television shows some awful pictures of war, people dying, and other such calamities. I am very surprised that this is even allowed, as there are children on the plane.

This somehow forces us to watch the news so I look at it sometimes. Yet I just think it is interesting because for me it is like a theatre of life. It is not different from the theatre I see for example when I go to a big city, into a situation that has lots of dynamics of people rushing around, in a supermarket, in an airport, or anywhere else. I see it from the perspective that it is just another set of dynamics rather than getting shocked.

If the news can clearly impact on our psychological state, what about the influence of the contact of other people we are interacting with in life, our direct social environment? Sometimes we get people's mood: we feel sad because they are sad, we feel good if there are well, etc.

Being in the space of people that are depressed, agitated or disharmonious brings the same effect than the news but it is even stronger because you are in their presence. The news only requires that certain senses interact with what is going on but being with the person, at least if you have to be physically close to him or her, requires much more of you, even if you are not conscious of it. Often, we will go to a place and think, "I was happy when I left and now that I came back, I am strangely lacking energy, I feel depressed, tired and with a headache". However, everything seemed all right when we were there. It was not like it was an immediate reaction where you feel that you had to leave on the spot, "Oh my God, I feel terrible, I have to go!". The unease comes later as it does not work like the news where you are shocked by a picture immediately. It works on the subtle energy – usually the solar plexus – on a cord that connects you to that person. The process is very slow and normally appears four or five hours later but it can be ten hours later, or a day later.

I am not saying that we have to avoid people who are feeling bad and then start being paranoid about where we go and always wonder if we should go there, but it is good to be discerning. Discerning is different from being judgemental. It is to know what is useful for you at this time. "Do I need to spend time with this person, just because it is what is expected, what is polite, or what is necessary?", or "If I do not, then what are people going to think, or what am I going to think about myself?". Many factors are implicated in this whole complex game, especially if you are sensitive.

There are different periods where people are more sensitive. During full moon or during new moon for example, women and children are especially more sensitive. In traditional societies it was understood that you were more sensitive at these times. Often there were taboo, certain things that were not possible to do or not expected to do for a mother in the first three weeks after the baby birth for example, or if someone is very sick or dying. In our society, the whole rhythm of life, the reference point is not traditional in that sense. It is about masks, expectations, politeness and money. So your question was, "Would we get affected?". Yes. We will get affected, without a doubt.

It is important not to get affected by these processes. People often wonder how can I deal with the dynamics surrounding me from morning to evening during retreats, "How come you do not seem to be affected?" they ask. I am not saying this to claim I am not affected, but simply to show that it is not necessary to be affected

Of course, sometimes people are very strong in their projections, whether it is conscious or not, and these projections are directly aimed at the person. If you are conscious, you know what they are doing. Now if it is unconscious, it is even more complicated because it really catches people off guard and it is difficult to remain detached from it, just as it is difficult to remain detached from your own thoughts, and your own feelings.

To say and believe that it is possible to remain detached from this process and proclaim, "I will go there and I will cover myself with light or I will just think happy thoughts and feel good", is a game. In less than ten minutes, your mind will pick up on a negative thought produced by yourself and if you can do that with yourself, you will definitely do it with other people. The discernment is to say, "What is the balance? Where is the balance?" I feel the balance is to not hide from the world. Being a hermit and escaping to the mountains and having nothing to do with anyone is useful during certain periods. It cuts out the picture of relationship that is important with the mundane, and that helps you to see things.

To go to the other extreme and be very social all the time is based on western individualism where we need entertainment from other people. We constantly gravitate towards some other form of entertainment, occupying ourselves away from ourselves and preventing us from being in our centre, in our own space. What matters is finding a balance. If you have a family, the balance usually swings towards it. If you are single, then it swings the other way and, usually, you are more social. There are different points of development.

If you are together and in love then the balance swings towards your partner and if you have been with your partner for a few years, your group usually extends. This was always natural for human beings, but we now live in a society with lots of people very close to each other and interactions are much more intense than they should be. In my opinion, cities are not natural. Big meetings and celebrations are interesting but not natural. What is natural is for us to interact with nature, with small groups that we feel comfortable with. This is our human trait.

Selecting the kind of activity and social environment we involve in is a necessary part of the spiritual discipline?

Of course. Why put yourself in a situation that does not bring consciousness to who you are? Selecting the outside space we want to live in is part of discernment. For this, one simple thing can be to ask ourselves: "Do I need to go to the crazy supermarket that is really busy to go shopping and save perhaps five euros a week? Or are those five euros better invested by going to my local supermarket where I feel calm, I have time and I do not have to be agitated, just being in the space which supports me more?". I this see a lot in times when there are sales. Rather than the traditional way of going to the local market, people are rushing around with their "I want to buy" madness and pushing other people aside, focused on not loosing much money but totally losing themselves in the material game, not recognising that it is just a game.

In America they have this interesting thing called the farmer's market where you can meet the person who produced the food. You can relate more deeply to the whole situation rather than just buy an item that is cheap. Then you have much more and when you are spiritual that surely becomes where you need to go. You move away from just buying things that are cheap and fulfilling material needs into a space that fulfils the material needs in a different way, so you select your environment. If you do not do it, ask yourself, "Why aren't I?" What is the game that you are playing with yourself, to put yourself in such a situation where you have no choice, or where you feel that you have no choice?

Are you aware of your spirituality when you are shopping like mad, as I see people during Christmas? Of course you are spiritual because every person there is spiritual but where is the awareness of anything? Surely Christmas has something deeper than the presents and what we are going to buy, making sure that we have got everything before the shops close. People have to be aware and you can be aware of your spirituality even in that situation, so I am not saying that by not doing the shopping you are spiritual. If for you that space does not affect you, what you are giving to people is a profound sense of sharing your spiritual love, your spiritual presence, rather than just focusing on yourself. Then maybe you really are Santa Claus!

Does spiritual awareness influence the body in terms of health and diseases?

Totally. Without a doubt, I believe that spiritual well-being can change physical structures. I cut myself once and of course, there was blood and someone asked me "Surely Tony you can just look at your finger now and change it. Why don't you do it?". This was my answer, "When you live in the circle of life you honour that circle and whatever is happening in it. You do not have to change anything. The divine wanted my finger to bleed so all I am doing is watching my finger bleed and have the experience of pain".

At other times I know my service is needed and everyone else is sick, then I use the spiritual energy that is communicating and loving the viruses around and say, "Hello, thank you for coming and joining me". I know this sounds childish but I embrace them totally and there is no sickness. You cannot, however, say that spirituality means that you transcend life, because life is everything and it is not simply transcending what we believe to be negative.

Sickness for me is like suffering. It has a place and it is not bad. Sometimes I even say I need to go through this experience and it is not a negative experience. If you are detached from it and see the whole cycle behind it, then it is a beautiful part of life. If, however, we are separate and if sickness is creating suffering to yourself and to other people, then sometimes it requires spiritual work to transform the physical level of suffering. This is what sometimes happens with people I work with. Yesterday, I knew someone was getting sick and I sent a message to them the day before yesterday, before they were sick, to send them greetings – which I rarely do. They replied, "Thank you very much".

This was a spiritual work to help the whole process of sickness that was a very bad one. It was some form of virus which affects the brain and gives you a headache. I did not want the person to not experience the pain, because it is possible to change this pain for it to be less dramatic so that consciousness has a greater possibility of understanding the space that is in that pain and in the suffering of disease.

For example, I worked with someone who had cancer and a lady said to me, "If you can change everything why don't you change the cancer now? Surely you can see that this is not very nice. He had a child and his child is only four years old and he had a wife, look at the pain!...". I said, "If you start to do this, you are playing with dualism, with the ego of good and bad, with what is right and what is wrong. You have to trust". All I do is speak to the spiritual essence of that person and from that spiritual essence that person has a deeper connection to the physical disease that is manifesting in the body. Then the comprehension allows consciousness to grow. It may be necessary because it allows for the feeling of suffering to be less dramatic, to make more sense and to become a natural reality.

When I was working with a person who had cancer, I worked with the comprehension inside, on the spiritual level rather than on changing the physical aspect. We worked together and there was a spiritual understanding. I felt some peace in this person and this is what is important, much more than changing. Then the cancer is not such a big problem and it becomes less acute because it is understood.

What is "working on the spiritual level"? You said you worked together and then this person felt peace. But what was the work?

Spirituality is coming back to the present moment and seeing everything as it is. It is not going to the future and saying, "I am going to die and my wife and children are going to suffer". It is not going to the future and feeling the pain, because the recognition of pain somehow entails that on some level, your body has to go through an experience. Your idea of pain is either in the future or the past, therefore the body is not recognising the present moment but moving in the forward or backward dimensions. When a person comes to the space where he or she recognises what is beyond that, to the centre of oneself, that to me is spirituality. There is not one word because it is unique to each person.

It is acknowledging the present moment...

Exactly! I think that changes physical reality. This is why when you do meditation or spiritual work, you are recognising more than just the mundane, you are recognising what is beyond the mundane and your body changes its chemistry.

Is acknowledging, a kind of letting go?

Acknowledging is letting go.

But is letting go not being passive too?

Letting go is active and passive because being passive, doing nothing, will not work, so it requires activity, like meditation requires focus. But if you are too focused then you are too active. The focus is to help you to be passive.

It is letting things be expressed...

Exactly.

What do you suggest to do to face or avoid sickness?

We can talk to every aspect of nature and change its specific form so that it has a different form. For example with bacteria and viruses, if we acknowledge their form as it is, then it becomes terrible and gives you the cold or the flu. We can instead treat them with love and speak to them in a way that changes their form so that they change from being a virus to something else. This is my view of what is going to happen in medicine in the future. Unlike the modern medicine, it will not be so much trying to kill viruses but rather invite them to change their form so that their form does not affect our own form anymore.

This is a long way from modern medicine but I would say that in fifteen years, people will start working on this, communicating directly to the virus. The virus will not just be seen as something that you get rid of through antibiotics, but something that you can actually deal with and work with in a way that was not possible before. This is what I do. If the virus is there and I am not wanting to get the cold, I say "no" and then we speak, but not in words of course…

Some theories say that our immune system is reinforced when we feel love inside, when we feel happy. It produces more killer cells that attack the bacteria.

If you speak to the bacteria and you say that there is no need for war inside of your body, they will understand. Intelligence is not limited to human beings. This is a very Western thing to think that only human beings understand. We also think for example that children do not understand, but it is wonderful to see how they develop and all of the sudden they are able to communicate to you in language. It is not that they have just begun to understand what you are saying, they have understood all the time. It is simply that they have not had the senses nor the possibility of communicating this to you before. The same can be said about the virus. I am not saying that a virus is like a baby, but it is another organism, just like a human being. They just have different ways of communicating than human beings.

If we communicate with anger or conflict or aggression, it becomes like the ancient times where there was survival. Now if we follow the potential that I am speaking about, if we listen to that potential, we realise that harmony and love are much more powerful than aggression, fighting, war, differentiation or dualism. I think in the future we will realise that this harmony can also be heard by all aspects of nature, including viruses. When you speak to them, you can change their form. One of the reasons why there are a lot of viruses attacking certain places is because of the thinking processes that go on in people's mind.

In a place like America where there are a lot of people who think and worry about certain things, this communicates not just to people but to all aspects of nature, to the plants and to the viruses, so then the viruses change their form to adapt to that thinking. This is why they become stronger, more aggressive and more difficult to handle. They adapt not only to the antibiotics but to our whole environment of the mind and feelings. Yet, we do not have to create this environment, we can create a different one.

If we create a different environment, we can affect it in an amazing way. This is how spiritual teachers could communicate to particles, like we hear about some of the ancient people in India, and perhaps in the Middle East. They could communicate to particles and things that are not seen except in today's advanced microscopes, because they did not communicate to them by speaking in words but by focusing in a specific way, so that that communication avenue was open.

I personally avoid getting sick because this is what I do. I am not saying this is the best way to deal with the situation but it is an amazing power because sometimes the virus do not want to do this as they are like a hungry tiger, needing to eat something. Even so, most of the times you can direct the virus to go to other situations so that they feed and survive in a different form and in a different way. This is what modern medicine can do. Everything in life wants to survive, so instead of destroying them, we can invite the organisms to go to a different space and to change their form. When they change their form, they are harmless to the human organism.

How to invite viruses to change their form? By meditating?

This is a difficult question because there is not a simple answer. There are many ways and one way is to make sure the unconscious aggression that human beings have is taken out of the picture. Sitting and visualising good things is not enough but it is actually removing the aggression that is inside of human beings. Once we remove this, there is a peaceful and harmonious state created around you. That becomes a kind of defence mechanism for things that cannot fit into that picture because they simply cannot come in.

If people are unconsciously aggressive at something that happened a long time ago for example, and cannot express it because they do not even know it is there, then they of course do not now that they are unconsciously aggressive. No one else knows either because they are very nice, they are very kind, they fit in and they smile, but all of a sudden a little virus comes... The virus "sees" that there is a space and starts feeding on it. Then, as the environment invites it to replicate itself, it replicates itself in the organism and so becomes part of the organism, of the body. This is what we call cancer today. Cancerous cells then grow and grow. Now if there were no aggression in the body, that virus could not find that space inside of you. How to do this? The first thing is to work on oneself to change all aspects that create the possibility for that to happen.

Like expressing love?

Expressing love. Being love. But we are human beings and of course we are much more complex than that. I guess modern medicine will soon work by creating the healing atmosphere in a different way.

Breath & Fear

During your retreats, you very often mention the importance of coming back to the breath as a way related to being present to oneself. Could you say more about this important aspect of spiritual work?

Breath is everything. It is the gift that we receive when we are born into this world: we take our first breath. What we are doing is manifesting our physical being into this world through the breath. The breath then enables the body and all the senses to be active and alive so that we can interact on a material level as well as on other ones. The breath is our experience in this world. In this dimension it is everything, our psychology, our personality and our feelings. The formation of the ego and the formation of our actions are related to all those senses, to our social environment, to our family, to our destiny, to our genetics and to our history – the genetic history.

The breath brings all this into manifestation and allows us the freedom to act in a conscious way. Not only is it a potential, it becomes a reality because potential is prior to the breath that enters the body. When we take a breath we make that potentiality or possibility real, in action. This is why we are here in this dimension. We are not here just to breathe but we are here to take the breath, which then extends to everything that we are relating to.

Breathing is connecting?

Exactly. It is union. That is a good way of describing it. Breathing is what assists this union to be manifested in reality, in this dimension. The breath is not just a technique according to which if you breathe in a specific way then somehow something happens. The breath is allowing consciousness to go deeper. It is to be more aware of the whole picture that you are and to be able to act in a certain way from that space of consciousness. Most of the time the breath is limited because our experiences in the mundane prevent the breathing from being complete. If our experiences lead the mind to believe that we live in a fearful environment and that fear is a reality, we breathe that belief system into ourselves.

Why is breath important? Because by breathing deeper we can release the essence of that fear, which is held in the way we breathe, out of the body. We can then realise the energy of the temple that is behind. Realising that fear is just an idea, we can go deeper into the ecstasy of the body, the joy of breath and the joy of being. The potential that we have to do things is so strongly coloured by fear that we are unable to act out that potential, so instead, we act out that fear. Breathing is a *mantra* to that union, to that connection and this is why breath is one of the essential and primary works that I focus on.

It is not, however, as in yoga or in Zen Buddhism where breath becomes a technique. It is much broader than that. You do not have to sit and breathe in a special way or count your breaths because it is beyond that. It is much more connecting the breath to something deeper. It has to do with consciousness rather than a technique and consciousness can be approached in many ways rather than just a physical aspect of breathing. It can be approached psychologically or like in Zen Buddhism, through a parable to confuse the mind so that the mind can see a different picture. It can also be approached through what I do a lot with people which is to really push them to ask themselves, "Is this my reality? Is this important?". I encourage people to go deeper into the limitations that prevent them from seeing what they are doing to themselves through holding the body and breathing in a certain way.

Your point is that breath and fear have connections. So going back to the breathe helps overcoming the fear that spoils life and prevents spiritual development?

Fear is a human trait, is not just cultural. In a sense or on some level, fear is in our genes. Biologists like to say that fear was useful because it made us run away from the animals that wanted to eat us. Fear and evolution… I do not believe that to be truly the case but I do believe, as biologists say, that fear is an inbuilt mechanism. I know that from experience because I have children and I see how fear is still present even though they grow in a very pure environment. It is not that fear is negative in itself but again, it is how we use fear that becomes negative. Society has latched onto fear as a way of controlling and manipulating people to be in a certain way so that things are steady and do not change too much. A lot of change creates chaos of course and for most systems, chaos means upheaval, which does not help society to function in a certain way.

Fear can be useful. You can use fear to grow spiritually or you can use it to control and manipulate people. I believe the problem is that most cultures do the latter strongly. It is not conscious because there is an undercurrent that most people are not even aware of. Everyone believes this to be a reality. We do not even see that there is an undercurrent nor do we see the manipulation and the control that is going on because it is not outside. It is not something that one can easily identify as, "This is controlling me", because it is actually inside of ourselves.

We have unfortunately become culturally socialised by our parents because they are themselves culturally socialised by the environment and by the atmosphere we live in. It is not direct in the sense that society says, "No, you cannot do this", but the atmosphere has an expectation and on some level, people fulfil that expectation. Scientists have looked into this by studying how if you teach one mouse a trick, the other mice learn the same trick much quicker simply because one mouse has already learnt it, even if the other mice are not genetically related. On some invisible level that information is passed on to all the mice and they have noticed a statistical difference. That is what culture can do.

There is an expectation and a fear in the atmosphere and even if you do everything right, children and adults are socialised and controlled. This of course produces fear because part of socialisation and of control's purpose is to take away your power. This is the opposite of what I attempt to do. I remind people that the power is innate, inside of them, and that they have the freedom to touch it and to work with it, but socialisation takes a little bit of that power away if it does not suit the culture. When that happens, then our fear is internalised in the body, in the breath and in the way we feel and that changes our breathing.

Even our breathing becomes a way of reinforcing that fear without us knowing it because it comes from a situation that is so far removed from our perception that we can not relate to it. Every breath that we take with that attitude of fear says, "Yes this is my reality" and it is almost like we are playing a film that keeps going on and on. Every breath that we take is playing the film that, in the end, prevents us from believing that anything can be different. We are so much in that movie that our breath, our mind and our body say it is real, so we wonder, "How can it not be real?". To bring people into an awareness that is away from this fear is the most difficult job in the world. Even when you bring people away from it and they glimpse this other reality for a moment, they fall back because the breath is there reminding them that the fear was apparently real. And society is there, pushing that control mechanism so that it makes sure everything is stable.

Spirituality is a revolution. It is not a political revolution but it is creating a new culture, a new way of living. I tried this for example in the experiment of an ashram and I realised how incredibly difficult it is. This is why I have always felt it important that spirituality is put into action. It is not enough that we do things individually for ourselves, we have to be beacons of light to other people in the way we do things. When many people breathe in a harmonious way for example, I believe we change the atmosphere and we change the culture by osmosis.

We cannot change things by holding a gun to someone's head and say, "You have to change!" or by controlling and manipulating people. Amazingly, many people who say they follow spiritual traditions do precisely that and say to others, "If you don't do this you will go to hell, or you will suffer!", or "It is your bad *karma*", or "You need to feel bad because you are not doing the right thing". By natural osmosis, we learn that our actions lead to more freedom, to a sense of power and strength where we are able to go into that freedom and honour it. We do not feel that we are alone or separate from everything. I am not a sociologist or an anthropologist to explain this in the correct language so I hope it is making sense.

You suggest that losing our breath, not breathing correctly is largely culturally produced...

Yes it is. The way we breathe is totally cultural.

Breath is excitement, stress and so on...

Yes, but it is interesting to observe how people react to the same situation of stress or excitement in their breathing, depending on their consciousness, their culture and their belief systems. What will stress someone may seem funny to another person. I am not saying that the breath does not change of course, but the essence of the breath and what it teaches you is different from one person to another. Let us take the act of walking in the forest for example, which I like to do. I remember walking with someone in the the rainforest in Costa Rica and I watched the way he breathed. He was totally connected and totally excited with everything that was around him so he breathed in a certain way and it got reinforced as he got more and more excited going deeper into the forest.

His attitude was very different from the other people walking in the forest who think of the danger of a snake for example. The fear comes to the surface and the breathing reinforces it, so even if there was no snake, people were reacting to the forest as if there was something dangerous and their breathing changed. Maybe if a snake would have appeared this person would enthusiastically say, "Hey, I have seen a snake!", while another person would say, "My gosh, is it poisonous?", and would breathe differently. I can relate to that example because I have seen this and it is the same with everything in life. Someone who is being driven very fast in a car could get very nervous and his/her breathing almost stops, the whole body tenses up and they may say, "Slow down! Slow down!". Another person might have another reaction and enjoy the speed. Why? It depends on the belief system.

The cultural production of emotional states and of the breath imply that coming back to the breath, taking the control of one's breath is a way of not being "out of oneself" and of resisting these automatisms of fear...

Exactly, and this is why it is a like a *mantra*. The breath is the best *mantra* because it will make you more conscious, even if it makes you more conscious of your limitation.

Acting consciously... Breathing consciously...

Exactly.

As we address fear, this leads to the topic of money and possessions, of the ego being at work to consume and to compensate for something. Money is a cultural imperative of the material life in most societies today. But it is also quite related to fear. Some people say that money is energy. Do you agree with this?

Money is an amazing spiritual work. Is money energy? That is New Age rubbish in my opinion because it is a justification to make materialism seem spiritual. Many New Age people justify fulfilling their emptiness by buying whatever is materially comfortable. If you are "spiritual" you may want to buy some nice Indian dresses and clothes that people like to wear when they are "alternative". Money is actually a strong aspect of fear, it is a manifestation of it. Possessing money means to possess more burdens and more problems than you normally have the consciousness to deal with. I find places like Polynesia wonderful because instead of money being a central theme such as, "I have to have money to pay for my food, to build my house and to do whatever I want to do", people live a daily life much more in the present moment than in the fear of the future or of the past even though it may not be like this anywhere nowadays.

I find that money is a very interesting way that society created to control us. It is part of the cultural manipulation that I was speaking about. People, whether they are aware of it or not, believe that money equals stability, happiness, or some form of security. On some level this is correct, but in the essence of reality, it is not. I believe this is why people are like slaves in our society and unless they do what they do for love, most people work for money. This is another form of controlling someone's life, controlling and wasting time, which is so precious, to fulfil a belief system. If you took money, put it on the table and tried to do something with it, it would give you nothing in essence! If you went out and bought everything that you wanted, you would see that it has no value. This is why some millionaires give away a lot of their money to charity associations. What they realise is that in giving, you receive much more than in holding.

Most people in the West want money for themselves. They do not want money to give to a charity, to Africa, to a school or to a wonderful project, but for me, this is the only reason to have money: to give it back to some form that creates joy for yourself of course, but also for other people. I am not saying that eating and sleeping is not important but most people want much more than that. The idea behind it is much more subtle because when they have enough to eat and they have enough to sleep, meaning that the basic needs are covered, they always want more and more.

I see people working with me and I am amazed when they say, "All I need is enough money to live a very simple life, to have a very simple house, to have enough simple food, not even complicated food..." and when they get this, their ideas change and they want more. Money is a problem because the more you have, the more you want and the more justifications the brain and your culture create to take you down this road, which is such a waste of time. It is this moment that is important for me. It is not that you work very hard to do whatever for the future.

Now I enter in a very difficult arena because of course, I am not saying that we should all move to Polynesia and go fishing like Polynesians. What I am saying is that perhaps by changing our focus and seeing the real value of money, by seeing what the essence of money is rather than the money attached to the ego and desire, which is how most people picture money, we can realise it is an energy. It is an energy because it can be useful to create positive things for ourselves but mainly for the future, meaning for our children and for the environment. Then the whole culture has a different reference point, it is not about making more money but it becomes about using the money or the energy that there is for creating joy and happiness in the sense of freedom, beyond control and slavery. This allows people to not feel obliged or connected to a system that wants more and more.

In modern society we need money but we really need much less than we believe. I am always cautious when it comes to this because some people working with me could become irresponsible and say, "I am going to leave my work, drop everything and I am just going to follow my dream!". We cannot do that because even if we leave everything, we do not leave the control mechanisms that are deep inside ourselves and acting in the background. These mechanisms are part of us and this is why we have to transcend them by doing what we are doing rather than escaping from what we are doing and trying to find a place where they do not exist.

If we leave the horrible job that we are working in and we say "OK, now I am free to live the moment", the fear of not having enough in that moment is still present. We take that fear with us and we have not resolved anything. All that we have done is created more fear because we realise that there is nothing coming in to support us in that moment. We have to find the real support which is to trust. It is not just trusting a vague idea because this is also a New Age attitude such as, "If I trust then money will come to me". Many people working with me say, "All I have to do is trust and then somehow the money will fall of trees…". They believe that they have the right to have that money coming their way, but we have to change many things… It is spiritual work. We have to change what prevents the flow of money to come through. The best place to change it is where we have trapped ourselves. It is not about finding another trap that becomes exotically interesting.

Transcending is not escaping the problem. It is dealing with it…

Exactly. Dealing with the money issue, whether you are rich or poor, whether you are hungry for materialism or you do not care about materialism. It is dealing with that present picture that you have. It does not mean passively dealing with it but actively dealing with it, by challenging the control mechanisms that may be from within yourself and not necessarily from the outside. Let us take shopping for example, which for me is such a bore but I sometimes agree to accompany someone, just to see what happens. Looking at people's eyes, I can see that it is almost like Christmas when people go to a shop and get into an "I want, I want" mood. In that moment of "I want", are they remembering the people in Africa? Are they remembering that suffering exists everywhere?

I do not say this to make people feel guilty but when you are in that "I want" picture, which is a future picture, the desire is so caught up in that moment of control that it has nothing to do with this moment anymore. You forget everything else. You even forget the people you love because this is what "I want". This is what the ego space does. It focuses so much on the self. You forget compassion and you forget love. If your children are with you, they also follow into that "I want feeling" of course, and you have the whole family "I want", buying and buying. I often ask, "Why are you buying this? Is it because you really need it or because it is an idea?"

Same with eating…

It is the same with eating! If I am around when people are shopping and they put something in the trolley, I say, "Why is this in the trolley?" The answer is usually, "Because it is organic". Then I ask, "OK, it is organic, but do you really need it?" They answer, "It tastes very good!" and I say, "Do you really need it or is it the cultural idea?". A good taste is supposed to bring happiness, to make you feel good and happy, but it is a whole mechanism that is not recognised in that moment where you grab the object that fulfils a form of need. You do not recognise it because you are so much in the "I want", in the action of the future, that you are not in that moment.

To shop consciously means that you walk into the shop or supermarket and you only buy what you really need. Then you do not waste any money and you are completely free, not caught up in the materialism or in the history of your family materialism. Perhaps your family never had the opportunity to buy all these things because of poverty and of course you act it out, "I want this because my parents could never have it". You do not even know you are acting this out but you do it because that is why society has created, a great big wonderful Material God. The general belief is that the *mantra*, "I need" and "I want" will make people happy, and of course nobody wants to lose happiness. "The more I work, the more money I have, the more I want, the more I have, the more happy I can be" … No one questions this *mantra*.

People think, "This is life. You need clothes, you need this, you need that". But do you really need all these things? I challenge people to live for less money, not to live poorly, but to live with just the basic needs and to be happy with what one has, to appreciate what one has, the rice and the vegetables that we are eating, rather than to look for complicated foods and to look for complicated gadgets... I am amazed when I accompany people to go shopping with me and observe the whole feeling of this "I want" game into action. I see the whole game unfolding and people wanting everything for themselves.

I do not want a house. My main thing is to build a temple, to build a space to allow people to work spiritually in this space. A house for me is unimportant because in a house there is no happiness. Happiness is only there when you invite the love, not just for yourself or for your children but when you invite the world into your space. This is what native people do for example when they invite the whole community to explore and experience happiness, to sing, dance, and transcend limitations. For me the "I want" has to be "I want for the world" rather than having money selfishly.

A way of spiritually dealing with fears, money and possession seems to develop a feeling of gratitude.

Exactly, gratitude and appreciation. I bring a personal example. Some people living in the apartment building I am living now were going through a very strong process. They wanted a garden, which is a natural thing to want, especially if you have children because living in an apartment is claustrophobic. It is not that easy to walk out even though we have the forest right outside the door. Things are not connected, you have to leave the apartment, you have to walk through a gate, you have to go up the hill, etc. They were going through a whole process about the garden, "I do not have this and I need this and when I fulfil this need then my happiness will develop and I will be happy".

I laughed and of course this made them even more irritated. I said, "Come on this is just another game that your mind is playing". They answered, "No, a garden is … you know, when you have a child it is easy". I know this of course because I have four children so I said, "What about appreciating what is here? What about walking in the forest and looking at the trees and appreciating the beauty of the trees, rather than not seeing the trees and wanting something and ignoring having gratitude and appreciation for the beauty that is around? You can have that appreciation now, not only if we have trees. You can even have it if there is a rose on your veranda. You can have that same feeling", but this is complicated to put into practice because the mind tricks, justifies and takes you down the path of the whole control mechanism where what we do not have becomes more important than what we have.

People never appreciate health when they have it. It is only when they loose it that they say, "I wish I were healthy again". Then they do not understand why they did not appreciate those moments where health was vibrant and alive. Your mind and ego play this game where what you have is unimportant and what you do not have becomes your whole driving and pulling force. This is how materialism works. What you do not have becomes more important than what you have, so you have no gratitude for what you have.

People never know the amazing possibility there is to work with a spiritual teacher until they leave. One of the people who worked with me got very irritated at one point. Many people do because I am always pushing and playing a little game. The person said, "It is so easy and so wonderful to be with you". Then I pushed a little bit and I made it more real. As a result, this person decided, "It is easier to work away from you!". She did not find a reason but simply said that it was easier to work away from me. I said, "Great, please do, I am not wanting you to be here. Whatever is best, please follow your heart and work". That person decided to leave for a year and a half and not work in such close proximity to me. A month ago, I talked to her and she said, "You know, it was very good for me to take some distance because I appreciate more now than I ever have before what it means to work with you. After a year and a half, I can see. But in that time when I was working with you, I took everything for granted, everything was easy and fell into place and I did not see it because it was there".

Some people get irritated and they just leave forever and justify in their brains or in their mind why it is important to do so. That is also the case even with children. When you have children, you have children. You do not appreciate your children because you have them. They are there in your life. They are your experience. You have unfolded them into your whole picture but when you leave them, after a week you think, "Oh, I miss them, I love them". Then you develop gratitude and appreciation. It is a pity because if you appreciate what is there in that moment, then it is much more beautiful.

Is having gratitude acting consciously?

Exactly.

... and gratitude is somehow related to humility, which seems to be a very important value for you. I remember a Native American saying that you quoted one time: "Walk lightly on the Earth" ...

That is exactly what humility is. It is gratitude and consciousness for what is. People who are driven by the ego lack humility. In Germany it is interesting because there are a lot of spirituality centres and spiritual teachers who are doing what is called a Satsang, a Sanskrit word meaning "in the presence of a teacher who answers questions". I do not know what Satsang for other people is but for me it is just a meeting. I am told there are hundreds and hundreds of teachers doing Satsang. It is interesting because I have met a few of these people in a direct or an indirect way and what I noticed is the ego at work. This is not to judge anything but the ego is present when someone says, "What I say is so important", "What I am teaching is the right way" or "This is the way". That shows a lack of humility. People who like this sense of self-importance from these teachers follow a kind of dogma.

I recently did a Satsang in the north of Germany and was asked, "Do you have any formality for people to sit in and approach you a certain way? Is there a certain timing to follow? Do they have to give a gift?". I said, "Why? What is the reason for these? I just have to be approached like anybody else". I was also told, "Other teachers consider you have to do this and wish people to follow a whole ritual". I replied, "That is only if the teachers are not sure of what they are teaching". Why do we have to do all these things? Everything is a teacher. I am just another aspect and manifestation of reality that is manifested in the tree and in the reality that everyone is free to approach.

There is no need to approach me in a specific way. Yet, many people like this. Actually, if I adopted this ritual, I am sure more people would come to me, because they would think, "Ah, it should be important. If we have to do this, it must be that we are approaching something that is greater than ourselves". I do not want to have this sense of greatness. I want the people to feel that greatness for themselves rather than having to see it as an external aspect of themselves.

The value of humility is not yet obvious for everybody. For instance, a person was walking with me and told me, "It is so strange to walk with you because I am just talking to you like a friend. I am able to speak to you and reveal everything to you. It is like an intimate relationship". I said, "That is what spirituality is. It is an intimate relationship. It is not having to develop this sense of superiority or "aboveness". Spirituality is having gratitude for this moment that we are sharing together". He said, "This is not the normal way of approaching other spiritual teachers. It is very difficult to communicate on a mundane level about the fears, the pains and the sufferings that happen in daily life". I think that this explains humility very well.

Humility is just being yourself and just acknowledging that everyone can be the same. Nobody has to create another situation. Spirituality is about being who you are. It is not about creating another ritual, another dogma or way of being so that what we are doing now is "spiritual work". When I say this, on some level people do not take me seriously because the way I speak is also a little bit strange. It is very basic if I compare to other teachers who bring interesting Sanskrit words and sometimes confusing concepts. I do not use any of those. I bring life as an example all the time – my experience, other people's experience – and just say, "This is the way it is for me". I do not need to use unusual words to make my teaching sound great. People may find it basic without seeing humility in it. Unless they work with me for a little while, I think they just say, "OK, it is just another person. I have heard it before and it is interesting but…"

Humility is very complicated, for instance. A child came into a meditation once and sat in, but she was a difficult child to have sitting in the room quietly. She was there and then at one point, when I was explaining a profound concept and saying, "I am going to do this now with you as an experience", she said, "Oh Tony, stop talking so much and just do it!". I said, "Great!" and everyone laughed because it was so real and without that formality of having to keep the direct communication away.

Everyone laughed and that situation expressed a good feeling of humility rather than a pretentiousness. Maybe people laugh because they realised how their created concept of me got broken in that moment and then they saw the directness of humanity, of the child seeing me as a person and working in that wonderful way. That is humility, but it is not that easy to see it in action all the time anyway. Most children always want to be in the presence of that mystery and simplicity, because for them that is what they enjoy. That is what all children and everyone enjoys, but it is lost in the controlling and "mundaneness" of society where other things fit into that simplicity and take over of it.

In his phenomenology of perception, the French philosopher Maurice Merleau-Ponty explains that silence is primary and the knowledge of man will remain superficial as long as we do not go back to this origin. Mahatma Gandhi also said that silence was the language of the heart. The more the heart is connected, the more we speak lower or keep silent, like we do with a baby with whom we can connect easily without language. We are right now using words to produce a book, but in silence there is this deep mysterious simplicity that is also part of your teaching. You sometimes say that you would prefer to not to speak basically…

I tried it and it does not work…

Yet you value silence…

For me, silence is the most profound meditation. Silence is not a lack of noise, silence comes from within silence itself. It is not like Vipassana meditation where you escape from the mundane noise because for me, the mundane is part of us so there is no escape. Silence is much deeper than that. It is going beyond all those aspects, but silence can also be found in a noisy environment. Silence is not a lack of communication. Sometimes communication assists the mind to understand what silence means. Silence is almost like a path to itself, yet that path needs communication because we are social beings.

Is being silent a way of being present to oneself and to be conscious of who we are?

Yes. I also think silence is honouring all aspects of who we are and bringing them into union. When that union happens, it is a bit like when you love someone. The words are important and the actions are important, but sometimes the energy of love is beyond words. It is beyond doing anything. It is just there. For me, the most enjoyable aspect of love can be expressed through silence. For example, if you have a sick child who is sleeping and you just stand there for a few minutes looking at them, just feeling love in that moment for them, because there is nothing else happening. They are silent, everything is silent. It can be so amazing, and in that moment, you can capture something and I am sure in their sleep, the sick child also captures something that is beyond having to do anything, such as having to buy toys, or having to go out and do something in action. That mysterious non-doing moment, that union, is very precious. I feel that is what is lost in relationships between people.

Often people ask me, "What you spend your time doing? Do you go to restaurants? Do you go out to the theatre? What do you do? ". I say "Nothing!" and they wonder, "But do not you get bored doing nothing?". I say, "No, actually in moments where I can just walk in the forest and do nothing. I do not have to say anything, I am just silent together with the nature around. Those are the most precious moments". It is the same when I sit at home and simply eat or do whatever I am doing in silence, but with a sense and an atmosphere of love. To me, that is all that is necessary. Most native people understand this. There are actions that are required to mean there is a more dynamic relationship, but for me, the actions are only required if there is a sense of emptiness. This is not to say that listening to music or going to the theatre, say, is unimportant, but if everything is so full of other things, then those things are less important. The silence of non-doing, of just being, is precious.

That is why during retreats, you sometimes invite people to remain silent, to go deeper into the understanding of themselves.

In the ceremonies also, I invite people to go back to the silence before there is more action, external action. That is the most profound connection to union.

Masculine, Feminine & Spiritual Awareness

Discretion and assertiveness seem to be two important qualities for you...

Yes, and this was very obvious as a child. I also remember that my respect for women was quite important. I grew up in a culture that respects women but in a different way than what we normally understand because in Egypt, men have the first role whatever they say and whatever they do. I grew up in that environment and those family dynamics, even though my mother and father were quite liberal in ideas. People can think that they are quite liberal but it is interesting to watch how society creates a whole set of dynamics that end up leading the women to clean up, to look after the children and to cook for example.

I am not saying that this is wrong but that was basically what was expected in my family because the men of my family and around were considered to be important. As for me, I related easily to both men and women but I found it easier to relate to the more feminine aspect than the masculine. If I related very well to my two parents, I had a lot of respect for the feminine aspect, so of course I related more to my mother and to my grand mother, and later to my grandfather. I am saying this because it has a chronological significance as to why I see certain things in this way.

I also remember falling in love with a very beautiful Egyptian girl when I was eight or nine. What I really liked about her was her feminine qualities. It was not so much that I fell in love with that person but she was expressive of these feminine qualities that I did not have around me, since I only had brothers in my family. Only my mother expressed these qualities but she was The Mother, and I liked to have this deep friendship with someone. It was not being in love in the sense of boy friend and girl friend, but it was being in love with the feminine aspect and she was my best friend. Interestingly enough, I think she was the daughter of one of the top generals in the military. We lived in a cosmopolitan neighbourhood, next door to Egyptians who were usually working in the military or political spheres. I liked this person so this is when I started exploring the feminine aspect and what it means, rather than the masculine. The masculine aspect was the family teaching me, "You have to be a strong and educated boy".

That was important as I was the first-born with two brothers. In the culture I grew up in, there is the father and then there is the first-born son, so the masculine was even more expected of me. In spite of that, I was very gentle and rather than seen as honouring the feminine, I was seen as romantic and easily falling in love. There were also many girls falling in love with me because they found that I was very easy to be with, even though at that age group, girls normally stay by themselves and the boys also normally stay together. I found it easier to be more connected to the feminine, not to say that I was not connected to the masculine because I had many elders that I respected very much, but it was more the knowledge of that person that I was relating to rather than the masculine aspect.

I just thought this is interesting because that has been very much a thread through all that I have done. Zen Buddhism is not very ritualistic and most often, the monasteries do not have pictures of Buddha, unlike Tibetan Buddhism where there are a lot of images. In Zen Buddhism, the monastery is very dark and plain, with nothing to attach to, but in the monastery I went to, there was one image, a very big image, which was at the core of this monastery's philosophy. It was Kuan Yin, which is the feminine aspect of the Buddha in Zen Buddhism. I did not know this when I went there and I found this very interesting because Roshi spoke a lot about the feminine aspect of the Buddha, or Kuan Yin, in Zen mythology. In the spiritual sense, this somehow created an understanding for me as why I was attracted to the feminine, not just as a personality or as a human being but beyond that.

Today I explain to people that the feminine aspect is not that you can divide the oneness of everything into feminine or masculine aspects, but if you look at things, you can see certain qualities that you relate to as an individual within yourself and also within a certain aspect of the universe, as having more of the quality of one or the other. I see this as the reason why for example our DNA has two strands that link into each other and create the DNA structure in the cell. I see the feminine almost as a space that is created like the cup that holds the content, the sacred vessel. It holds the form, it holds the consciousness, it holds the meditation and holds the space and the masculine is what fills that space with activity. The way I understood Kuan Yin was the same, it is the feminine that holds the space, and the masculine Buddha aspect is the active one that goes out to the world, reaches and touches. I honoured the Kuan Yin aspect, or the feminine aspect. Some people whom I have worked with have said, "Tony you could reach thousands of people. Why are not you more active like certain teachers and use that masculine aspect to go out more into the world?", like some Indian *gurus* and people who go out and reach many people. The answer is that the place I am trying to reach people from is not from that space but from the space of the feminine. People have to come to me if they want to work.

Would you characterise your spiritual work as "intimate"?

Yes. It has to be in the space that holds the connection rather than me going out in an active manner and reaching out for the world. When people say to me, "You are very gentle and very feminine and very soft", they have not seen some other sides because I can be very strong. Some people would even say that my approach is almost too feminine, too gentle. It is not. I actually see the feminine not as feminine, in the sense of girl or boy, but as a quality that is what touches the divine more closely.

Listening is feminine?

Exactly. Listening is feminine. Being still is feminine. Being receptive is feminine. Touching things from an awareness of that stillness is feminine. Those are the qualities that I am working with, the qualities that come across in the world more strongly and this of course started with many things, but I think that one of them was falling in love with this wonderful girl in my childhood. I never knew what happened to her because I left Egypt when I was twelve. Interestingly, my parents did not keep contact with any of these people so I believe it is a karmic thing: we met for a brief moment only.

That feminine quality becomes expressed in my relationships, even to children, because my work with them is to be quite passive rather than active. I see American family movies portraying families who are actively doing things together and having a good time, with the father being the hero in an active role. It is absolutely not what I do. People may wonder what I am doing but it is simply holding the space for children to be there, to be present and touch the quality of love beyond having to do things so the feeling that they are loved is there. It is quite an important difference. This is what I find difficult in countries like America where the recurrent question is, "What did you do today?". Would it not be more interesting to ask, "How many times did you connect to this beautiful part of yourself – the heart, your centre – and feel love, ecstasy, and joy today?", rather than, "What did you do today?".

"What have you been today?" would be better than "What have you done?" ...

Exactly. That passive role is not close to depression, although I often find that people who are depressed feel that they have got that quality. Actually, it is the opposite quality because depression is that you prevent the feminine from communicating to yourself. It is a lack of communication, a lack of being in touch with your centre. When you are depressed you are the masculine, but the masculine without action.

The masculine trapped and falling apart...

Exactly. The masculine that has almost collapsed. Some people misunderstand this inactivity, like with mental sickness for example, about which they say, "It is bordering spiritual insights". I have been told many times that mental problems, psychoses and schizophrenia are very similar or border on deep spiritual experiences that may have a whole dimension of crisis around them. When I was a child, because my spiritual crisis seemed so unusual, people wanted to see if I was mentally sane for example. I actually find this to be almost at the opposite end of the spectrum.

There are many dimensions that are similar of course, but the opposite dimension of the spectrum is that schizophrenia or psychoses put you totally out of touch. You are not in contact with anything, except with a mind that has gone haywire. In my opinion, this mind has connected so strongly to the ego and to its own functioning that it has lost its connection to reality and to this world. It has lost its connection to the heart and to the centre, focussing completely on one side of our personality – the mind-ego. It has lost its connection to stillness, to the feminine aspect of embracing, and has almost gone mad.

The opposite is spirituality, where you drop everything. You drop your connection to the mind, to the ego and you embrace the whole of who you are. It is almost as if you let go of the mind. Maybe it has some similarity with depression, but the difference is that you do not let go of the functioning of the mind. You let go of the madness of the mind to come back to the essence of functioning from the centre. The centre has the higher aspect of the mind inside of it, the higher aspect of emotions, the higher aspect of connecting to family, to community, but in a transcendent sort of way. It is beyond what is seen as socially acceptable or culturally normal. This is why it is the opposite end of the spectrum. People who diagnose mental illness as a form of spirituality – or spirituality as a form of mental illness! – have not understood spirituality in a complete sense.

When you go through spiritual transformation, there is a high level of stress because the whole movement of your energy system speeds up. Everything quickens inside of you. You are becoming more still because you are coming to your centre, but everything is activating. You see that more things are happening much quicker than they did before. In the beginning, the body is not use to this quickening so it cannot hold that space. It cannot hold this new transformation that usually happens much quicker in the energy body than in the physical body because the physical body holds on so much more to the past. Then, the physical body of the past starts to fight back and reacts to this whole situation with stress.

The stress is for instance that the body becomes a little bit more nervous. You become a little bit more sensitive. If there is a loud noise, you are more sensitive to it because your senses become more acute. Your mind becomes more aware of things. The stress is not coming from the transformation but rather from the space where it is not able to comprehend the whole change. Yet slowly, that change happens in the body. We feel strength to be able to listen to sounds, to listen to people, to listen to the activity that we now see much more consciously around us and to hold it in the body without it reacting to this.

I feel that this is why I went through moments where my body health and my need to be a little bit isolated, away from the masses of activity, was very important at the different points in my life you asked about. From the outside, people may have seen it as something going psychologically wrong. I was not displaying any problems but there was an obvious agitation and a movement in me that I could not comprehend. When I was nineteen or twenty I was remembering a lot. I had left the Zen monastery and had gone back to England. I had a strong memory of times in my childhood, I think at the age of one or two. I was remembering a car accident that my family had when I was a little child and it was a very bad accident I was part of. Luckily nothing happened to me, at least physically, but my mother was terribly hurt and stayed in hospital for many months. The car was totally destroyed. It was a miracle that she survived, a miracle that my father was only superficially hurt, and a miracle that I survived, as it was decades ago when the safety standards were not like they are today.

This of course had energetical impact. People think that a two-year-old child does not comprehend, but the child does in fact comprehend and it all stays in the body energetically. I was releasing that energy, that fear and that whole situation that I did not logically comprehend. When I was in England after having left the monastery, I was still working just as strongly as I was in the monastery and this was a very strong and traumatic moment of my life. My mother came to visit me and she was a little bit worried, as mothers are, because she could see that there was a certain agitation in me. She thought that meditation should have made me calm and peaceful and most of the time it does, but sometimes it does not, because it is not just relaxing and doing nothing. It is an active participation of the inner world in being aware of the invisible space, holding a consciousness that there is a direct communication to that space, which I was doing at those different points.

Would you say that the people who have developed the feminine aspect inside of them are, in a way, protecting themselves from the sudden shock of depression?

Definitely. It is the most important thing. I am not a psychologist but it would be interesting to see if depression is more prevalent in male dominated societies than female, maternal types of societies – and I would imagine that would be the case. There can be chemical imbalances that cause depression of course, but I am talking about general depression rather than specific types. For this general kind of depression, the reasons are psychological and we feel bad without even knowing that we are in depression.

Many people try to keep that sense of depression away by entertaining themselves, watching movies, drinking, going out, talking, and finding as many activities as they can to keep themselves away from themselves and from that sense of depression that is lurking in the background. It can easily and very powerfully be changed by allowing this feminine side to be part of the communication with yourself and with the world in your activities and actions. This is why, out of that masculine/feminine tension, the search for feminine peace is a natural step. I am not saying of course that peace – or feminine – means inactivity, but peace in a sense of coming from a different space rather than actively feeling threatened by, reacting to or fighting, certain situations.

Let us take anger as a practical example. There is a masculine and a feminine way of dealing with anger. The masculine way, which can sometimes be necessary but is done too much, is that we feel threatened by the situation and we react to it. We use our mind which then judges the situation and causes a strong feeling creating in its turn a sense of anger. That is the masculine way we are taught to deal with this emotion in the Western culture. It is how both men and women deal with the situation. So rather than coming to the space where we embrace what is around without accepting it as part of ourselves, peace is embracing this space so that we feel what it is like to be in it, together with that activity which may cause the reaction.

Another way that would be very interesting would be through the breath, which is the spiritual path; breathing in deeply and with the out breath, embracing that situation completely. Doing so we expand to that space. We connect to it rather than alienate ourselves from it and create a sense of dualism where that situation outside – a feeling of injustice for instance - is making us feel this situation inside – a feeling of anger. I am simplifying things, as it is of course difficult to completely explain what is something that is a practical experience but I think it somehow gives an idea.

When we do that, the energy comes back inside and helps us to move to a higher perspective of what is going on, rather than being thrust out actively. This higher perspective then gives us knowledge to watch what this whole situation is really about. We then have more compassion for ourselves and for the situation. We can react, but we will react from a different perspective. That reaction can be masculine or feminine. It does not really matter anymore because it comes from a different reference point so it does not have to be quiet. It can even be quite strong.

In a depressed person, the feminine is not even acknowledged. People in this situation are not aware of the feminine. They are not even aware that they can breathe out and embrace things in a more complete sense. What they have done is reacting to situations or to the emotions so many times, that some part of them has said, "It does not work", and they have given up. The anger has been internalised. Instead of being outside, it has come inside but they are not aware of it because it is in the unconscious. It is not even something one can see, it is done without knowing. Instead of going up and transcending, which is the feminine way, that energy is regressing down to the more material aspects of the body. Instead of it being energetic, it becomes physical.

The body is then bombarded with this energy that activates certain hormones and chemicals in the brain. The body does so because it is all it knows. That then creates a physical depression. The body reacts as if this energy were no longer even real but it is real inside of itself and therefore we do not even know there is anger. We know that the body feels terrible but we do not know why because we do not know there is anger. We just know the sensations. The body feels totally fatigued, not enthused to do anything, and sees the worst and the most negative in everything. There is nothing positive. Problems are found and worried about, whatever they are.

At that point, the person has lost the ability to communicate with the feminine. Society has succeeded in destroying another human being by not honouring the feminine in our culture, by not showing that the earth is feminine and that we need to touch the earth with our hands so that we can feel the feminine in our body. We need to breathe the air from the trees so that we can sense the feminine in our lungs. Instead we have put children in a classroom in front of the desk, in front of the teacher and we have told them to listen to words that activate the mind and to be quiet. We have told them not to worry about the emotions or the creativity. I am saying this in an extreme sense, but in reality it is almost like this.

For most children, at ten, at least in our types of society, there is no communication with the feminine. It is all about homework and getting good grades. The communication with the feminine is when you play with other children in the playground, but then the bell rings and you are back into your routine. You forget, because the routine becomes part of you. The strong ones survive but very sensitive ones become depressed. On a superficial level the first ones become successful but later, at fifty, they do not have that same joy that they had in life. They look to communicate to a deeper meaning and the deeper meaning is always the feminine, one part of it being compassion.

Many people then become compassionate not just towards their goal and drive but also towards the world. They become more giving. They give money away, they give time away, they give love to children, to helpless people, to people in Africa or to something. Some part of them knows that to communicate to this feminine, you need to be compassionate. This is one of the aspects of Kuan Yin: compassion.

If the affirmative part of a person is more masculine and the doubting one is more feminine, isn't a person who is continuously in doubt about things in a way protecting him or herself from a sudden falling down of everything, beliefs, cultural models, and consequently depression? Doubting – the main concept of anthropology, which constructs its knowledge on the relativity of models – could then be a very a positive scepticism, questioning things without falling into disarray but as a humble way of observing and being in the word. Doubting in the sense of being self-critical and not too much assertive about things. Doubting as a psychological state of mind protecting a person from the sudden collapsing of the ingrained program, which can lead to depression. This attitude towards everything (religion or any dogma) is obviously not too valued in most societies and we generally meet people who are convinced of everything. Does it make sense?

It makes totally sense. Doubt may be connected with humility, so it is not doubt in a negative sense of judgement but more in the sense of openness to many possibilities. It is the beauty of doubt. I think this is a very important quality because, in the end, to say, "I have all knowledge", or "I know everything", is very masculine. This is where I feel that some religious leaders change the quality of religion to have such a masculine aspect that it misses its beauty.

In the Catholic Church for instance, they have forgotten the feminine aspect of Jesus, the humility of Jesus and instead, portray him as this strong masculine figure who is actively out to save the world. Then the priest, the pope, and whoever in the Catholic religion, have to somehow conform to that image. It is almost as if they have to replicate this strong form. That does not show much humility but a little bit of arrogance with a sort of a sense of "I am better", "I know more", or "You are stupid", in a subtle way. I think this is a definite sign of our sick and totally destructive society today. For me, the doubt is important. Doubting about what we think is real and what is supposed to be essential is spiritual work. If something is important, why it is so? It is necessary to put the cultural program into question and completely go to the point where we look at things with clear consciousness, not with the idea that we know everything.

It is about having a clear consciousness that we do not necessarily know...

Exactly. How can you know before consciousness shows you the knowledge? If you go in with the idea that you have that knowledge, then consciousness cannot reveal the beauty of knowledge that is only found in humility.

Is it developing attention?

Yes. It is pure attention as you do not need to know things in the normal way. Some people say, "How I am going to know this?". You do not need to know anything. You know when that attention is totally there, without any other knowledge of you knowing something. If you say, "I know a little bit of meditation" and you go in the meditation knowing this little bit of meditation, you do not let go of that knowledge so that the meditation shows you the meditation. You only have that idea of meditation. I saw this a lot in Zen Buddhism and some people did it for twenty years. It was amazing to watch Japanese or Europeans sit there and adopt this very masculine form of Zen Buddhism where you sit in an almost militaristic disciplined way. You breathe and you follow certain ways of doing things very strongly. Yet it did not come from humility or from doubt but from a sense of, "I know how to reach knowledge, so I am going to pursue it and find my way there".

You have people doing this on other levels also and this is the most dangerous. That happens a lot in families but especially in spiritual groups. It is like a spiritual competition, where people want to appear in a way that they have knowledge about these things. They blow up their ego to a point that all the other people around them can sense and see the importance of their spiritual accomplishment. In a way, that happened a lot with people working with me. This is the trap that is possible when people believe they have reached a certain stage. That knowledge then becomes a setting for yourself beyond the sense of humility and beyond the sense of simply not knowing. But there is truthfulness in "I do not know".

Knowledge may be real on some level but it is not real enough to have anchored itself in your being in the total sense, detached from the ego and from the mind. Instead, you have this vague perceived idea that some knowledge is attached to a certain competition, to a certain blowing up of the ego, which prevents you from really facing the deeper aspects of yourself. You cannot communicate to the deeper aspect of the feminine because it is too scary. It is much easier to communicate to the masculine aspect, to relate to the mind or to the thinking of the mind or even to the thinking knowledge of the mind, whether it be logic, whether it be spiritual knowledge of logic, whether it be cleverness or whether it be the acting out of knowledge.

Many people do this in spiritual circles. They even dress up in special clothes. This is why I refuse to have people wearing specific distinctive clothes in the work around me. It does not matter for me if you have a T-Shirt or if you have an orange garment. Yet, some people around me would dress up in white – white is a very popular colour around me – to sort of portray the purity of their mind. I always laugh quietly in the background when I see these wonderful spiritual clothes...

People do many other things, acting out in the same sense, not just with the clothes but also with their voice and their words. To have a spiritual voice also makes people have this more "*guru*" like talk, using esoteric words that sound very "spiritual" because they are part of the current spiritual language. People would also frequently use the word *karma* to explain things – "Ah yes, of course, this is your *karma*!" – but that word is something so lightly used and it has absolutely zero meaning because it has no depth in it. It then becomes a language that is talking by itself amongst an almost insular group of people.

In a way, this is almost preventing the real world from coming in to touch your experience, because it is safer to agree upon a culture, a social setting or a social idea of how it is to be spiritual, rather than to be spiritual. This happens without fail around every spiritual teacher. I found it even in the Zen Buddhist monastery where it was very interesting to watch the games. Yet it is important not to judge those games but to see them as a reflection of ourselves, reminding ourselves that, somehow, we are also here to learn from those games.

People's external games and conscious or unconscious competition in the spiritual domain are particularly irritating...

When someone is dressing in white and says, "How is your *karma* today?", or do whatever people do these days, there is no need to judge and come out strongly by saying, "Do not be stupid!", "Go deeply and be more full of humility!". If you do so, then you have caught onto that same energy level where you are all of a sudden reacting in the same way as that person is interacting with you.

In other words, focusing too much and reacting to these games means that you are also yourself close to them. The best would be to remain a silent and non-judgmental observer of what it awakens in you?

Exactly. Then it is just thinking, "What an interesting game and what an interesting mirror". Just wondering how that really fits into your world. In doing so, knowledge goes deeper. Instead of it being a judgement of the outside, it becomes knowledge and you develop compassion for the outside. Then rather than attacking the outside, you bring more of that compassion in action to the outside. That is the feminine. This is why the feminine aspect of spirituality is not popular. It is more popular to learn "*karma* in twelve steps", to do this special ritual and then go around saying to people, "I know the secret words for letting go of my *karma* of my life two thousand years ago!".

I am joking here but in a sense it is easier to skirt around the truth than to jump into it. Most people will do this without knowing it because when the mind is playing a game, you think you are doing the best ... and when the mind is there, what else can you hear? What the mind is creating for you as your own reality may be totally crazy but for you and for other people it is not. Since everyone falls into the same circle, it almost becomes like a comforting family unit. It is almost like you do not even have a reflection from the outside to say, "This is crazy!". The only person that would say, "This is crazy!" would be the spiritual teacher but he or she will do it in a way that is not out of judgement but out of compassion.

But some spiritual teachers may also say nothing, just observing what they see.

Some spiritual teachers would say it in a different way, not words but...

They mirror it?

Exactly. They mirror it. They act in a way where the person can feel the madness or the mad circle that they are going through much more strongly and experience it much more realistically. It does not always work because sometimes we have to go through an entire dimension of transformation before we can understand the whole picture. Sometimes we have to go down. We have to fall into the fire and burn, like Dante, to go down into the core of the earth, somewhere down there, and it is very hot, very uncomfortable. In a way, that is also spiritual work. That is why we cannot judge, because in the end, no matter what, every soul is bringing more light to itself, every aspect of our essence is expanding the light within ourselves. It is done in different ways and everyone has different destinies and a unique path to follow. Some people would get lost but getting lost is also part of learning.

There are no detours...

There are detours. And there can be very silly ones too, but maybe we need those silly detours to learn. There is no way not to learn. I am hesitant to go deeper because this is one of the points where the spiritual teacher can actually do certain things that speed up the process. But that is a whole other dimension of the talk...

The idea that Masculine is the mind and Feminine is the heart is a little abstract. Some people would refer to the left and right brain, the left side being logic and the right more intuition. Do you agree with these conceptualisations?

Everything is useful to explain when it is too difficult to see directly. Yet for me to say that the thoughts are masculine and the heart is feminine is not really the picture. I am not medically qualified to really know how that works but I see the masculine and the feminine as two aspects of the universe, which are the universe as the macrocosm of our internal world that is the microcosm. This internal world is in the DNA structure of every cell, of everything that makes us physically present in this dimension. The DNA structure has two strands that join, of which one is masculine and one is feminine.

It is the same as the universe that is made of two parts, but you cannot distinguish them. They are not actual entities separate from each other. They are completely part of the same aspect but can be related to differently. The universe has a masculine and a feminine aspect and as human beings, because our sense of relationship comes to the senses, this can be related to the thinking, to the feeling, to the intuition and to all the senses that makes us perceive the world in the way we perceive it. Yet, this is not reality. Reality is bigger but our perception of reality is that the masculine has certain attributes and the feminine has other attributes. The masculine is the expansion, it is the ever-expanding aspect of the universe, and the feminine is the contraction.

This is an esoteric way to describe the universe but we can take it to something more practical, more useful in our daily experience and associate the masculine with the mind and the feminine with the heart. This is why I use those analogies to explain expansion and contraction. When you let go, you have the sense of union in a space of oneness, the heart. The heart is the centre, and the centre is the union, the sense of oneness, so then that could be understood as feminine. On the other hand, the mind is ever expanding, wanting to perceive, to analyse and understand things, wanting to be part of whatever is going on. The mind is expansion.

If that expansion of the mind expands to a degree that it is too expansive, it loses the feminine quality, which is the heart, and loses the point of being centred. When the mind expands from a reference point that loses its basic structure, its basic holding, it goes crazy. If you bring that expansion to the heart then what we have is the mind, our everyday normal mundane thinking, connected to divine thinking. If we want to consider the divine, the macrocosm, the mind of the divine could actually be seen as the masculine, while the heart of the divine is the feminine, but of course, the divine does not have a mind nor a heart, so this is just to make my point.

Dreams and certain feelings, like love, compassion, listening, being still, having a sense of humility, are given a feminine quality. The masculine is more related to action and to doing things that are outside of that centre, but if it carries that centre within it, if it carries those actions of stillness, of humility, then what the masculine is doing is expanding the feminine to reach the space where the feminine needs to be. This is a little bit esoteric, so let us see that in a practical sense. Why this is important is because in the world we live in we have man and woman. Without a man and a woman coming to a harmonious understanding we do not have children. When they spend their time being angry with each other, it is very difficult to do what is necessary, which is to love each other, to create a child.

Regarding relationship, the masculine and feminine are important aspects of the work I do, which is to create the sacredness of the man and the sacredness of the woman in our actual being. The woman then becomes a goddess. I use the word "goddess", which is an interesting word, to mean that a woman is more than just a woman, and "god" to mean that a man is more than just a man in the masculine traditional sense. It helps to see the dimensions that relate to the macrocosm inside of you as a man and as a woman. It also helps to relate those aspects to each other in a relationship, to bring those divine qualities in union and to create the possibility of a new life, which is the birth of a child, not necessarily in a physical form, but the birth of something.

If you do not have children, when a man and woman bring those divine qualities in union together in the energetic form, they are creating what the universe is naturally doing, a sense of expanding love. That is what a child is in its physical form, a product of this love. For that love to be real, it does not mean that you need to have children, it is actually also in the etheric level that this union brings this sense of connectedness with the macrocosm. Once that happens in sexuality for instance, what we are doing is realising that this union brings the sense of ecstasy. The two opposites complete the union to create an expansion, like the heart being part of the mind, expanding to a space where both aspects touch this ecstasy.

To be more concrete, let us look at the physical dimension that is sexuality, because for most people this is the easiest thing to relate to. For the majority of people, sexuality is totally strange because on some level it is a physical thing. Teenagers and youth today and actually society in general, focus very much on the physical and this goes to the point that to sell a car you have to have beautiful models being part of the commercial ads. Therefore what we forget is the inner beauty, which is of course what I am speaking about in the masculine and feminine, not the external beauty or the external sense of gratification often associated with sexuality.

When we bring the divine aspect into sexuality, it is important to understand that the complete sense of masculine inside of you, if you are a man, has so much more than just the body and it is important to express that to the feminine, the feminine in the feeling which is receptive to that. The feminine realises that you are not abusing because you are not focusing just on the physical aspect of the woman but you are actually bringing in the other qualities, the macrocosm into the sexual relationship that you have with your partner. Then the woman is able to open up also in the same way, and her opening up opens up the relationship with the man. It becomes a whole domino effect.

In a relationship, do you consider that the opening to other qualities than just sexuality – like the feminine aspects – should start from the man?

Well, I did say it that way but I did not mean it that way. It starts from... I think it starts from love! Because the woman is the heart, love is usually felt more acutely or more deeply usually in the woman. This is generalising, and I do not want it to be a dogma but we could say it starts from the woman, but not really. It is the sense of love. Yet, the woman is like the vessel that is able to pull the expansive space of the man into that centre point. It is almost like the woman has to embrace this whole relationship in the beginning. Does it start from the man or the woman? In a practical sense, I believe it is the woman who needs to invite the man into the heart.

Why?

If the woman does not do this, then the man can only touch the physical aspect of the woman and he is lost. Just like the mind is lost without anchoring in the heart. I am not putting all the responsibility on the woman of course, but on some level the love needs to be focused much more than just on the physical – which is the tendency in the western culture. To really go to the depth of the divine aspect of the heart, love needs to be focused on the beauty, the essence, the divinity and the light within, not just the feelings, otherwise sexuality loses the quality where it brings up energy to release old patterns.

Some esoteric schools – and this is what I also do – talk about the woman being able to release energy in a man. I am trying to find the right words because I have not really spoken much about this before. It is almost like the woman can be the battery – the battery being what holds the energy for the man – and recharge the energy that we call the *kundalini* or life force energy of the man and of the woman. There are certain things that a woman can do to assist with this. One of them is embracing the love of a man but inviting that love to be more than simply directed towards the physical or the emotional. It is inviting that love to go to touch the macrocosm, so that it is equal in meeting the macrocosm and this is maybe why the woman needs to take the first step. It is not just a meeting of physical senses as it carries more to it.

This meeting is done through the breath. I am still talking about sexuality here in a practical sense, so to clarify, the woman can breathe in a certain way, which was perhaps taught in the old days, where the breath is not lost in emotions or lost in the physical senses. Instead, the whole breathing technique is done in a certain way where there is an invitation for the energies, and for the life force energy of the man especially, to be directed to a certain point rather than the mundane. This, I believe, creates a whole sense of ecstasy, which is missing in normal sexuality because sexuality has just becomes a physical matter.

Actually the ecstasy is not physical. The ecstasy is where the woman embraces so much of that expansive energy within the battery that this battery, which is based and actually has a physical space, expands. It is almost like the battery is "activated" to produce energy. That energy definitely changes the sense of the woman in the sexual act, which, when that happens, activates the same in a man. It is not that the woman has to actively do this but it is more like the woman has to feel comfortable enough for that situation to happen and of course, that depends on love. If the woman is not happy because she feels that there is something else and thinks, "It is just my body that you love", or "It is just this part that you love in me", then that battery becomes closed because the heart is not functioning. Other aspects are functioning, like the physical body, the survival mechanism, and the survival mechanism of creating a baby. These aspects are at work but not the ecstatic one.

Ecstasy is completely connected to the macrocosm but it is also connected to the DNA structure in the cells. In that point of ecstasy there is a certain light that travels between the two strands of the DNA structure and it is almost like electrical charges that bind one to another. This is what is happening in the macrocosm when the two aspects meet and that is like an incredible surge of energy that we call "ecstasy". It is not just physical, it is physical, emotional and energetic. It is not simply contained in one experience.

This ecstatic experience then activates the battery in the woman who feels her goddess-like aspects, as an individual, as a personality, but also as an extension of the divine. When that happens, the heart of the man is activated completely because his mind recognises the whole thing that has unfolded. The experience then dramatically pushes his mind straight down to the heart, and the whole body expands from that space. The reference point is changed.

This is why I believe that relationship is one of the easiest ways of practising meditation. Sexuality is of course only one part of the relationship, but what I have just explained is more easily experienced in a practical and tangible sense in relationship to a woman or a man. It is of course possible to directly be in touch with the divine without a relationship because the universe is doing this all the time, and you are part of the universe, you are the universe and the universe is you, but in a tangible sense that you can relate to, it is easier in a relationship. This is why a relationship is so vital and this is why I speak a lot about the masculine and feminine, even though they are one and equal.

There are qualities that have gone to man and gone to woman. When those qualities meet, they complete a sense of union. The man then finds aspects that are inside of him in the woman, and the woman finds aspects of herself that are important for that completion in the man. That union brings that sense of oneness which both are in essence. We can experience it more easily and in a more tangible way in a relationship but only if the relationship is made of love. It is not the woman nor the man but the love that starts this whole sense of union. The *kundalini* experience, which is part of ecstasy, directly relates to what I have been speaking about.

What is the "special breathing" you mentioned for the woman?
It is something that cannot be so easily explained but when the breath is connected to the heart, it changes frequency. It goes deeper and goes inside, not outside. With a deeper breath, the feminine aspect goes inside to the point of contraction. If the mind is thinking, the breath then of course brings the mind into that point that is where the battery is. This battery is at the base of the spine, at the point where the perineum is. When you bring the heart, the mind, the thoughts and the breathing to that point, it centres the whole experience much more than getting lost in the breath or the breath getting lost in the thoughts, or whatever normally happens in sexuality. There is much more and there are so many other points that you can pick up from but I was just relating it to man and woman.

Some feelings can be masculine and others can be feminine. This is why a woman is a mother and has motherly feelings for example, while a man is masculine and has fatherly feelings. Some people believe today that a woman can be a mother and a father at the same time. Many women are single and believe that they can complete the job by themselves, which I do not think is possible, unless the person is totally enlightened and free of attachments of personality. It is difficult. I believe that those two figures need to be present in a relationship to a child. A mother has certain very deep motherly feelings that are instincts, that are genetic and have been put into our body as a survival mechanism. A father also has genetic things but men's genetic binding functions somewhat differently although of course, they are very much influenced by genes in their actions. It is necessary to understand that perhaps women have feelings that are difficult for men to understand if you just perceive them from a masculine point of view.

Nature has created us, our senses and our perceptions, differently and this is often one of the main reasons why relationships go wrong. It is not that there is a difference in understanding but just that a man sees certain things and a woman sees certain other things. They do not meet because they are different. I see this very often in relationships, once the mundane has taken love over. Love is then in the background. We remember it is there but when the ego intervenes, or when something else comes into the picture, we forget.

It is a trick of nature to bring this sense of love and attraction to each other so strongly. Then Nature leaves it to man and woman to find their way through the mundane. And often the masculine way of thinking, which is expansive and sometimes outside of the space of the feminine, carries the woman to a point that is not so feminine. The woman then feels lost, somehow abandoned, or not nourished in the way that a relationship is meant to be. This is very much how relationships in modern western culture happen. The woman is forgotten because we focus on masculine aspects of our culture which are expansive, like driving a car to get to work, making money, creating things, competition, shopping – and of course, it is also women's fault, not just men's.

On the other hand, the feminine emotions are contractive, like communication and being. Just being in the space together, perhaps without saying anything. For some men, this is difficult because it does not seem like you are doing anything. This is why nature created woman as a mother. It is not always the case, but a woman will often be able to hold the baby quietly and not do anything other than simply being a mother. The space of that silent communication which is a very feminine aspect, could be in a man, but it is usually more in a woman. It is a vital part of communication between a mother and her child, especially for the first two or three months.

The woman wants this in a man also, not to be mothered or fathered, but to have that same sense of communication with a man. Unfortunately there is not time for it because our society is busy. We have the washing up to do and we have the clothes to hang up – that is what the woman, sometimes, ends up doing, if it is a traditional sort of masculine-feminine role – or going to work, etc. In doing so, we forget the feminine qualities and the man supports that forgetfulness by also doing other things. By the time there is time for communication, there is anger in the woman because that quality has not been honoured. Then that anger is unexplainable.

It is a bit like the moon, which has a feminine quality. The anger just touches on non-logical words, emotions, and situations. It simply attaches to that and then it is expressed through this dimension rather than directly expressing what is really going on, but it is not crazy. It has a meaning and a whole connection. Angers appears because, in essence, the woman has not been able to have that period of deep silence and deep communication with the man, which is necessary on all levels.

It is necessary to have that time together before sexuality for example, but most of the time sexuality is much quicker for men than for women. Sometimes it is the other way around but the expansion happens mostly for men whilst for women, the expansion has not happened because it needs to come to the point of contraction before it can become expansive. This requires more time and our society does not value time. It does not value that quality of silence, of not doing, of being inactive to create activity in the space that creates poetry and art. Poetry and art are only seen as important when they are activated. Poetry only becomes important once the poet has created poetry. Yet everything that happened before the poetry, all that was prior to art is never written about... That is the feminine aspect that is not honoured in our culture but honoured in some traditional cultures such as the Australian Aboriginals. Time loses itself and has a different quality. This feminine aspect is very important.

Coming back to an idea of feminine, kindness or being nice for instance can, as you mentioned, be mistaken for weakness. We sometimes think that when we are kind we are just weak. The strength in the feminine expression of ourselves is not always clearly located...

I think we are all kind. Deep inside we really all are kind but if we pretend to be something, like to be nice, and on some level that pretence is hiding a more subtle feeling, which is not so nice, I find that a bit deceptive. It is more confusing for children and for people who are sensitive, because it is as if there were two things being said at once and we do not know which one is right or wrong. One is the superficial kindness and the other is the element of deception behind the kindness because there is another feeling that is stronger but not expressed.

It is not that I believe that kindness is wrong but I believe that kindness needs to be direct and true to how you really feel and sense yourself in that moment. Often when that is the case, when people are very kind from their centre, it does seem feminine. Some people say to me, "You are soft Tony, you are very feminine, you are very gentle". I do not see this in the same way as people on the outside. I think it gets perceived in that way because I embrace the feminine quality which, if you can differentiate between the masculine and the feminine, is much more like a mother, much more able to express that softness.

For some reason, these feminine qualities are perceived as weak in our masculine society. I do not find it weak. I actually find that the feminine quality is the strongest. If we look at what women actually have to go through, they have to be very strong. This is of course on a physical level but for example all the hormones change every month and it is very strong emotionally and physically. Giving birth for example, is not as easy at it looks. In Israel, which tends to be a very militaristic society to preserve itself, women are seen as the most amazing soldiers because they can endure much more pain and suffering than men, so they are respected as fighters. I am bringing this up just to clarify that the feminine is not weak. It is strong, not in an external explosive sense but more in a passive peaceful sense. It endures much more than the masculine aspect can. This is what gives patience. A mother who is really honouring her motherhood needs to be patient with children. Without patience, it would be very difficult to keep going as a mother, so for me, the feminine quality is actually stronger than the masculine quality.

This is why I find that today's society has chosen a wrong path to be a masculine society because it has lost the quality of strength that sustains it. It is rather an explosive external strength that seems to have the image of being strong but lacks depth and inner strength. We see this as soon as anything changes. In societies where things are more complicated, it is usually the woman at home, the mother, the maternal part of the family, that holds the family together, that gives it strength through turbulent times, through difficult times and through dynamics that are external or internal to the family. I find that quality to be very strong. I am not judging it as better or worse. I am just saying that the judgement is a little bit mistaken when we say that the feminine is not a strong quality.

In my work, I need to expand and strengthen the feminine quality to a degree that most people perhaps do not see as important. This is why patience is a natural aspect of the work. I need patience, because I need to listen, I need to be present and I need the strength to keep going. In a way, if I wanted the masculine part of myself to express and change everything, it would lose track of what is important. The ceremonies that sometimes happen require for instance the feminine aspect to work more than the masculine because it is a very feminine ritual. For some people, it seems like I am doing nothing. If you look at it with your eyes only, I am very still and quiet. It is like a quiet meditation. That is because we are looking from the masculine perspective and do not see all the subtleties that are going on. This is where the feminine strength is important. When you are free of the masculine and the feminine, this means they are in union. Then in one way you go beyond ingrained cultural limitations.

The Substance of Destiny

Many cultures value the concepts of destiny or fate that invite people to accept their present situation in life. India has particularly developed this idea through the caste system and the notion of *dharma*. This is an easy way to justify human differences and unequal opportunities in life. Is explaining differences in people's opportunities and interests in spirituality in relation to astrology, or to some cosmic aspects that transcends their person, a relevant approach for you?

This is an ancient philosophical question, why are we so different? Maybe the best way to speak about it is to take India as you suggest, that offers an extreme explanation of this. It is supposed that in the caste system, the untouchables accept their destiny because on some level they believe that their *karma* has created their situation and they cannot do anything but live with it. I totally disagree with this and see it as a very clever way of controlling the masses. This was perhaps necessary at some point for the Indian political structure to survive, but today, in the world that we live in, it is a hindrance rather than a help, even to the political structure of India.

I do not believe that the western model is any better but the Indian model, stating that you are born in a situation that can never change, definitely stops people from recognising who they are. I believe we can change any situation on one level and nothing can stop that. In other words, if you are born in the wrong astrological time or if you are born with a certain *karma* or in a certain situation that limits the possibility of change. But that is not an unavoidable limitation. It is only a limitation if we believe that this limitation is stronger than the possibility of change.

For most people, the problem is they do not believe that the possibility of change is real. They know it as a concept, they try to practice it in their mind, but reality means that you have to put it into practice as if it is here and now, not an idea tomorrow. Yet, most people cannot live that experience. This is why after wining the lottery, there are people who just cannot live with the new situation because in themselves, they still live in their old sense of "I don't deserve the money" or they maybe feel they deserve the money but they live that lifestyle in a way that comes from the fear of not deserving the money. They spend all of it, they abuse it or they pretend that it is not part of their experience by doing certain things that seem very outrageous. Psychologists have analysed these difficult situations where people who were previously very poor become millionaires from scratch and that totally changes their whole world. What they see is that the problem is not the money but it is the person who just does not know how live with this new possibility. That is the problem. It is not destiny but it is the person who has so many possibilities.

The person is divine but the divinity cannot be recognised because so many other aspects get in the way. The mind, which is our experience in this world, is so focused on those limitations, on trying to resolve or go beyond them that the concept of the divine is far removed from the experience the person is thinking about or feeling in that moment. Then we can ask the question again, "Why is a person unable to move beyond a certain limitation and another person who has a totally different situation, which on some level on the outside looks much more negative and much more limiting, is able to move beyond that and utilise the negativity to become more conscious, to become happier, to become more present to the divine within oneself?"

My answer to this question would be that destiny does exist. It exists so strongly that, on some level, things have already happened. This idea does not work in the normal timeframe of beginning and end. Things have already happened and all we are doing is re-living what has happened. It is not like some New Age philosophies where you can create your reality and blame the person for not actually taking the initiative to fulfil a conscious aspect of their destiny. One cannot say that because actually, on some level, the destiny of the person is already formed on many levels in the moment when conception happens.

Is it astrology?

No, it is not astrology; it is beyond. I cannot really say what it is because there are no words for it. When a man and a woman create the possibility of a new life, there are so many dynamics that inter-flow together, that create a substance that is present even beyond the personality that is there. That substance follows the being during all of his or her life. It is there when the cells mix to create a little baby, when the baby grows and becomes a person. Behind all that is the destiny that comes when the mother and the father build the atmosphere that creates the possibility of a new being to be born as a body with a personality, with the emotions and with the senses to be present in the world. Behind that, there is something else – destiny – that really controls a lot, although it is invisible. This is energetic work that I do with people. It is something so beyond psychology, so beyond anything that is obvious or tangible that I call it "destiny", but it is not astrology. It does not really have to do with the moon or the stars being in a certain alignment.

Things that are written...

Things that are written or things that you have done before... It is much beyond and much more complex. People like to create simple pictures to understand the world. In India the caste system and the *karma* philosophy explains the world too simplistically. There is a much deeper essence behind everything. On some level, *karma* is true but it is not that if you have bad *karma* you have to be part of a lower caste and you have to live in suffering for the rest of your life. This whole idea was changed by the political structure but it goes much deeper than that. People have misunderstood the whole philosophy, just like in Christianity.

Jesus' wisdom was passed down to the disciples and was changed to fit into a structure that became political, social, and institutional. A lot of what Christianity speaks about today is not Christianity. It has nothing to do with it. It is the same with destiny. In my opinion, a lot of *karma* and destiny, as explained by many spiritual and religious traditions, only simplify and move us away from the reality of what destiny is. Destiny can be understood more as magic, in the sense that there is a mystery. When we accept the mystery of life, we do not need to question or try to understand why certain things happen in the way that they do. We accept the mystery and we flow with it rather than try to explain why this suffering happens.

I keep circling around the same theme but you mentioned this idea of a "substance" behind the personality. Does it explain what makes these differences in opportunities between people – being born in specific place and experiencing specific situations, etc. – or does it mean that everybody has the same opportunities, whatever the experiences are?

There is a judgement when people say that they are born into a negative or positive situation, lucky or unlucky. In the end, there is no negative situation in the complete sense. There is of course more suffering for certain people, but everything is an opportunity. I feel it is a western attitude to judge certain things as "good" and other things as "bad". For example people always judge Africa as a terrible place where people must suffer and of course they suffer, but on some level there are opportunities and work that happens that you cannot see unless you are there. How can we say that it is better to live in apartments in Germany?

All people do is go to work and come back home and turn the television on. They have no friends except for their television, but it is important to have human contact. They go to work and on the surface they have everything, they have food, they have a car, they have all the things that make life easy but on another level there is deep suffering. To me it is the same suffering as in India or Africa but it is not on an obvious level. It is a deeper psychological level. People say, "It's not as bad as in Africa" and they will focus on the external picture of suffering, which happens in Africa or India. Actually, no matter what the situation is, people are learning something that is of more value than the suffering.

We are not here to remove suffering from our lives, which is the concept of the western culture. We are here to embrace our experience of life. Removing suffering does not make us happier even though people think that by having more material wealth to pay for more food, more television and more cars, they will be happier than in India where most of these things are missing. For me it is not like that. Both types of cultures are suffering in different ways. We have not addressed the problem, we have just changed the picture of the problem.

In India, during those moments of suffering, some very wise and amazing people are born, so suffering can give birth to genes that are lost in societies like in Germany for example. Everything is organised and functions, but it is not really fulfilling because there is no aliveness in the living of that experience. How can there be less suffering when a person has spent ten years living in a small apartment watching television as their best friend? To me that is totally isolated from the reality of experience. People have made themselves immune to life rather than going deeper into the experience.

Destiny is beyond suffering, beyond good or bad. Destiny is the opportunity that is given to people so that they can embrace life more completely. Some of us have an intense possibility for that transformation and some have less. It is not good or bad. If you are born in Africa you have an intense possibility to transform, to understand, because you will have to question life. If everyone else is dying around you, for sure you will come to a deeper understanding of death, suffering, life, love, pain and the experience of humanity, than someone who watches a soap opera.

Every culture provides "spaces" for spiritual awareness but in these same cultures there are so many spiritual inequalities at birth, inequalities related to social status of the family, physical health, cerebral disease...

But spirituality is beyond this.

What is beyond? Is it the substance behind the personality?

Exactly. There was once an article about a child who was born with some very major physical disease and everyone on the outside would see this person as living a lesser life because "something" was missing. This child was intelligent but he did not have the same capacity as others to create art, music or other things that society values as important. The mother loved him very deeply and said that for her, this was the biggest gift because she understood life more through this child than she could ever have without having him. Then he was a beautiful gift, not a lesser gift. Even though she did not want the child to suffer, she did not feel sorry for him because she understood the depth behind his physical state. She said that since it was very difficult to communicate with language they have communicated beyond language with eye contact.

They have created an atmosphere that is difficult to put into words but that is of greater value than the outside understanding of it which is based on the spontaneous definition of things as being of more or less value. Let us look at Stephen Hawking who has a degenerative disease preventing him to speak and who has to type everything he wants to communicate through a computer. People could have thought that his disease was terrible because it would prevent him to communicate anything of value to our society, but he learnt how to communicate something that is recognisable and of immense value in physics. Maybe he would have never got to that point without that disease... Who knows?

How can we judge what is suffering and what is not suffering? I feel that in my childhood I suffered immensely through teenage years. I would not want to suffer like this again but, at the same time, I would not want to not have suffered like that because that is what changed my whole life. For me it was a gift. It was destiny creating a space where I believe possibilities happened that otherwise would not have happened. Without that intensity, I would not have crossed onto the more subtle substances that are around. Maybe everything would have been all right and I would have just done something totally different, so I am very happy for my suffering.

I am sure that in that moment it would have been very difficult if a spiritual teacher came up to me and said, "I do not care about your suffering", because I would have thought it to be a little bit naïve and not recognising the pain of that moment. Of course a spiritual teacher will recognise that, but he or she will also acknowledge something beyond that. We need to recognise the whole picture, so it is not that it does not really matter but it is sometimes difficult to see in that moment. That is destiny.

But sometimes the pain and suffering is extreme, like some parents who lock their children in a cave for twenty years. The children then have just no space to express themselves. It is therefore difficult to think that there is a value of learning in these situations. In other cases, the children are born with a disease in the brain and preventing it to function...

Yes, I understand totally. It is because we are looking from a limited perspective. It is not that there is no value or that there is value in what may seem very difficult situations of life but it is that certain things have to happen for other things to happen. I am not saying that the suffering needs to happen in that way. Obviously, the example you are bringing of the parents locking their child in a cave is terrible, but it happens. So what is the value in that? Of course there is no value on one level and that does not need to happen, but there might be a value that we will not see.

The person who is locked can in no way see the value of this kind of situation because the suffering is strong.

The person who did this for sure will not see it, and the victim for sure will find it very difficult to understand.

We are back again to the different opportunities in life...

We are speaking about something very difficult here. Suffering has no value in itself and I cannot see any value in it, therefore I am not justifying suffering. There is no justification in someone crying, starving to death, dying, having a disease, being abused, or any kind of suffering. There is no value in itself and this is of course not what I am saying but we are speaking about destiny, "Why does this happen?"

I am not saying that destiny justifies the suffering either. What I am saying is that instead of looking at the suffering as a limitation, as a point where people think that the world is so negative and therefore there is no need to understand it, we can move beyond that point of limitation and wonder, "How can I be in a totally different situation that gives a whole different atmosphere to that suffering?" like Mother Teresa for example, hugging people who were dying. For these people, that was a gift of immense value. It did not stop all the suffering but it was very important. It was the last moments where they were able to communicate a love that goes beyond eating, that goes beyond suffering. On some level the person who was dying felt this to be of value and Mother Teresa was awake to the importance of giving in that sense.

That does not justify that people are dying or have to die because they have no food. Yet, it beautifully shows that humanity can go above that suffering and reach a quality that changes the atmosphere and hopefully brings consciousness to everyone around. Parents often do not know what they are doing to children. They do not have the consciousness of the pain they are creating. Of course when it is about locking someone up in a cave we would assume that everybody is able to understand that this is not the right thing to do. The person doing this may not have the consciousness, or may be lacking the possibility of consciousness, in the same way that many Americans justify killing children in the Iraq war for whatever reasons they invent. How can that be correct in any way for a normal human being to understand this? It is difficult because on some level the war has been justified. The mass media and the culture have accepted this sacrifice and they support it but it does not justify the pain and suffering.

Perhaps this whole transformation that is happening in America takes place because people had to go through these negative experiences to get to a point of understanding. This could be said about any suffering. I am touching a very difficult point here because people can misunderstand what I am saying and say that suffering is justifiable. It is not! For me it is a lack of consciousness and the only way to transform it is to be more conscious. For a parent to love a child is to be conscious in that loving situation. It is not to be loving because that is right or that is wrong because then you cannot love completely. Africans are starving today because we waste all our money doing things that could easily feed all the children of Africa today. Why do we not change this? Why do leaders collect millions and millions of petrol dollars and do not feed the children who are right there in front of their eyes suffering and dying in the streets? It is a lack of consciousness. If they knew what they were doing, they would not do it. It is ignorance.

Besides ignorant behaviour, I would like to come back to inequalities between each human being regarding spiritual development. For example, while some are born in a spiritual family that facilitates their own spiritual development, it clearly brings suffering when someone is born in a family and loses his or her parents early. How can we put the fact that not everybody has the same opportunities

in relation with your idea that there is a substance behind the personality that is the same in essence for everybody? What is exactly this substance? Does it mean human differences are just formal while there is sameness in content?

No because there is no difference. It is like loving someone. There are different ways of expressing the love. You meet someone and you love that person in a certain way. Someone else meets another partner and loves that partner in an another way. In essence the love is the same but it is expressed totally differently. It has what I call a substance, an atmosphere, a presence that is different. If you go back to the depth of the love that you have for each other, that love is not a unique experience for you, it is a human experience.

We all have a heart that is able to open up and love in this way. I am using this concept – the substance – because for some reason it is now able to manifest between you and someone else in a certain way. But why only now? Why not ten years ago? It is because your destiny was to meet now in this way. Ten years ago maybe you were not ready for each other to explain and to communicate this love that you have for each other. The atmosphere would not have been right to communicate this. Your destiny was to meet at the exact right moment.

So something is written?

Something is written, for sure. This is what I mean by "substance".

Is it an equal potential for everybody?

It is the same, there is no difference. My love is the same as your love!

So whatever people experience in life is an external expression of something that is identical for all. This is the case even in someone who would be called "crazy" because of a brain dysfunction: although the consciousness is not there, the substance is the same...

No, because the atmosphere is changed by the external. People called "crazy" – since you bring up this example – are not able to open up to that substance deep inside of them. That is why the external is not harmonious with the depth that they are not able to communicate. What they are communicating is their lack of depth. I would not call someone "crazy" because some people considered so are not.

I actually meant "brain dysfunction" ...

This is why I previously brought the example of the mother with the child. Maybe this child was autistic – I do not remember – but even though there was apparently no communication, there really was a communication going beyond the spoken communication. It took time to create the space of recognition that there is a communication because we are so used to the senses, words, and feelings that we judge those experiences from those senses, but we forget the substance that is behind all that. This is why babies are so amazing because their substance is alive. When you hold a baby, that being is very present. The baby does not say "I love you" but there is a connection.

This substance is not so obvious in people who are suffering because a baby is alive with all the senses. Someone who is behind that space of so called "craziness" still has a heart that is full of that substance, even if he or she has done the most awful things that people just cannot understand how there can be any space of love in them, like mass murderers for example. On some level there is still a space of love but it is deep behind the attributes.

The idea of common substance suggests that spirituality is for everybody.

It is for everyone. This is why I cannot understand the caste system because for me you cannot quantify a person as being better or worse. No matter what the actions are, the divine is present in everyone but just expressed differently. In some poetry and music it is recognisable in a very obvious sense, but according to your value system, it is not seen in others. Western people for instance who went to Australia almost considered Aboriginals as animals because they did not recognise their language. They did not see the inherent quality in their heart and in their way of interacting with the world because they did not share the same language. This is where we create this sort of dogma of better and worse, this person good or that person bad. Ultimately you cannot judge, you have to embrace, no matter what you are embracing. When you do this you create a connection to the substance that is deeper than the actions outside.

This leads me to another question related to the substance. It is about spiritual awareness and health. Spirituality is often associated with health. To get and maintain a healthy body we must have our consciousness. But the consciousness we can raise at some point in our life may apparently totally disappear when sudden physical diseases happen. I am thinking about Alzheimer for instance. What happens to the spiritual awareness of the person who has been involved in raising it and has been trying to act consciously in his or her life when such a biological disease appears?

If you are asking if people who have done lots of spiritual work and all of a sudden get Alzheimer's disease have lost their consciousness, then no. The only things that have gone are the senses. Nothing has changed deep inside but the expression of consciousness did. We judge Alzheimer as not a nice thing, which is of course true. It indeed creates a separation because in the world that we live in, the senses are of primary importance. Yet it does not mean that the essence of the two worlds is different. It is still there, totally alive in the same way. It has not changed in anyway. The persons have not lost their spiritual consciousness. They are not able to express it to us with senses as before but they are able to express it to the divine inside of them in the same way. In actual fact, the experience of a person with Alzheimer is as valid as someone without Alzheimer.

But people around can hardly understand this...

From outside, it is impossible to understand what the experience of the person is.

... and what about the person experiencing this?

They understand but it does not mean that there is no pain. The senses are what cause pain or the lack of experience through them. When people start loosing the possibility of remembering things for example, it is a whole process of disintegration of the senses in the physical body. What they are left with is just their essence, their substance, and that is different.

This essence is not expressed externally anymore?

It is not expressed in the senses anymore but it is expressed. It is not that their expression stops, although it does stop on some levels. The nervous system begins to disintegrate, which stops that method of communication. That communicational bridge no longer exists but the other bridges that are there remain. For example when I am working with people I am not always working with the senses, I am working beyond them. The other bridges are still there. I can then work with someone who has Alzheimer because that level of communication is still open until physical death. I do not need to speak to them. I can work and then the other bridges to the essence open to another dimension.

Karma, Reincarnation, Soul & Attachment

You often use the term *karma* while you practically do not use the term "reincarnation". But as you know, it is practically a systematic reference in all New Age and spiritual activities, and people working with you are no exception. At the same time you do not really acknowledge the notion of "soul". Would you clarify your position on these matters?

When I use the world "soul" it as a reflection of the divine, sacred, Godly soul, but sometimes we need words to simplify things and make things more sensible and understand on a conceptual level what is going on. We are not a specific or separate item from the whole, even though it looks like it is the case, there is no personality within the soul. I mean that there is personality in the practical sense, so we do have a personality, but if we die there is no personality. This is now reaching into philosophical points...

There is no personality that says, "I am Christian, he is John, and I am Tony" and when we die, somehow that identity of who we are stays in a certain format, like a ghost or whatever. I absolutely do not see any of that. That may seem very sad because we identify very much with that specific aspect of ourself and we want that to not disappear. In actual fact, there is much more to us because beyond the personality there is a light that shines that is not personal. I am using the word "light" because that is the easiest way of describing it. You cannot give an identity to the quality of light. It is beyond identity. It is part of the complete light that is everything.

The idea that when you die the soul goes somewhere and finds another body to reincarnate into is humanity trying to make it nice for itself, trying to make death more agreeable. "If we do not do it now, we will come back. We will never part. Our love will never be separate because our souls will meet again in the next life", is how some people think. It is all very romantic and beautiful but I do not see it that way. Now, I know I will enter into a point where many people will be disappointed because, of course, people want things to continue – and something does continue – and that is that our consciousness disappears by melting into the great consciousness. That can never happen because our consciousness is already part of the great consciousness, even though it does have an aspect that gives it a form (soul).

I know I am contradicting myself but that is impossible not to do. You cannot say that the moon is not divine, but you cannot say that the moon is the divine because that limits the divine to something specific. You cannot say that only one person is the divine like some dogmatic religions believe. Many religions of course will disagree and say that their aspect of devotion was the only divine aspect to manifest on this earth. For me that is not true. We are all spiritual beings, there is no separation in the divine, but at the same time the divine has many aspects and many forms.

Each star, for instance, has a quality that makes it unique. As human beings we have that same uniqueness but our essence is not the physical form. The body simply goes when we die. It disappears and even though we would like to hold on to some precious feelings, there is nothing left of the physical body or the emotional body. Even the energetic or etheric body that is around the physical body goes. What is left is pure consciousness. The pure consciousness is of course this bigger aspect of the divine. It has a form but it is beyond personal identity.

Not a human form anyway...

It is not a form that can go somewhere, wait to reincarnate and come back here, as various religions advocate. It never goes anywhere. It has never gone anywhere and has never changed. Its form is exactly the same. It is not that we can qualify it into an aspect and say that because the body has died, this form will come back into another body. This is where reincarnation, in my opinion, is totally misunderstood. I am not saying that reincarnation is not real because that form actually never dies and carries on forever. Just like if the moon disappears, even though the physical aspect of its energy has gone, its energy is still there. If everything disappears, if there is a catastrophe in this world, it does not mean that things stop. The physical form has disappeared but the energy of life is still there.

If we go back to reincarnation, the essence of each person, can never die, no matter what you do. It can never die. If you believe and understand that this aspect can never die, then on some level, that is reincarnation, but the doctrine of reincarnation says that there is a beginning and there is an end; that we begin at a certain level and we end at another, so that essence changes to become better. But the divine cannot become better. The divine is perfect so it never changes and, rather than evolving through reincarnation, that aspect simply has a different experience.

In the common idea of reincarnation of some Hindu denominations, if I am correct, is that we start as an animal, and then there is a hierarchy, the dog somehow is a lesser quality than a human being. Then there are different levels of human beings, the Brahmans at the top and the Untouchables at the bottom of the scale, and these qualities are supposed to have happened through reincarnation. This is where karma is totally misunderstood in my opinion and actually used in the same way that Christianity has sometimes done in the past. Indeed, misunderstandings within some denominations in Christianity have created this idea that if we are good we deserve a place in heaven and if we are not good then we go to hell, but the divine can never go to hell because the divine reflection within our soul is part of the heavenly realm. This is what Jesus spoke about in the Gospels.

The divine in itself is pure, it does not need anything and does not need to go anywhere. It loves this game of maya, where it becomes conscious of itself in different forms. One dimension of that form is this world that we live in. Another dimension of that world that we live in is the human experience. Another dimension of this human experience is the mind. Another dimension is the body. Another one is the feeling... There are many levels to being human but in essence, what is feeding humanity is that divine aspect that Rumi spoke about, which feeds our heart with a fire and then gives life and passion to everything else.

Once we realise that passion in our human form, then there is no fear of death. We realise that what gives life, real life, cannot die. It is never ending. So in that sense, there is reincarnation because the divine aspect will create itself in another form, constantly expanding. It does not stop at one form but it will create forms and expand into its game of recognising itself in different forms. In words, this is the best way I can explain it.

In the way reincarnation is traditionally seen, everyone wants to be something nice, like a pharaoh or Cleopatra. How many people have been Cleopatra? I do not know but no one wants to simply have been a humble servant. In my opinion, this is an illusion of the mind, trying to preserve itself in some form and creating a whole philosophy. I am not saying that after death there is nothing either. When experiencing love, just like in the moment of enlightenment, there is actually more personality, more aliveness in the personality, in the mind, and in the body than any mundane experience of life.

In that moment of awakening we feel more alive than we have ever felt. This is why it is an experience that people desire because they want to be more alive than they have ever felt. That aliveness does not stop when we die – how could it? – because it is beyond the body, beyond the emotions, beyond the chemistry of the mind. It is our essence. That is what carries on in reincarnation. This manifestation carries on, it never stops and continues to expand.

Is that divine aspect which has no form, awareness, or what some call "pure consciousness"?

It is awareness because it has an aspect that is like the mind. It has an awareness of itself, but it is beyond the mind because the awareness of itself is not related to what people normally have as an awareness. It goes much further, so the awareness transcends normal awareness. It goes to a point that is irrelevant to most people's experiences but at the same time it has the same quality. That awareness never dies. If you fall in love with someone and it is deeply touching to the heart, that love does not die when you die. That love stays in that awareness that I am speaking about because it has the quality of that awareness. It is remembered beyond the personal aspect.

When you fall in love with someone, it is not so much the face or the emotion of the person that you are in love with, but the being of that person. The awareness of that being never dies and is constantly remembered. When two people meet and fall deeply in love for example, even if they are separated through death, that love is remembered and registered, not as an intellectual or an emotional memory, but as the holding of a certain pattern in the whole theatre of live. This is so for any profound love to another person or to children.

I suppose that's what makes Jesus a little bit unusual is that his love went beyond just one person. It went to all humanity and expanded so that Jesus had deep love even for the people that were hating and hurting him. That is the divine love that can never die. Once he recognised that it was beyond death, that gave him eternal life, which is what Christian people speak about. When that love goes beyond anything else, it has eternal life as it is connected to people.

Does an awareness – a human being – that has been full of love in life have a different status than other types of awareness in this other realm of awareness?

No. Love is a very powerful bridge, but love as experienced by most people on a personal level is only personal while the bridge is not this personal aspect of love but the love that goes beyond the personal. It is a bridge just in the same way as compassion or any other human trait. It does not remain in that personal sense in any way.

I mentioned love because most people have the feeling that it might make a difference in the other realm for this awareness – if there is any. According to Christianity and the karmic principle, people's behaviours have effects beyond the material life. In other words does someone's action in his or her life (good, bad, immoral, etc.) produce different status and awareness after death? In your understanding, what remains of individual consciousness after this life?

This is where *karma* comes in. In the traditional sense, *karma* is that if you do something bad, then you will be punished and you will have to undergo certain suffering because of that punishment, like being reborn into a life where your reality has more suffering than someone else's. This belief states that you have created your reality and your *karma* has created your destiny in this moment, so your whole experience can be explained through *karma*. I do not see *karma* in this way at all, but your question of course is another deep issue; does consciousness remain unaffected by our actions in this life? No, because our consciousness is affected by every single action. This is why every action is so important. Every moment we live in this world is so precious and so vitally important to honour and to complete who we are.

Every action and every thought too?

Every action, every thought, every moment, every everything. It is a gift to be here in this form to experience what we are experiencing but we forget that gift and our actions then become negatively affected. I am not judging in a moralistic sense or saying that if our actions are good and we are saints in people's eyes, or in our own eyes, that we then reach a higher level of consciousness that takes us to more heavenly aspects of the divine. I do not see this. If our actions are negative, then the sufferings that we have through those negative actions are the sufferings and the consequences of our actions.

If we do not know how to love in a deep sense for example, the suffering is that we do not experience love. We do not experience the completeness of ourselves. We experience everything else, which is called *maya*, the illusion, the circle that I speak about, but we do not experience the joy of love, of being alive in that sense of love. If our actions come out from the space of hatred, from the space of egotism, or out of the space of wanting to hurt others, then the suffering is the consequence of our actions. We have not experienced our potential and that lack of love does influence our experience after death. It is not a punishment. It is just that we have to go through the same circle again.

To explain more, if we are going around in a circle going from point A around and around and always going back to point A, that circle does not stop just because we die. Some people say, "My life is so bad that the only solution is to commit suicide and to leave this world because my suffering is so great". This is many people's idea but that does not change anything. When we leave this physical form, the suffering is the same because our consciousness is limited in the same way. If the darkness, that means our hatred, our sense of injustice, our sense of judgements, creates all these pictures – which I call "the darkness" – and prevents the natural light from expressing itself because we are so attached to these pictures in life as a human being, when we die that suffering does not stop. It just takes on another form. That suffering is not on an emotional level, not on a physical level, not on an energetic level but it is still on the level of being incomplete, being unable to manifest the full potential. It is not that we die as a lesser human being, but we die with a lack of consciousness of what it means to be a complete human being.

And then...

I have to be very careful because it is not to say that when some people like Jesus die their death means that they died in a better way than a criminal who could only see the suffering and negativity of their experience in that present moment. The divine aspect is the same but we are not able to relate consciously to that divine aspect in different manifestations. This is where *karma* is very important. *karma* is the experience that we need to go through to release that darkness so that the light comes into that experience. If there is hatred for ourself or for someone else, it is important to release the karmic hatred so that light has the space to go to that space, instead of the darkness of hatred occupying that space. When we die, if we do not do anything, that hatred, which is emotional, or that we experience as emotional, still remains but in another form. The darkness remains there. It is not released.

This goes in contradiction with Christianity where the soul is supposed to go to heaven. In my opinion, there is no heaven in that form. There is no place of light that we travel to and where we live happily. Heaven is made real through our actions as a human being. It is made real through actions in this invisible world, through other forms and other dimensions that we are not aware of as human beings. It becomes clear when we die that what we are doing here and now has a karmic thread that carries on and does not stop, so every action that we do has an influence, creates *karma* and influences our experience after death. When people who are depressed, or who feel that life is too difficult, say, "It is easier just to kill myself and then everything will be OK because I will be free", they forget that things are not that easy. We have to be free in action. We cannot be free by killing our body, by killing our emotions, or by killing our energy points. Nothing changes because nothing has changed.

So we are here to work and to clean something...

There is no other possibility. We have to work, whether we do it consciously or unconsciously. That is why we are here. This is why we are human beings. Even if what we do is totally wrong, that knowledge of what we are doing becomes part of our evolution so that we become able to see what is not useful and let go of what is wrong. If we realise that hatred does not serve a purpose or does not serve anyone, this is because on one level we needed that hatred to realise that. We cannot judge it in a moralistic sense. That hatred opened the space for light to come into itself and that light expands and goes on forever and ever. There are so many degrees. It is not as if we reach a point where we are free of everything. Actually, once we go beyond our human experience, that expansion goes beyond that human experience to other levels and other dimensions. It is unstoppable. When we complete our human experience, it goes further and further.

But with a different status for this awareness...

With a different status because at that point it is not necessary to be a human being. You can be a planet, you can be a star – I am using symbolic words here – you can be anything. Our human experience is only essential because this is where we have reached at this level of evolution, so we need to go through the human experience. This is why to kill ourselves because we do not like the human experience does not mean that our human experience stops. It comes back. That is reincarnation. But it does not come back through traditional ideas of reincarnation. It comes back in a different way.

Not a new body on earth?

Yes and no. Yes and no...

Is it yes or is it no? Sometimes you say that if we do not learn our lesson "we have to come back". Who or what is it that comes back?

This is a very big question so I will try to make it clear. I am just trying to differentiate from other traditions, that I do not think that it happens in the manner where when you have done something bad, this bad comes and reincarnates in a physical sense. If it is really, really bad, some people say you come back to a lower form of life and if it is really good, if your *karma* is free from so many things, then you are a higher human being. This to me is just misunderstandings, and I do not see it in this way at all.

Karma – I use the word just because there is no other word in English – is really the aspect of consciousness that is always growing. It is not bound to good and bad or to the dualism of what we see as good and bad because I see that as a very cultural and sometimes very mental thing. This is why I say "yes and no". It has much more to do with something that is much bigger and that we only understand through consciousness itself. After you die, consciousness does not die, it carries on but how does it manifest? How does it carry on? This is the question that maybe you are trying to ask: Where does it go? What comes back in the body?

This is why I say "yes and no" because consciousness is not bound to come back to the world as a new human being. Consciousness is free. There is so much more beyond this world that only consciousness understands. It is free to explore many levels and dimensions of the world, which create reality for consciousness. Here we are in a manifested dimension where the physical limits our consciousness to a certain point so we have to integrate our consciousness into this world. When this world goes, it does not mean that the other worlds that are part of this world do not go onto other structures. Not onto physical ones but onto much larger ones; so consciousness goes to those and it is happy in those because it is part of consciousness growing.

Consciousness is expanding all the time to come back to itself, which is union with everything. Sometimes it becomes clear for consciousness that it needs to come back to the world but I do not believe that consciousness comes back as a personal aspect. I believe it comes back as a gift to another manifested being. It is not the same personal aspect that people think of when they die, "That's it! I'm going to die and then I'm going to come back as a new body, as a new person and I'll be recognised as this person". For me, that personal aspect dissolves. There is a personal aspect but only in the part of consciousness that is personal, not in the character or the in the personal dualism that we see and that we are attached to.

If you look at a child for example, it is not the personal aspect of the child that relates to *karma*, it is rather the deep aspect which is part of the child's incarnation into this world. This deep aspect is like feeling, but not feeling as understood in the normal sense of the physical world. It is more a sense that we have of a person's energy and of being that part of the child's manifestation in this world. Consciousness needs to learn and expand in this world and this learning depends on many factors such as social setting, time, and people, and spiritual teachers that are present in the child's karmic cycle. What we think of time these days is totally different in another dimension. Time does not follow linear rules. For me reincarnation is more subtle than what is traditionally understood.

It is the consciousness which comes back and I believe that this is connected to many things. It is connected to consciousness of course, but also to family genetics. Everyone has their own consciousness which is free from many attachments, but when you look at them, a lot of their consciousness can be seen in a very clear way. Some of the consciousness is a family trait, it is visible, as you can see similarities with grandparents, and so on, but they are not exactly the same, yet some aspect of them – of the consciousness – is repeated and this is a type of reincarnation for me.

Some people say it is just genetic material and the DNA structure but I am not talking about the physical. I am talking about the sense of a person which is beyond the physical structure of the DNA or the chemical structure of the body. It is that sense where you know there is something else that is connected to the past, to the family. Sometimes you will see that the child is totally different from the family and that they have a consciousness that has come from somewhere else. I do not believe that this consciousness just evolves out of learning. I do not believe that the child is born and then socialisation happens and that their consciousness simply appears...

The substance is already there, before?

Of course. Anyone who has seen children can see that they cannot express their consciousness in the physical form through talking or through expressions but they are totally alive in their consciousness. Sometimes they are even more alive. So where did that consciousness come from? It came from the mystery that could be termed as reincarnation, but that is just a concept that doesn't explain the mystery.

Not a soul. A consciousness...

No, not a soul, this is why death is not real. It is just like a blanket that gets lost or a clothing that gets changed. The consciousness just moves through different aspects because in the end, consciousness is everything. There is no separation. People who see reincarnation in a personal sense are still caught up in this picture that there are individual things. There is an individual aspect of consciousness but deep consciousness is not individual so it cannot be separate in the sense of, "You die and you're reborn. Because you've done bad, you'll be reborn like this". This is just the mental picture of people trying to make an understanding of something that is too complex to understand in that way.

A simplification, but close enough to what you describe... Then the popular concept of reincarnation is not so incorrect?

It is incorrect because there is no beginning and there is no end. There is no evolution of forms, as certain religions and people state. Everything started where it started. Nothing has a beginning and nothing has an end. Everything is. It is close but it is a simplification because dogmatic religions have gone back to institutionalising what was wisdom and what many saints, prophets and holy people probably spoke about. But for normal every day consciousness, it is nice to know that when someone dies, they somehow come back. It is a reassurance. The institution then carries on this comfort feeling, "OK, don't worry you'll go to heaven or you'll do this or that", but it is much more complex than that. I do not think that the person disappears and it is the end, that this is it and you have to live life here and complete things. Yet on one level it is, because consciousness is integrated into everything. I do not know if it answers the question.

Yes and no, yes and no...

I do not want to speak about it too much because people may start to tie me down and say, "You said this so of course then it's like that" and they will begin to argue and debate. I am not that clever with concepts nor am I like a theology master who tries to find the little things here and there. What I do have is a deep understanding of reincarnation and when I read about it or people speak to me about reincarnation from other traditions, it is not the same. How I see it is quite different because it is based on the union of consciousness.

Not an individual soul transmigration?

I do not see individuals. I see individuals only because they have to speak as individuals. It is a method of being in this world but that individualism is actually a concept that becomes invalid in a deeper sense. It is only at the surface. This is where reincarnation and *karma* do not fit into the picture because *karma* is always individual. Many people say, "I can't be bad because if I'm bad then it will come back and haunt me and I'll be reincarnated as this and then I'll have to repay". Of course we have to repay. Every action that we create stays forever in our consciousness. It never disappears and we have to work with it, but it is not that we have to pay for it or suffer from it as an individual. It is rather that it limits our growth to the space where everything is union. This action actually keeps us in the suffering, in which no one wants to be. When people are suffering, they want to be in the union of love and ecstasy. We know deep inside that this union is what is important, but the individual sometimes gets caught up in the games that then repeat themselves and create more suffering. That is called *karma*.

Ancient Greek philosophers talked about reincarnation and called it metempsychosis. While some remnants of this idea are found today in Hinduism and legitimate the caste system, it is not obviously present in Christianity and Islam. Was is it never there? Did it disappear?

It is a very important concept and maybe the institutions found it too threatening because on some level, institutions like to control people. To control people and keep them in the dark, you have to go down to the level of consciousness where you satisfy their needs and desires. I was reading the other day that terrorists had blown up something somewhere, and if I think about it, of course I can understand the situation. But do these fundamentalists or any other extremists actually understand their religion at all? If you understand their mind, this act can of course be justified politically, but can it be understood clearly? Could they truly understand what they have done if they understood that every action that they create carries with it much more than what they believe they are doing?

Extreme Muslim sects today have created this sense of conquering and pushing and it is the same with extreme Christianity in the past, for example when the Cathars or other religious groups were persecuted for their beliefs or different belief systems. This brainwashes people to such a degree that often people kill themselves in the name of religion, as we see today in many of the extreme situations. Not only do they kill themselves but they create suffering for other people. In the end, those people living wherever these terrorist things happen, are really in the dark so it does not help to create light by blowing them up! Everyone that lives in the mental picture of religious fanaticism believes that he or she is somehow fulfilling something important. These are the people who have changed the whole philosophy of religion to be so simplistic that they have brainwashed people into following these doctrines.

Christians are the same. They went on crusades with their swords, "taming the barbarians" ... How can people believe that picture and then relate it to Jesus speaking? It is so far removed from what he was saying! These crusaders believed and were encouraged to believe by the Pope that they were doing a fantastic thing, as do all the fundamentalists still today. The problem with what I say about reincarnation is that it is so complex that it cannot be put into simple doctrines. It does not fit.

And you make a point to use the words "awareness", "light" and "consciousness", instead of the word "soul". Why?

I don't believe in a personal physical soul, because, at least in my understanding of soul, it means that there are some aspects of you that are separate from the body. It is like a form that survives and lives with a quality, but I do not believe we have a soul in a traditional sense. I believe we have light and that it has a personal aspect, if you want to use the mind to understand it.

Do we have or are we light?

We are light. It has a personal aspect but it is totally impersonal to what we understand.

The idea of soul would be too personal?

If you believe in soul, then you believe that we are individuals. But we are not. We are just manifestations of the same. For me, there is no individual aspect suggested by the word "soul" because we are all the same. It does not mean we are the same as the tree or the same as the dog. There is a form to the divine, just like the stars, the moon, the earth and the universe. Everything has a certain element of expression, but that expression is not personal to a soul that migrates through different dimensions and then comes back to earth as a dog, as a pig, or as a human being, a man or a woman.

On some level it does, however, come back to another form. This is very complex to put into words because the way to understand it, for me, is to move beyond the linear into the circular, and to understand that in that circular there is no beginning and no end. There is only a point that is in this presence of now.

Now we enter another complicated thing. If we look at this moment, if we think this moment is seen in the same way as people say, all this moment disappears and then there is another moment that happens. We look back, and this moment that we thought happened actually took place in nineteen seventy-six, January the fifth, and I was twenty-three years old. That creates a whole concept of mind, which is simplifying the whole experience of reality in order for it to be perceivable but actually, that moment never happened in the past and it will never happen in the future. It is happening continuously. We somehow – and again words complicate things – have an awareness of that moment, but that moment is endless, so to speak. It is metaphysics. Metaphysics is difficult because it is like you are trying to describe a reality that cannot fit into this program of understanding.

By describing too much, there might be a risk in your teaching to say things that people want to believe and follow, which is not the point...

Exactly. For me, this present moment is never ending. It has no beginning, no end, no evolution, no quality of being better than something else. It is so present. It is like when we look at a star. We might think, "The star is out there". Then we see its light and to understand that, our mind thinks that the star's light has moved down from where the star is and touched our eyes, so that our eyes are aware that there is something out there. In actual fact, the light of the star is the same light that is inside of us. This is what recognises the real light that is coming through.

The other light, which is just the picture and the senses, can of course be explained in scientific ways, but the light is the same light as the light inside and that is what recognises the light that is outside. That light is not dependent on time because it is beyond time. That light is at home in itself and that self is in this moment that never dies, but our experience of this moment takes many forms, so we choose different forms. At one moment of that form, we are looking at the beautiful person and we say, "This form is my son. It is ten years old. It has a certain personality. It is like this or like that". Yet, that is only identifying certain aspects that we see in that moment and believing that those aspects have a reality, believing that the moment is then contained within that picture, rather than that picture being a partial picture.

We do have the need to focus on partial pictures to be able to understand the bigger picture though. This is why for example Jesus said, "You are not my father. You are not my mother", letting go of that personal identity of time and recognising that there was more than that personal aspect. The mind is always trying to comprehend things in a personal way but the divine is not personal, it is beyond personal. This is why *karma* is not personal, it is beyond personal. This is why reincarnation is not personal, it is beyond personal, and related to this moment that cannot be explained in a linear fashion. This is why I say it is a circle.

If we do not allow the light to express itself in our human form, this prevention of expressing that light gets repeated moment after moment. Our consciousness attaches to that experience and remains in that space because it does not know that there is any other reality. That is hell because we cannot move beyond a certain experience. We die in that moment because we do not see that there is more. This is why any dogma or any belief system in itself is limited and, in a way, not spiritual. It actually kills the possibility for us to see reality, which is much bigger than that narrow view.

When you love someone, if you identify that love as personal it becomes limiting. Of course that love is personal on one level because you are feeling this, but it is more than personal. People get confused when I speak about this and they say, "But of course you love some people more than other people, don't you Tony? You cannot love everyone the same!". I answer, "Everyone is the same". They insist, "But no, you love your son more than you love a criminal!" and this puts things in a space that makes no sense when you are in the space of love. It is a judgement and limited to the darkness of that concept of suffering, which is that limited space, and not seeing beyond it.

Love is not your son or a person. Love is recognition of the divine, when you recognise the divine beyond the personal in the person. You recognise the divine aspect of that person and you recognise the divine in everything. That opens up your recognition, your union to be open to union with everything. This is why a mystic like Rumi went drunk with love. His love was not just to one aspect of manifestation, it was to the divine in its complete sense, to the reality that is beyond limited perceptions but is in everything.

Yet human beings naturally create attachment to significant others (friends, lovers, parents, children). According to you, it looks as if the whole purpose of this journey on earth is to extend this attachment not to these special beings but to the whole life that is surrounding us. That seems to be also the main point of Hindu spirituality...

Let us take it to a more practical experience. For instance, a woman who has never been a mother but becomes a mother and has a child. Before that point she could not really understand other people's love for children. She could of course, but not in the same way as in her own experience. This experience opens that love to a point where her love is so intense, so deep and so connected to the child that it is personal, but personal on a level that is unique and special. What happens is that the mother then recognises that same love that every mother has. She has the awareness of what it means to be a mother, of the divine aspect of motherhood.

Then the mother is not just a mother out of ego, because "I want a child", but the mother becomes an extension of the divine loving this aspect of itself. The experience of the divine becomes more conscious in that situation, in that moment, and the mother never loses the love for her child. On some level, she gains a deeper understanding of what it means to be a mother. She has compassion and understanding for motherhood and in a way, this is more difficult if you have not been a mother.

That can be extended to all personal relationships with people that you are attached to, so rather than stopping at the personal attachment, it becomes the bridge that takes you to the points that are so profoundly enlightening that this personal attachment becomes deeper. It does not lose its personal aspect but rather gains a deeper understanding of what that personal aspect is, a bigger picture to that personal aspect. It is not like Buddhism, which can be perceived as quite cold, where detachment means that you leave everything of this world as an experience behind you and focus on whatever Buddhists are focusing on.

On the contrary, I believe that our attachment to certain situations is essential as part of the spiritual work. Our love to a partner is not moving us away from consciousness but rather inviting our heart to recognise consciousness in a way that would have been impossible without having that personal relationship. It has total value and deep meaning. That deep meaning and total value does not die just because that love extends to other aspects. It is simply that consciousness becomes more divine in its understanding of the whole situation. You then are not attached to the person being in a certain way, being kind or being nice to you. You just love people for who they are.

Love goes deeper and deeper and deeper, even with a personal relationship. It takes many years to love a person in the complexity of who she is, beyond expectations of what it means to be in that relationship. Even with children it sometimes takes many years to understand how to express that love without attachment to them being in a certain way and to love them unconditionally with a more expansive love.

But we naturally attach to a form of a being...

Of course we are human and we have to be attached. Our experience has to be human and social. We have to complete it.

... and during this human's experience the point is to be aware of our limitations...

Our human experience is not limited.

So to attach oneself to a special form is not a limitation?

It is not limiting. It is the gateway to being human. To completely put our love into a certain situation or into an action is not limiting. It is only limiting if we believe that action to be the point where everything stops, evolution included. Then we say, "I can only love the person when they are like this", rather than seeing that our love goes beyond the person being this or that.

What you say makes me think about a situation. I met an old man a few days ago who is a friend of our family. He is eighty-five and just lost his wife after sixty years of marriage. They apparently really loved each other, but the feeling I had when we met him was not one of peace but more one of contained anger and negativity. The beautiful relationship he had with his wife was not expressed to people around him and I actually found him a little dried out. If we love someone so much, it is kind of strange not to extend and irradiate this love outside of the person who created this feeling. Clearly, the sadness is understandable in this case but still, it seems that something has been missing all along...

This is because he identified with his wife as being the cause or the reason for his love, not fully realising that what was driving that love was that they gave each other enough time to recognise their beauty, which is the inner quality that he discovered in sixty years with this beautiful being. This is also what can naturally happen in relationship because of course our whole awareness is connected to one person. It is very important that it is connected with one person but if it becomes exclusive to that person and it is not able to show that quality of love more freely to everything, especially to yourself, then the attachment can create a limitation.

That limitation is what it means to be a human being. It is not a negative. It is just what is natural for human beings: to contain their love to certain situations, to their children, to their family, to their closest friends and to their partners. There is nothing wrong with this. It is totally natural and it is wonderful that he had the opportunity to be able to do this for sixty years. Then, of course, the pain and suffering of losing that focus, what created attention for that person, is what creates the dryness because somehow it creates turmoil, which is also natural.

This is what happens when people lose the objects that they feel are making it possible for them to feel that way. They identified with the personality rather than the being of that person, which is beyond the personality. For example your children are of course the object of your love but surely what gives life to that love is their divine being, which can never die. The suffering is therefore not necessary because that aspect – the being of the personality – actually never dies. It just changes form.

... and it is our work to acknowledge that forms are transitory?

Of course it is, because we are in our human experience.

Is it the whole purpose of the human experience?

It is not the purpose but when we recognise that we are just in one temporary form it reduces the suffering. There are many aspects of the divine that our human perception cannot comprehend at this moment.

Yet there are not many spaces in societies and cultures to help people do this work. Everybody has to understand that alone.

Exactly. This is why it is important to have a reference point. What I see as the important reference point is the divine itself, but in our human experience that becomes very vague and we can be so lost that we forget to connect to it. If we have connected in a relationship with someone that we love for sixty years and we lose that form, we can get lost. It is natural.

Why did not you stay in touch with the persons you have met along your spiritual path?

I never stayed in touch in the sense of writing letters or going back to visit, but I feel I am in touch with everyone, in a different way. It is interesting because other people, who are more "in the world" would have liked to meet some of the people who have been on my path, like the Zen master, because he was alive until not so long ago, and it would have been very easy for people to go and visit him, but I say, "Why? What is the purpose? We have things to do. Life goes on". Many people, cannot really understand this logic.

Is it a logic of non-attachment to forms?

Yes. I did not say "No", but simply questioned the validity of anything in that situation. I could not see the purpose because for me, the person is alive in my actions and in what I am doing, so there is no need to go back and do something specific. It is the same with my family. I suppose when you meet someone, one of the first things you do is ask about their mother, their father, etc. Yet, I never had that feeling to do that with people.

I am not of this world of attachment. I do not have the drive to seek the contact as people do, or to hold on to an aspect of a person. To me, this is less important than the contact that is real, that is always there.

I do not feel that I am distant from what is going on. I do not feel separate just because physically and time wise I am distant. I feel that I am totally present, and although at times, it can be important to come and speak and be present physically, for me, it is just as enjoyable to be present in a different way.

Enlightenment & Meditation

You are obviously very cautious with words as they convey projections and ideas that take people away from the experience. There is one word, often used among people on the spiritual path, that you sometimes also use: "enlightenment". Is for you a "glimpse of enlightenment" very different from "enlightenment"? And is there any way back once someone is enlightened?

That is an interesting question which I will answer from a human perspective. I say this because I could be answering it from another perspective that is not so easy to relate to. From a human perspective, the idea of enlightenment is an illusion. My experience is that we are all enlightened. It is not like school or University, or even normal actions in the society, where we have reach a point that we were not at before. We are there. We are totally there.

By being? By simply existing?

Exactly. By existing. Because without that sense of enlightenment we could not be here as human beings. I know this is esoteric and difficult to understand. People will say, "That's a nice picture but it's not my experience of reality!". This is because "the veil" or "the mask" prevents that picture from seeing itself. That veil then becomes like darkness, not in the negative sense, but a darkness that separates this sense from our experience of the world. As we do not see this sense of enlightenment and as we do not recognise ourselves in this space of enlightenment, what we acknowledge is the mundane, again not in the negative sense, but the mundane as in the mind, the emotions and the body for example, into acting with the world.

Sometimes the mundane can be seen in a very enlightened way and sometimes in a way that is hidden from that sense of enlightenment. This then becomes the human dilemma. I suppose that this is what the Bible speaks about, falling from our sense of grace into the space of this mundane world which does not have that deep connection. But that world is not real. It is just a sense that we perceive as being real. That is not reality. Knowing that, when we have glimpses of enlightenment or glimpses of our essence, we can ask ourselves, "Is this any different from enlightenment?", "Is there any way back?".

If you have a glimpse of something, there is usually no way back. It would be very difficult to go back because your senses would grasp onto this reality and never want to let it go. It is not like it will discover something other than itself. It will remember and re-discover itself. When you come home to that sense of self, how can you move away from that space of being at home? All that happens is that the desire to come back home becomes much stronger. This then becomes a path to enlightenment.

Is the enlightenment different? Not really as there is no difference. There is no difference because if you are enlightened you have not added anything else. All you have done is let go of your attachment to this veil which prevents you from seeing your sense of self. Nothing has changed. Is enlightenment different from the everyday mundane human experience? Yes, of course. It is totally different because your reference point is totally different. It is just like asking, "Is a baby different from an adult?". Not really. On one level we are the same, but on another level if you want to go down to that perspective of seeing if there is a difference, of course yes. A baby is a baby and an adult is an adult.

Is there a big difference between glimpses of enlightenment? I think in that moment when you have a glimpse of enlightenment, there is no difference. The only difference is when we fall back into our attachment, into the mundane. Then we wonder why that glimpse is no longer there. Sometimes glimpses can be more painful because we know something more or we understand that there is something more than many people consciously understand.

Some people will just say, "What you are talking about is just esoteric rubbish. All that exists is my work, football, the weekends and my beer and I am happy with my children. That's all there is. That's reality!" and of course, that is reality on one level. But if all of a sudden that person glimpses another reality, it can be quite a dramatic shift... This is why I often ask in the retreats, "Are you really ready for that?". It is always easier to just go back home, drink the beer and watch the football.

It is easier too because if you really want more you may find it...

Exactly. If you really want something it may happen and once it starts happening, it is very difficult to turn back. It is like once you start falling in love, you cannot say to love, "Sorry, I cannot fall in love anymore", and stop. Actually, you can say this, but there will always be a part of you that will remember that it has fallen in love and this part will always want to fall in love more. Once you have fallen in love, you cannot say, "Love does not exist". Your memory of love will override any other distortion of reality. So is enlightenment good? It is a good question...

Is it the aim of life?

No. Because I think enlightenment in a way is neither good nor bad. It is just what it is. In the end, enlightenment is inevitable. It is the essence and we will come home to ourselves, whether we like it or not. Some people will do this very very slowly. Others will do this very dramatically and then we will say that they have become enlightened. It will seem that a miracle has happened in a very short time. This is just because, from the outside, from people seeing what is going on and even for the person that is sensing the experience of enlightenment, the reference of time in that moment makes no sense to that experience. But that experience has not simply happened in that moment. For example, when I say that I realised many things at the age of twenty-seven, I am saying this to relate to people in this world but actually, that moment never happened. It was always there. It is not that this moment happened at twenty-seven and then "Bang!", something exploded and I became more enlightened than I ever was. No. That moment was always there.

The window was opened...

The window was not even opened because the window was always there, open. Nothing changed. All that changed was certain aspects that are not even real. Nothing really changed because the *maya*, or the illusion of what we are identifying with, the theatre, the film, whatever you like to call it, is not really there. It has no real essence. It gets very confusing – and I am taking it deeper into a more esoteric realm – because then, some people ask: "Why meditate? Why do any spiritual work? Why do anything? Why not just sit and accept that whatever happens, happens?"

You cannot look at it this way because then you are coming from the space where you are not seeing home, you are only seeing the mundane. You are having a fatalistic attitude because everything is so beyond what is comprehensible. But it is not. It is totally comprehensible and actually so simple that it is laughable how simple it is. If you compare it to mathematics or philosophy, these sciences can seem quite complicated, but it is actually much simpler. This is why we can only imply certain things. Glimpses of enlightenment imply something, but it is not really the complete picture, and it is the same with enlightenment.

The problem with the idea of enlightenment is that it puts things in a judgemental way. A person is enlightened and he or she has understood something that we do not understand, that we have no concept of or even any relationship to. But it is not like that. The word "enlightenment" is totally deceiving because if we look at it in a practical sense, it means that something happened in that moment that is not there. But it is not that way at all.

You often use the word "essence". This concept clearly refers to something that is already there and goes with your point according to which there is nothing to reach through a process, it is just about being aware of what we deeply are. But you also use techniques, and techniques are related to processes. Could these techniques not disperse the seeker who uses them in a space-time frame where the goal is more in the future than in the present moment? Would you say they only help to unveil what is already there but hidden rather than bringing something really new to – or into – the person?

Exactly. Techniques are there because the mind is so tricky. By mind I mean the intellect of course but also the emotional mind, the physical mind and the body mind. It is so tricky that you need to have a way so that you do not fall into the games that we all create for ourselves. I call this spiritual discipline. One of them is meditation and it is a vital part of our spiritual practice, because in a way, it creates clarity as to what is happening in our lives. Without meditation, I feel that we easily get lost, but meditation is very open ended, so we need a technique to inform us of what is really happening. If we sit and meditate for example, what happens for most people is that the attention becomes much more focused, much more aware, much more clear, as to what is really going on. The energy comes back to the body and we sense it more easily. It comes back to the emotions, to the mind, to the sense of who we are, some people say to a centre and this puts things into a real perspective.

It is wonderful to sit and meditate after a sense of being disturbed by a situation, like an argument for example, or something that happened that disturbs you and disturbs the equilibrium of who you are. To sit and put it into perspective is not resolving it or changing it. This is not what meditation does. What meditation does is just allowing consciousness to experience this moment and see where the energy needs to flow. Does it need to flow into our attachment, into our reaction to the situation? Does it need to flow into identifying ourselves as a victim? Does it need to flow into our sense of guilt? Does it need to flow into anything? There are many ways the energy could flow.

Some people want to go around this circle. There is no problem to get angry, to feel a big turmoil or to feel guilty. It is not bad but in the end, once they have experienced this hundreds and hundreds of times, most people get bored of it. It is really boring to go back into the same old program of feeling like a victim, feeling angry or feeling guilty. It is too boring and so we want more. That is what happens in meditation. The consciousness creates that sense of expanding beyond the space of victim. It shows you directly where it is possible to go, where we can expand. In the beginning, it is a slow process, or at least it seems to be slow. It is like anything. When you look at a tree growing, the tree does not just happen overnight, it grows and grows and grows... It is the same with meditation. It becomes more profound, clearer. Consciousness slowly expands to a point that becomes obvious for what it is.

This is why the practice of meditation needs to happen more than just once or twice. Spiritual discipline is needed to start the work and for some people, it can be over years. Meditation is one of the core aspects of what I do. Without it, there is space for a fatalistic point of view where one considers that there is nothing to do if things have to happen. Without it, things will happen, but they will not happen as you would like them to, because we will tend to attach to life, to react to life and to lose a lot of valuable possibilities. Sometimes this is important but I have found that at this point in our human development in the world today, at this point of our human evolution, it is not the right thing to do anymore, so to speak. We have reached the point where possibilities have never been as clearly and profoundly powerful as they are now. This is because evolution, not just physical evolution but the evolution of human beings, has taken us to this point.

Meditation does not have to be dogmatic and I want to clarify this. It can be holding a child, a baby for example, and just sensing what that means in that moment, being conscious of the body, connecting to another body from the heart and opening to another human being in a very profound way. That union allows transcendence to happen. Our sense of transcendence then bypasses our normal mundane human reactions to the world as it is and to ourselves as we are. That transcendence then allows the meditation to become deeply spiritual. Then it is almost like the key or the bridge to come back home. This happens without a doubt to everybody in meditation.

This is why I emphasise with everyone who works with me that it is not enough to just come to a retreat. It is not enough to practice meditation during a retreat in the weekend, or even, for five minutes a day. It is essential that we practice quite a lot throughout the day, everyday. Meditation does not have to be half an hour here or half an hour there. It can be in many actions that we undertake. It can be during a period where we would otherwise do nothing, like sitting in an airport, waiting for the plane, rather than getting caught up and stressing because of time constraints. In these situations, we can practice some of the meditations that I use, and that changes many things.

The work of being present to oneself seems more important than any technique for you. In this logic, meditation cannot go with expectations. Would you say a meditation with expectation is a missed meditation?

Yes, because if you have expectations, you are putting pressure that the meditation has to fulfil something, and the meditation does not fulfil anything. It does not add anything. It is just like a key that you slowly get used to using. In the end, you do not become a better person by doing meditation. Rightly or wrongly, I think Transcendental Meditation has emphasised that by doing it you become quieter and more relaxed, that your immune system becomes stronger, that you become kinder and that your intelligence grows, but these things are totally unimportant. If that is why you are doing meditation, then it is very selfish because you are looking for extra gifts to fill in a space that does not need them. Meditation goes much beyond that so there is nothing that you gain from meditation in that sense.

Meditation should not put time and expectations into the picture but our time should be put into the meditation...

Yes. If you do it with expectations then you will be disappointed. Before meditation takes you to a space that will seem more complex, you would have said that it does not work for you, because in the beginning your expectations of being more peaceful are not met. You will then say, "I thought I was doing meditation so that my mind quietens down, but what is happening is that I am realising that my mind is very active and very busy. I do not want to do meditation anymore". If it is as simplistic as that, we tend to lose faith. Meditation is much more than that.

The discipline is required for it to be clear and in the beginning, meditation requires perhaps a little bit of trust. It is about trusting yourself, trusting the process of love to go deeper into this process. That requires trust and maybe even risk taking, since you do not know the steps that you are taking. It is diving into the unknown, into a space that you have never been taken to before, and it is not always very nice because it sometimes makes you feel uncomfortable. In the end, the step itself gives you much more than the idea of taking that step – the giving of love to someone for example – even if it is a risk.

You will realise that in that sense of giving, you have received much more than what the expectation of getting from the outside could have given you if you were simply waiting for it to give you that sense, waiting for it without giving anything. The self-discipline is giving time to that work and once you enter this path, it is not a part-time job. It is not something you do on the weekend, or like going for a beauty treatment once a month. It is a complete transformation of your life. All focus changes.

So meditation is to connect to our essence. You mention giving love as a meditation. But to be more specific, how to connect to our essence, to this inner space that has everything, when doing meditation? How to deal with thoughts?

How to deal with thoughts? For most people that is where we start when we start with our mind and in the beginning, we think it is just a lot of noise. In the end we realise, however, that a lot of thoughts are very interesting. It is a whole journey in itself. It is a whole television program, with many programs, sometimes interesting and sometimes very silly and crazy, but it is there. There is no easy way out really. How to deal with that? As every moment will require a different action, it is impossible to establish a single system of how to deal with our thoughts. Rather than trying to specifically deal with the thoughts, it is important to come to the space inside of yourself which recognises how to deal with the thinking or with the mind. How do we do this? There is only one way. Come back to love, to your centre.

When you say "love" it can be a set of ideas related to possessions, jealousy, the ego...

In the beginning love is only an idea. It is like someone who has never had a child. Having a child and giving love to that child is only an idea until you have the experience of having that child. Then you realise what it is to have to really be present and loving to a child. No one could have explained you that situation because it only explains itself in the moment when it invites you to act out in that way, or to see the reason why you are not acting out in that way.

In the beginning love is an idea, but trusting in the idea is enough because it is connected to reality. Even though it is very far removed from reality, it still is connected to it. Our essence is speaking and the words or rather the sound of the essence is floating through many dimensions, slowly being heard by the mind that is crazily going through all the pictures and ideas that it usually goes through. In that noise of this television program, love is heard in between spaces of the thoughts, in between ideas that are happening. Whether we can catch those glimpses or we cannot catch them, some part of us still recognises that space, so it really is an idea in the beginning. For me, the only way is coming back to the centre, to the heart. There is no outside technique. It has to come from inside.

But isn't the process of "coming from inside" originated with the thinking? Or would you say that the thought is itself originated by the process? Consciously at least, the thought starts everything.

Of course it starts with a thought, but where did the idea that we can be something else come from? When we connect to that thought, even if it is not recognisable in the beginning in an obvious sense, that becomes the gateway to our heart, which is our centre. In the beginning, it is a little bit superficial, I agree. I remember sitting in the monastery and thinking, "I sit here and I want to be there but I am not there because as soon as I am centred then all of a sudden I move over there, thinking about this, remembering that, feeling that, even forgetting that I am meditating. I am somewhere else". This is natural because the centre requires all things around it to be clear before it can shine through its meaning. It is from that point that it comes clear to the inside. It is not from the outside. So where do we start?

In the beginning, sitting in meditation is discipline. We sit down quietly and that is all very good but after a while, usually after a few weeks, we realise that we have embarked on a journey that is much more complicated than we thought. Then we have to have something more. It is faith. I think we have to have faith that the process will show us very clearly where we need to go. If we do not have faith in that beginning point of the process, we will just say, "This is not working for me". We have to have faith.

This is where a spiritual teacher is very useful. Every time you say, "No. This is not right", or you lose your reference point to your centre, the spiritual teacher will say something, do something, or mirror something to remind you that this is real, that your centre is not an idea. That feeling will then create a notion of wanting to go on, to continue to go deeper and deeper. Once you open your centre, it guides you in the meditation. The knowledge then slowly becomes conscious and what is revealed from the essence, from the heart, moves and expands to the body. Usually you do not recognise it but people see it. They may comment, "Oh, gosh! What are you doing? You look different. You seem much more peaceful", but they will see the physical resonance more than the rest. What happens is that the body, the temple, needs to change to sustain the other changes that are happening at the same time.

When this change is happening, the body is the first point that begins to be obvious for you and for other people. This is why sometimes it will be painful. In meditation, there will be certain pains, certain sensations that will come up because the body is letting go of programs that have prevented this sense of self, this heart, from expressing itself. When this happens, the emotions also begin to change and they speak to you. You have moments of inner stillness. We enjoy these moments of inner stillness profoundly in the emotional aspects of ourselves, so we want more in the meditation. We want this experience to go deeper and to be much more part of everything that we are doing. When the mind understands this knowledge of essence from the heart, it comes first through the body, then through the emotions and then through the mind again...

From the mind it goes to what I call the "energy level" – some people call it the "etheric level". It is the level that is not as tangible as the mind but is even subtler than the mind. When this happens, we change the energy around us. We do not change just the physical body but the energy that is really connecting the body with the outside world, which is explained in quantum physics. Once this begins to change, it is like a domino effect. All the particles – the physical particles, the mental particles, the thought particles, the emotional particles – resonate at a totally different rhythm or frequency than what was normal before. This then attracts to it situations that are similar and the resonance connects to the resonance that is all around because it is an etheric level. When this happens, the domino effect gets very strong. This is when we have movements of deep spiritual experiences, when the *kundalini* energy is moving and rises all of a sudden very quickly. Some people call them glimpses of enlightenment or profound insights. This is a very important stage.

At this stage, and at any stage really, I feel it is very important to have a spiritual teacher, because in those moments the ego can inflate, as it always wants to control everything. This is the thing when we sit in meditation: the ego mind wants to always grab on, to try to see, and even to take the experience away. It is a bit like love. You have the experience of love, you fall in love and then the ego comes in there and wants to understand everything. It creates a whole set of new dynamics around this experience of love because it is a little bit further removed from the spontaneous action of being in love, which then becomes something else. Then the ego sometimes gets caught up in it, in the same way as with spiritual insights or *kundalini* experiences.

This is where a *kundalini* experience can be dangerous, not dangerous in a bad way but dangerous without guidance, because rather than having the reference point of your heart and of your centre, it starts having the reference point of power, of strength, of betterment and of the sense of dualism. This is what happens for many shamans and spiritual teachers. I have seen many spiritual teachers – and it is not a judgement, I just find it amusing – who believe that they are very special and amazing beings. The ego then controls that knowledge to move completely differently than where it can move if you are centred in your heart.

But you asked about techniques. There are so many techniques and they are so individual to a person that I never really say that one technique is better than another, or that this is the right way and this is the wrong way. In the end, the technique is your heart, your essence, your centre. It is not what I tell you to do, or what you tell yourself to do, or what other people expect or tell you to do. It comes from a much deeper space. The only thing I put out is the vehicle to create that space, or the situation to create that space, and that can be done in so many different ways.

Peace, Inner Light & Attention

The value of being non-judgemental is understandable but how to deal with violence and really mean actions that destroy and kill other people without being judgemental?

We enter a very difficult space here. To have the concept of how to deal with it is not as important as dealing with it, so rather than trying to understand how to deal with it, let us deal first with ourselves, our mind and our own sabotage, and see how we deal with this. Then, maybe let us think about a wise Saint in India, a *guru* of the yoga tradition, who was sitting besides the holy river Ganges, meditating in a place where it was not so safe. In this place which was not good to sit and meditate, one of the worst known criminals came up to him and said, "Give me everything you have or I'll kill you!" Now in that moment how do you deal with that? It is impossible to know how to deal with it.

The story continues so that we have an idea how this enlightened person then dealt with it. His reaction makes no sense, unless we understand what is going on from the depth of that story. He asked the criminal, "What are you doing? Is what you are doing out of habit or out of need?". With this utterance from the teacher, the thief realised that what he was doing was something totally stupid because he was not dealing with a normal person, he was dealing with someone in total peace. There was no place for him to disturb that total peace. There was no feedback. There was no expected reaction to his action, therefore he was not willing to kill the master and became one of his disciples instead. One of the most aggressive and violent thieves in India of that time changed because the space that the other person was in was one of non-violence.

Now Gandhi of course understood this idea that consists of not giving violence the space to flourish, of not giving violence the possibility to multiply. This is very much central to what I teach. It is not so much avoiding action but it is rather being active so that the peace inside of you produces the peace outside. This is, in my understanding, what Gandhi did. He approached violence from a totally different space, not acting with the ego, nor being angry, upset, or saying, "We are justified to do these actions because what is happening on the outside is so wrong!", but rather show the world that it is possible to approach it from that different perspective. As I believe human beings are good, then the goodness of every human being will be touched and will be encompassed. This is what happened with Martin Luther King in a very difficult time where most Americans saw Africans and Black people as inferior and yet, instead of him feeling inferior and angry, his actions showed the world that he was not inferior and did not give any truth to that.

So your question of how to approach violence and real violence is a good question. Of course you cannot act it out by simply pretending that you are peaceful and go to Harlem, saying, "I am all peaceful", walking down a drug ghetto where you may be shot because of habit. You have to approach it in a different way. You have to find real peace, but when you have that real peace, you do not walk down the ghetto of Harlem. You do not attract certain situations that push you to understand what is going on in a deeper sense. Your sense of peace then touches the good in humanity, rather than the bad aspect of what is going on, which is violence. Your action speaks much louder than your ideas about the action. If you are peaceful, then your thoughts and your body will touch everything around that is peaceful. Even if the people who are violent towards you are not peaceful, some part of them will be touched.

This is the same in war. If a soldier shoots at your children, which is the reality in some countries, it is very difficult to understand this concept and say, "Everyone is good", because you react in a way where you feel hatred. Even so, if you show love to these soldiers – and this is very difficult to do, I am not saying it is easy! – they will be disarmed in the heart. Their actions will be totally naked and they will have to face themselves. I remember an amazing picture of the Vietnam War, where Americans believed what they were doing was right – saving Vietnam from communism, which meant the evil, the destruction of a country – with a soldier running down a street and this six or seven years old child in total fear, because what was happening was horrific. She was trying to escape, because her parents were killed, and this child was so totally naked in her emotions of vulnerability, fear and despair, that you could see in the eyes of the soldier that he was totally transformed in that moment.

I could almost guarantee that he could not continue doing what he was doing because in that moment, everything became so clear that it was a total game, which is called the illusion – the *maya* in Sanskrit – that he was part of. He could no longer in all honesty be part of it as his heart was transformed. To be angry at a person who is the soldier at that time is of no use because he actually has good but he just cannot see it. This soldier was not aware of it, because half an hour before, he was part of the action that was destroying everything around him, receiving orders and perceiving in his mind that he was doing something to create order and get rid of evil.

Your question is complicated because in the end there is no simple answer. Every action requires a different reaction. If the essence is coming from the space of not reacting to evil – because it does not exist – but rather reacting to what is divine, then everyone around you will be naked of their thinking process that justifies negative action. They will have to come back to their heart and they will thank you and the existence. This will help them much more than a reaction that could come out of hatred because they are harming you, your family, or your culture. This is, in my opinion, the only way forward for humanity. I am not saying pacifism or war is good or bad. I am not saying that military is bad, as that is up to each culture to decide. It is just their attitude of military or violence that is negative. Military can be useful if it is done in a way that stops certain boundaries from being pushed. What I am saying is that we just have to act from a space of inner peace.

The idea that what we are is part of the situation and may change the situation makes me remember a sentence of Sri Aurobindo who said something like: "We put ourself in situations which reflect our state of counsciousness. When we have reached a state of wisdom, violence naturally disappears in front of us". Yet people like Gandhi and Martin Luther King, although they have reached a state of wisdom and non-violence, have been killed...

I actually believe that many saints and people who have reached a high level of compassion, like Jesus, then do put themselves in situations that put a threat to their life when it is necessary. Buddha was not killed but I think this is because of the cultural difference in India where the whole philosophy is slightly more peaceful – or can be slightly more peaceful – than the Western culture, except for the fundamentalists, who are usually Muslims, but there are also Hindu fundamentalists in India of course. Interestingly enough, Buddha was not part of a lot of turmoil.

Buddhism was actually expelled from India. Although Buddha was Indian his spirituality contradicted the Hindu notions of *dharma*, *karma* and reincarnation with the message that freedom could be attained in this life, here and now. That position did not go along with the unavoidable religious cycle of reincarnation.

This is true, but even so, it is interesting to watch that in India they can encompass a lot of belief systems more harmoniously as a culture than in the West, where it is believed that you have to follow certain paths. At least in the past, secularism was not really part of our culture and the Catholics fought the Protestants, so that the State would be one religion only, even if it was Christian. These manners reflect a more violent aspect of our culture.

The scholars of Hinduism always point out that it is absorbent. It does not really leave room for proselyte attitudes – except for the adepts of a religious movement especially exported to the West, whose followers want to convince people in a somehow Christian ways, like the Hare Krishna movement for example. Hinduism being a culture, a way of life, nobody can really be converted to it. One is born a Hindu but one does not become a Hindu without the whole cultural package coming with it. On the other hand, Christianity and Islam are based on the idea of conversion. This leads to another question. You clearly make a point in your teaching to avoid dogmas and belief systems that are reducing people's freedom and potential. Would you say that all beliefs should be suspect? If so, isn't the idea that going into oneself to find answers in itself another belief?

I think all belief systems have to be looked at, not suspiciously but deeply, to see if they actually have meaning for you. In my way of understanding things, a belief system is only a belief system if you do not understand what it is. If you say to people, "You have to go inside to discover the truth", it is legitimate to wonder where is "inside"? Unless you have an experience to show you what inside means, it is a belief system. Actually "inside" is just a word because where do you go "inside"? Do you go to your kidneys or to your bones? Where is "inside"? It is just a word.

This is a belief system for me because I am not actually saying to go inside into a specific space inside. I am just saying this as a method of understanding that certain belief systems on the outside can be put away. Then as you put away certain belief systems, you come back to who you are, you go inside, but whether this is inside or outside is a belief system also. It is not so much going "inside" but coming home to something bigger than the belief system, something more valid.

Everything is a belief system. Even that thought is a belief system. This is where the work that I do is questioning everything. We enter a very complicated topic here. On one level we cannot really touch our "inner space" – I call it this way – without some form of bridge to take us to that inner space. All the bridges on the outside are too dangerous because they are constructed with human ideas, so the best bridge is the bridge inside. It is reached in many ways but one of them is critical thinking, really being aware of socialisation, programs, emotions and ego that control your perception of the world.

So psychology, sociology, and anthropology are good tools to start with...

They are very good tools because they question many things. This is important because that is somehow our hook into going deeper and exploring the world beyond a framed perception. Are all belief systems negative? They are all negative if they come from a belief system that becomes dogmatic and fundamentalist in its point of view.

Everything that says "you must", "you should", "you should not" ...

... "You should", "you should not", without allowing the person to explore that understanding and replicate it from a space that comes naturally rather than from the outside. It is the same with children. Disciplining children is not a negative thing. It is only negative if the discipline comes from programming the child to be in a certain way, because this is the way one feels the child needs to be, rather than allowing the child to be free. Being free does not mean that discipline is taken away. Discipline is part of whatever a child needs to grow. In my opinion, if you do not create anything around children, then they have nothing to touch upon. They need discipline but the discipline has to come from a space of inner freedom.

This is not saying, "You must sit down and listen to me speak", but rather, "If you want to hear something, it is good to try to sit down and listen". There is a whole difference. The whole school idea that we have today for teaching children is wrong in my opinion, as we do not allow the children to learn from listening rather than from being taught. It is the same with belief systems. If you listen to belief systems, then what are you learning? Are you just learning to replicate those belief systems or are you learning to find your real belief systems?

Listening is being active.

Of course! It is also being total and critical, being strong. It is not critical towards everything because it is fun to be critical, but critical in the sense that you question: "Does this have validity? Why does it have validity? From what does it come out of? Does it come out of my emotions because I react in a certain way that is programmed from my evolution with my family and my grandparents? Do I think in this way because it comes out of socialisation as I live in America or in Japan?", and so forth. You begin to question what it is to be human beyond those aspects. All belief systems are negative for me but they are also guidelines that help us because in the end we are humans, so unless we are born with a deep understanding, with a deep wisdom, we get lost.

We need guidelines to pull us through the spaces where we get lost and spend a lot of time going around in this circle. I tend to try to make these guidelines as vague as possible so that they do not become dogmatic, but one of them is what we have been speaking about: peace and what that means. It is not a dogma where I say, "You must not do this". It is rather finding a state of peace inside which we know exists. When we fall asleep we are peaceful. The work is to replicate that in our actions with children as a parent, in our actions as a soldier, in our actions as a politician, as a teacher, as whatever we work in.

But the ideas of "inner light" or "the light inside", although beautiful can also be part of a belief system in which we want to put faith...

There is no darkness inside. The darkness, in my opinion – and this is a belief system – is the ego-mind creating a picture of duality, a picture that separates us from our essence which is the inner light. This is the terminology that I use. The inner light is expanding all the time. It expands from the moment we are conceived and becomes material through the embryo becoming a baby, the baby becoming a child, and the child turning to an adult, etc. It is the slow manifestation of that light in the body. We also have another aspect that stops that manifestation from being complete which is the mind-ego. That comes for many reasons and it becomes the battle of a person. The mind-ego battles to understand why, for example, a child cannot pinch and tease another child. It needs to do it to understand, so to say "It is bad" just creates a sense of fear and represses that action. Then to show the child why it is not so good because there are so many other factors involved helps the child to understand that there is an inner light and that it is possible to express it rather than express the other aspect that is sabotaging it.

The idea that we have an inner light is beautiful and it is easy to want it to be true. But again it may also be a kind of tolerable and acceptable belief because it is not harmful to anyone.

I understand what you are saying. This is where I suppose it is very difficult because in this way it is a belief system. If you are depressed or if you are not feeling that there is any inner light, then you will say, "That is a belief system. I do not see it, I do not feel it". Definitely not everyone feels an inner light as part of his or her everyday normal life style, so it can be a belief system. That is where that belief system then has to change from being a belief system to trusting. The act of trusting is the same as trusting a child. It is interesting when you have a baby who cannot speak and you say "speak", "speak"! They do not speak and you have to trust that slowly, through their attention, through their love of family and communication, their trust changes to words and the words become expression and language. That language then communicates to you and reflects back to you what is there. Did the child learn the language or was the language there all the time? The child could not speak! When a child cannot speak, we have to trust that the language is the essence of humanity. Every child is born with that potential but has to manifest it. The same with the inner light…

It is interesting that you mentioned the word "attention" as this is a key notion for Krishnamurti who kept inviting people to always go back to a full presence. For this philosopher, the spiritual goal is to have a vivid attention without – or beyond – the limitations brought by ideas. He was carefully avoiding words such as "God" but rather valued attention to find answers. It seems quite in the spirit of your teaching…

Yes. And for me attention, deep attention, is meditation. Meditation is not what most people think it is because it is not a way of doing certain things. It is rather creating the space where attention is invited more than is usually possible in mundane life. A space of attention, deep attention, is a space of meditation. Even if you do not know that you are doing meditation, you could be doing meditation. For example, if we are captured by beauty, like a sunset, we have moments of deep attention, which is meditation. We can see ourselves in those moments where the deep attention focuses and our consciousness expands beyond the ego. We can see all aspects of who we are in that moment and that is vital. That is the central core of the work that I do. I often use the word "meditation" however, then people think that it means you have to stop everything to meditate. Of course, you can, but meditation can be done while you are cleaning the nappy of a baby. You can have deep attention in that moment so you do not separate yourself from your action. Any action can have a deep attention.

So attention is not only in creativity, like in arts, that may produce a feeling of being beyond space and time. When the creator, be it a professional artist or not, is involved in his or her work, time flows. To create may imply a spiritual experience. Yet your point is to not be limiting our spiritual life to moments of creativity or to meditation. It seems rather to develop an inner state of being…

All the time. This is of course for people who want to practice spirituality. What I advise for most people is to understand how to go to that space, because there are steps, just like with language. For most people, meditation needs to have a formal setting in which their mind can become tranquil enough to have that deep attention, that space, and focus on that deep attention space without being distracted, and it would normally be difficult to have that deep attention when shopping. Since our mind is constantly distracted, some meditations are good to practice and in the beginning they have a formal setting and a time where you can practice. To sit quietly for one hour and do a technique of meditation is useful but to say that this is spirituality is to miss the point because that is only the beginning of spirituality.

That deep attention then has to move from that meditation to all aspects of your life, not just that deep meditation. That is the beginning, just like the baby learning the language when he or she begins to say "mama". That is the first word but it is not the complete communication. It is the beginning of manifesting a certain aspect of communication. It can go further, like deep attention can go to all aspects of your life. You can have deep attention even though you and your mind feel you are not there consciously. You can have deep attention while you are sleeping. This means that the spiritual work opens up your consciousness to embrace aspects of the unseen and of the invisible world, to become more conscious. Then you have the intelligence of that unseen being manifested in creativity, in action, in whatever form that is needed in this world to create great human beings, like Einstein for example. You have it because your action encompasses much more than just what is normal.

Deep creativity often comes when the mind is somewhat free of ideas. You said that words are deceiving but thoughts may be deceiving too. If I understood Krishnamurti, real attention to life is beyond words and thoughts. Do you agree with this idea?

Some spiritual traditions focus on words that are supposed to be more important than others, like praying, contemplation, ritual. For me that is not important. What is important is that the attention touches aspects of yourself that can create creativity, like you were saying, aspects that become real. It is not enough to have deep attention and do nothing with it. It is very important that this deep attention has actions related to it. Artists are wonderful because they have deep attention in the process that they are going through. They create something in the physical form that manifests that deep attention, and people are usually touched by it. This is what is important. Rather than replicating things like words, or even *mantras*, it is important that this deep attention invites a new aspect of yourself to be creative and manifest something in the world.

It is not enough to sit in meditation. There needs to be an action that takes the meditation further, and when you are sitting, this action also needs to be from that creative space. If you sit in meditation and stand up when the phone rings and it is your stepmother saying something that makes you upset and you shout in the phone, then that meditation has not gone further than just that space. It needs to carry on in all actions.

Your point is that spirituality is not only for some special moments of our life, something like "Now I am spiritual as I am meditating, then I will go back to my life" …

Yes, it needs to carry on further.

Attention is also close to what you learnt with Zen Buddhism. It is reaching a state here and now, beyond thoughts, as if the answers were beyond thoughts, a space where attention could lead us.

Yes, this is very true and this is why I was attracted to Zen Buddhism as a teenager. I read everything at the time, all the possible books about philosophy that I could find when I was fifteen, and I realised that philosophies are interesting and wonderful, but the deep sense of understanding that I was yearning for was beyond the words. Zen Buddhism then became the closest thing that I could find at the time to manifest that yearning in a real sense, which is to go beyond ideas in the mind and beyond the logical thinking to a space where intelligence gives me a deeper answer, an intelligence that I trusted was there. That was my attraction to Zen Buddhism, but at some point I realised that, just like any other tradition, even Zen Buddhism had got caught up in certain rituals and certain belief systems. They were much less so than many other traditions but still, it was there and I realised that meditation or deep attention was definitely my focus and this is what I practised for many years.

Would you encourage people who work with you to try to get rid of thoughts during the meditation or it is not the point?

You cannot get rid of thoughts or the thinking process, but during meditation it is good to not attach to them, when possible.

In Zen Buddhism people focus on a space between each thought and progressively try to enlarge this space…

Yes, Zen Buddhism has a lot of interesting philosophies and one idea for a Zen Buddhist, as you say, is to go to the space that is beyond mundane thinking. Zen Buddhism is finding that space of non-thinking and it is done in many ways, for instance as you said, choosing that point between the thoughts, or finding the space of quietness inside of a core. This is very important but it is not my way. Zen Buddhism is a very masculine method of meditation and it requires strong discipline, which is wonderful. The philosophy of finding that space is interesting but I have a different method of reaching it. Rather than forcing the mind to understand that space, it is to naturally fall into that space without the mind even realising that it is doing that. It is almost like a trick. Tricking the mind.

Would you say it is a space of non-thoughts?

It is a space of awareness that goes beyond simple thinking around the ego. It is not that there is no thinking but the thinking of normal daily life is irrelevant because it is not the same. It is not to say that you sit in a blank space, because that thinking is still there, but it is beyond the thinking being attached to certain perspectives and ideas. It is more like going into a space of floating and expansion. The thinking is expansive.

Simple awareness?

It is not a sense of, "How do I sit down and figure out how to do this?" where the mind thinks about the issue because this is how we learned in school so that we can think about it. It is not this way of thinking but rather like going into a space where whatever you need to know in the thinking mind just drops into it, without you knowing where it came from. You are not doing the work. It is actually being done for you because it is an expansive way of thinking, almost like a dream. It is strange because it does not have relevance to many other things that come to you without you really knowing where they are coming from.

That reminds me of a Hindu story about a master and his disciple who fell asleep during a meditation and afterward asked his guru if this state was bliss. The master answered: "This is it ... but with awareness" ...

Yes, exactly. It is not a space of nothingness. It is active consciousness, active awareness where there is actually more than ever before. It is not empty space. It is over flowing.

You often speak about the idea of being aware of what we do and of doing things with consciousness, like eating, even if we are eating something that is probably not the right thing for the body, doing it aware of what we do. Is this awareness a continuous state of meditation?

I do not feel that any activity in our life is separate from meditation. I actually believe that all activities are meditation so I do not differentiate between meditation being specific, following a certain set of exercises, and life being separate from those exercises. Often that meditation is infused in our daily activity, whether it is eating or whether it is walking, even driving, but sometimes you have to be quite aware of what is on the road... Meditation is attention to this present moment. That can be in any activity, even sleeping. What seems like a non-activity, such as sleeping, can be a meditation. Sleeping is not a non-activity for me, it is a very deep, profound activity. For some people that may seem like nothing is actually happening, but that is meditation. Awareness extends to every aspect of our body, our mind, our emotions, our breath, our energy and how we react and interact with all those aspects of who we are.

So it is related to the deep attention...

Yes. Attention is not an activity that requires willpower, it is more like intention. It is a more relaxed and joyous activity, not something that is strict like people think of Zen Buddhism where attention has to be focused and uses a lot of energy. It does use a lot of energy, yet the energy is used up because we have to let go of what distracts our attention from being present, rather than the attention itself.

You often point out the relationship between spirituality, food and eating, reminding people of the necessity to act consciously. But what precisely is "acting consciously" or "with awareness" for you?

You cannot be general and say that one action is spiritual and the other one is not, or that this action is conscious and that one is not. Acting consciously means that your reference point is not from the ego, from fear, from a lack, from a limitation or from socialisation. It is rather from the sense of connection and love that you feel for something, whether it be your country, your work, your family, or whatever you are acting towards. That connection is your reference point and what makes you act in a certain way.

It is very easy for someone to act consciously with members of the family because on some level – if we are in a relationship with a child or with a partner – we include them into our space. If we live in a house for example, we are not going to pollute it or throw rubbish around the house, but on some level, people feel that the house has walls and stops at a certain point. Then they go to the forest, the river or the sea and they feel it is all right to pollute it because it does not involve their small space. Acting consciously to me is to extend that space beyond the limitation that is artificial and part of socialisation or individualisation.

If we act consciously we cannot harm nature because harming nature comes out of ignorance of not understanding that we are harming ourselves. If we do not understand this, we pollute the environment, we pollute the sea, we disrespect the trees, we cut them down, we do not have a connection to the plants, insects, animals nor to the world that we live in. We do whatever we do because we are not acting consciously but rather out of ignorance. Acting consciously is a sign of maturity and development inside of us. We extend the experience of ourself towards our family and then towards all aspects that are part of the divine, which ultimately are part of us. I am not saying moralistically that this is good or this is bad, but if we act from a space in which we feel love, then it is difficult to do anything that is negative. Whatever we do is to extend that love towards us. Nature will be vibrant and will give us even more of its beauty rather than be polluted and depressed in its level of vibrancy, making us receive less.

There are many ways of acting consciously. Morals and standards of behaviour are unimportant to me and to a certain extent it is more the essence that drives people that I focus on. That is the space where acting consciously comes from. I do not say, "If you do this, you are not doing the right thing". For example, people talk about being good and helping people in Africa by donating money to charities. It is important of course, but if you donate the money out of a sense of guilt or fear then you are not really giving anything to Africa. If you do it out of a sense of love, then it shows that you care on a deeper sense. It is not out of the limitation of fear because if you saw the children in Africa as your own, you would of course feed them. If you had your own child starving to death in your house, you would not give food out of guilt, you would give food out of love. I just think humanity is caught up in its ignorance and does not see the larger picture. Acting consciously is moving into that larger picture and acting from that space.

Tolerance, Moral Values & Spiritual Discipline

One very popular idea today in New Age ideologies is that "everything is good" or "it's all for good", meaning that every situation we face or we are into, is a teaching situation. So there is no need to judge people, even those who hurt you. In this view, good luck and bad luck are just limited views of the mind. What is your opinion about this?

It is an interesting question but for me, it is not really a correct question to look at because only in the space of perfection and divinity is everything perfect and divine. In the world we live in, many things are imperfect and not very divine. If you say that everything is good, then somehow you are being a little bit superficial, not acknowledging the world and what is actually in the world: suffering. To brush it away with a flick of some nice philosophical words means that you have not really experienced pain and suffering. It would be good to see if that philosophy remains your philosophy when you are in the middle of something profoundly painful, so I find this attitude a little bit superficial. All suffering, for example AIDS or cancer, is very strong and very difficult. To help each individual to understand their journey through that, it is good to understand that what we are going through is not so good, but can actually be good if we go deeper than just the surface level of the suffering. That is the case with everything, not just AIDS.

We can go deeper even with feeling upset. If someone says something to you and you feel upset about it, obviously what that person said is not so nice. Maybe he or she said that you are totally stupid, or that you are too fat, or whatever. Then to say, "Yes, this is for the good", does not go deep enough. If you look at that picture and you detach yourself from what is creating the suffering to actually go deeper into it, then you have the strength to go and touch that point from a real sense of your humanity. You do it much more than by simply reacting superficially and saying, "I do not like anyone calling me fat". You could go to a point where you instead acknowledge that "Yes. I am suffering because I am actually a little bit fat and I do not like it, but what does it mean?" You can go deeper into that meaning for yourself.

This can be taken to war for example. If you are in the middle of a war zone, you cannot say that someone shooting your brother is right and that it is for the good... This is crazy. What you can do is acknowledge that pain and that suffering as real, and see how that pain and suffering can be used in a way that moves you beyond simply reacting to it. It is quite complicated because most people react to it and that reaction will attach to the pain and suffering that is not only there but that is everywhere.

It is the pain and suffering that is part of your personality, that is part of your unconscious, that is part of what makes human beings and what veils human beings from seeing the divine. Then you spiral down into a sense of injustice and difficulty that is just going to create more pain, depression and suffering. This can be useful for a little while because it allows us to acknowledge that there are many sides and complexities to being a human being, but in that moment, it is wonderful to go beyond that space; not to see what is good or bad but to rather see the picture that is really there. This is what is difficult.

How to see the picture that is really there? Someone for instance says that you are fat. What is the picture? You can explore that. You can decide that person is nasty but what is the picture for you? How can you use that picture to develop it so that it becomes something that helps you to see perhaps the more positive aspect of that person? Something that allows you to see that this person actually has a lot of pain and – just like someone in war – is defending herself from that pain by externalising it and pointing the finger towards you, so that you feel the suffering that she is avoiding to feel? This is something that human beings do a lot.

Look at children. Some children are very cruel and will treat other children in horrible ways which are actually dangerous. They do that not because they want to cause suffering but because they are unconscious of their divine. They cannot see their divine. They cannot see their beauty, so for them it is easier to point the finger and watch things from the outside, rather than trying to understand what is going on in the inside. That of course does not justify someone's actions. It does not justify someone being cruel or doing something that is unacceptable to someone else but if that happens, and we have no possibility of changing it, then what we do have is the possibility of changing our own experience. No one can take that away.

In this way, my concept is a little bit different from "everything is good", because no, not everything is good. Actually the world is not good, in the sense that if you look at the mundane, the world is slowly being polluted to death, people are dying, there is suffering, people are ignorant, not compassionate and selfish. You know there are a lot of things that we can look at and if we look at everything at once, it would be very depressing. Yet for me to look at that and to simply say this is reality, as it is not good, misses the point. We actually do not know reality, because we are not really in the space where we are able to sense reality in its complete sense. We only sense a little bit of reality and what is easiest to sense is the mundane, which is the suffering. That is usually good because, in the end, it awakens our deep yearning to find something else than just he mundane.

The idea would be to be aware of imperfections around us without being judgemental but rather being tolerant at the same time?

Of course. To go around and say "everything is good" but not to be discerning in the world is silly because we have to create a boundary where actions that harm others are simply not allowed. I use the word discerning in the sense of understanding that something or a form of action is unacceptable. This needs to be voiced in every way, individually, politically, and culturally. If something is unacceptable, we need to create a discernment, to say that it is simply not right. It is not judgement because we are not using a sense of good, bad, or morality. In my opinion, discernment is sensing what is unacceptable, because it is unacceptable to any and all human beings, not just a cultural group or a social group. It is unacceptable to kill and if any human being comes to a space of love, he or she will understand that it is unacceptable to kill.

Some people will justify their killing but in the end it is simply unacceptable. If someone is doing that, if someone shoots someone else, we cannot just say that what he or she is doing is all right. We have to set a boundary and say "this is unacceptable" because it is not a human action that we want to continue. It is good to be discerning and to see what people are doing, as long as you are not judging from a moralistic or egotistical perspective.

So there is a gap between the need to have discernment about what is acceptable or not, according to moral values that we culturally decide to consciously or not believe in, and the positive attitude in life, which also implies that one can learn from a bad situation. It is two different things...

Yes. I think it is quite different. I think many people act out of their sense of justice, which comes out of the ego and of a sense of being hurt or put down – sometimes related to moral or religious beliefs – rather than real values that are general to all human beings. What those real values are is for each of us to find out, but I think they are there because most human beings are born with certain things that make them human beings and then other moralities are added on. Children naturally want to learn. They are very loving towards babies, especially towards their mother. It is a natural instinct, they naturally want to please her and to be loved by her.

Children are not born with aggressive manners. They just change as they grow, because of many reasons. Sometimes love cannot be extended to anyone, not event to the mother, and this creates a vicious and violent person. This is probably the problem for people punished for crimes who are in prisons. Some say that this is why we have to be easy going on everyone and prisoners who have committed crimes need to be treated more humanly. I do not know if that is the truth because if they commit a crime they have lost some of their humanity. I am not saying that they deserve to be treated badly but what is important is that they become aware of what their actions mean. That awareness definitely does not come up by treating them nicely. It happens when the person in whatever situation, in prison or at home, is able to see what they have done in a complete sense.

I do not know if prisons today actually help the person to see this, because their logic is moralistic. I believe a person is punished because we see that he or she does not fit into a concept of what we see as right. In this respect, many prisoners today are innocent. This is not really a good situation for learning and becoming conscious of a problem, so I am not sure if prisons even resolve or create anything better for the prisoner.

Some Buddhists have gone into prisons and taught prisoners techniques of meditation to become more self-conscious of themselves and of what they have done. This, according to people who work in this field, has changed things tremendously, not for everybody of course, but the change was so great for some people that they became completely wonderful and worthy human beings who themselves feel that they are wonderful and not just outcasts in society. The best was stimulated in them.

This is what punishment should be in my opinion: to make a human being conscious, but in a very strong way, not in a liberal way. It can be firm and clear that this is the way it is – and it can be with love. I mean that you can be strong with love. Love does not mean you have to be kind and weak. This is a misunderstanding. We judge love as being associated to a certain type of person that is soft and gentle. Yet sometimes it is necessary to be clear and strong when things are not acceptable.

Good is not really about being good. It is being more clear and real with the person rather than putting on a mask of being nice and good. Some people think, because I am a spiritual teacher, that it is more important to be gentle and kind. But I am not always so. I am sometimes quite firm and direct with people because I think that creates a better space of understanding than being kind. Sometimes you have to be so clear that the person will take the time to really go inside and understand what is going on. By being kind you are maybe just doing something that they want you to do and end up entering their scenario and program.

You talked about activities and social environment and insisted on the need of spiritual discipline. Do you include moral values as an evidence of spiritual discipline?

Spiritual discipline is not a specific idea of what you need to do or that you have to follow certain procedures. It is just giving time to yourself to activate what is normal, for example, listening to your dreams and working with them, spending time with your partner, spending time in nature, breathing, eating healthy food, fasting or at least purifying the body through various exercises and meditating in the sense of focusing for example. All of this is part of the spiritual work. Spiritual discipline can be through walking or through whatever activity that helps you to focus. It is not discipline by exclusion but rather by inclusion of things that we normally do not have time for. In that sense there is no moral attached to walking or to the way you should be in relationship with your partner. There is no right or wrong.

There are human values that of course are, I feel, universal, which need to be taken into account. When you are in a relationship, it is based on love. When you are walking, it is based on respect of the environment that you are walking in for example. It is not that the moral values are not there, but they are not imposed in a specific format as good or bad, because these universal moral values come from the heart or from your centre. When you are at peace with yourself, the moral values become self-explanatory, self-realising. I feel that all human beings have universal moral values and one of them is compassion. It is not always expressed in life because we do not give time to our heart to express that compassion which gets covered with other things. Yet in essence, every human being is compassionate and the heart is the gateway to expressing that compassion. It has nothing to do with the spiritual discipline really, but it allows the heart to communicate more clearly rather than through imposed moralistic values of what to do.

That is not to say that I do not believe in morals. I think that as human beings we all believe in some form of moral, at least on some level. For example, we all feel that in essence, it is wrong to kill other life forms, whether they are animal, plant or other human beings. Sometimes we justify the reasons why it may not be so wrong but we know that it is something distasteful. It is a moral that may be important to look at: to not harm other life forms and to approach the world, its beings and its creations, in a peaceful way. It is not that it is so much a moral but rather that if we follow a path of peacefulness we create harmony and cooperation between all life forms, so that it sustains us and sustains nature in a more positive way.

This then creates a more positive atmosphere for everybody and every living being, whether things are right or wrong. For example, is it right to be vegetarian or is it all right to actually take life away from an animal and eat it because you are not vegetarian? I do not say it is more morally superior to be vegetarian because you are not taking life away. I rather implore that people look deeper into the situation so that they realise this for themselves than rather following a social structure – as their parents have never been vegetarian, that is the way they are – but it is interesting to everything else too.

I feel that once your heart speaks to you, you become more centred in your truth than if someone imposes that truth upon you, so I do not really have morals codes to provide. It is like with children. I do not think it is nice to impose anything on a child. I think it is much more interesting to create an atmosphere where they can grow naturally, creatively, where they find their own centre and they create their own space to see what is right and what is wrong for themselves and learn from that experience, which then will be more grounded and deeper within their being rather than imposed and superficial. Their moral will be a natural moral, a natural universal belief, rather than a superficial belief that comes out of fear of disturbing or creating a bad feeling for something.

Relationship & Sexuality

You insist on the spiritual benefit of getting involved in a relationship with a partner. In your opinion, which qualities should this relationship have to be part of a spiritual awareness? And what is the place of sexuality in this relationship?

I am not saying that it is absolutely necessary to be in a relationship with a partner, rather that relationships are important, but these can be relationships with your family, your children, and any other deep and profound relationships in general. It is of course possible to be alone, but if you are alone, I always question, "Why?". I believe that for most people, being alone – meaning that you are not in a relationship with a partner – is an escape and is based on fear. The typical old English bachelor that decides to never want to get married or be in relationship with someone, for example, is an escape. Relationship is the opposite of escaping because in a relationship with someone you have to face yourself, unless it is not really a relationship.

You cannot be in relationship without looking at parts of yourself that sometimes are not so easy to look at. You also cannot be in a relationship without adapting and opening up in a way that is not necessary when you are alone, because of course you only have yourself. Normally you are in relationship with people but not in that very intense kind of relationship that I like. This is why I also say it is important to have children as it brings another quality of opening up and facing yourself in a different but very intense way, depending on how you have children, of course. Not everyone has a relationship with his or her child in the deep sense of the word.

For me the attributes of being in a relationship are very simple. One of them is to be honest. By that I do not mean being moralistically honest, I mean being honest about who you are and opening that honesty up to the other person by being real and clear to the other person. When you do this, I think what happens is that all the dishonesty that comes from the cultural socialisation, the expectations and belief systems that are in a certain way dishonest, as they are manipulated into creating a certain picture, have to be challenged. That challenge is what makes a relationship complicated. We constantly have to let go of certain things because they can no longer be sustained in a deep and profound relationship. You can pretend to be someone to the world, like being a doctor for example, but you cannot play the professional status game with your partner. You have to be yourself. Of course you can play the game if neither of you are honest but it will not be a real relationship. You have to be who you are behind that mask of doctor.

This is complicated because our whole society is built on masks. "To the parents I am like this, to the society I am like that, to the shopkeeper and to whoever I am like this", with all these wonderful roles and belief systems... With a partner the tendency is also to fall into a role but it is less likely because those roles cannot last if you are going deeper in the spiritual sense. If you are working through those roles and wanting to find a more profound or honest picture of yourself, then you have to let go of the old pictures of those old belief systems. Letting go means having to bring them up because they are so deeply ingrained inside of you that when they come up they are projected onto the person that you love. That is how we deal with things.

To understand things we need to bring them up. A feeling, for example irritation, comes up and we do not know where it is coming from because of course, we love the partner. We are irritated and that irritation allows us to recognise that there is irritation, so we have to feel the irritation. It is no longer possible to just project the irritation onto your partner if we want to go deeper. We have to see what this irritation is about and then we may recognise that the irritation is really not about the partner but it is irritation at ourselves because we are unable to do an action. We are irritated at ourselves because we cannot do this and maybe also because we cannot put into practice how to be real with our partner in that situation without the role or the mask. If we take away the role, what do we do?

What brings love into a relationship is that you both discover a new role. You create a new culture that is more honest and you are more real towards each other, but first, before being real, you have to let go of what prevented that realness from being. Of course that means seeing it and working through it in whatever way that is possible and natural for the two people in relationship. The reality is the union, the closeness and the honesty that creates a new way of being. Every time you do this, love becomes more profound, more real, more deep and all embracing, not just of feelings but of personality, of ways of doing things, of thoughts and of belief systems. These aspects inter-link and create a sacred space that then becomes the space of relationship that you have. To explain what is important and what is not important is difficult because each person, whatever his or her process in relationship to a partner, is different. No matter what comes up is unique to that person. Yet, I believe one may consider that a relationship is very difficult and cannot go deeper without being real and honest.

I have seen many relationships that have lasted many years where people have just agreed to be "okay" instead of being honest and real. Understanding each other's space and working around the mutual roles and games without ever facing them may make a relationship last but it does not make it into a profound or spiritual one. In that sense, I feel it is worse than being alone because when you reach that point, somehow there is the sense of not being lonely but with the pain associated to it, and it is a state of "okayness".

I see this especially in the older generations where people just live with each other and the relationship has no depth because there is no honesty. It is obvious for the children or the grandchildren as they see the lacks and the games that are being played. Yet, it is not obvious for the two people because they have lived in that way for such a long time that it has become a norm for them. Then they need the challenges from outside to wake them up to this "okayness" that is really not OK. This usually happens from their children or grandchildren.

Honesty and appreciation of the qualities of a person are important although it does not happen often in a relationship because we take things for granted. We say, "Oh yes, this is all right, but I wish that my partner had this and that". Such an attitude is lacking that appreciation of the qualities that are right in front of us. What sustains a relationship is being able to say to the partner, "I love the fact that you are creative, that you are able to sing, that you are able to laugh", or whatever it is.

If you focus on the qualities that are negative, such as "I wish you could do this!" or "Why do not you do this?", it changes the atmosphere from being a magical union to a not so magical separation. Of course, if you focus on what the partner is obviously separated from, then you are honouring the separation rather than building the bridge of connection between the two of you.

I think this is what happens a lot in relationships after a while. The magic between the two people gets lost and we may not be appreciating the beauty or the quality of the person. Instead, we can start questioning, "Why? How can we change? What is better to do? How to do this in a better way?". Then the atmosphere harmoniously changes to one where it is more like brother and sister, to one where people are in awe of each other. I think it is important to hold that quality of awe to hold the relationship and the "specialness" of the relationship because too often people are not in a relationship but in a partnership, as it is much easier and this is what is expected.

Honesty and appreciation of the qualities of each other are the two qualities that I would say are the most important in relationship. Then we have sexuality but that becomes easily misunderstood. Let me take an example. I was invited to a Hare Krishna community after a 40-day retreat in Brazil and I usually do not go to such communities because I find them a little bit strange, but it was a beautiful and unspoiled place in the mountains and this community was vegetarian. I found the dogmatism quite uncomfortable, the way people dressed, the way they were doing things, the separation between women and men and even though it is much more alive in Brazil than in Europe, the physical aspect was also very regimented. I talked to a member of the community and I learnt a lot about the Hare Krishna movement, notably in sexuality matters. I was explained that physical sexuality is actually not allowed unless you plan to have a baby. In some ways, physical sexuality is seen as in some religions, as negative outside of marriage.

It is interesting that in some places sexuality is experienced more freely as part of everyday expression, not just for adults, but for children too. In ancient Polynesia for instance, sexuality was very open. There were no taboos and people could express and find out what sexuality meant in the physical sense. Children were allowed to connect their physical intimate body to their feelings and to their mind rather than separating sexuality as a mysterious, unique and strange experience far removed from communication. This was important for the people as it allowed them to find their partner, their real partner that they really felt connected to, not just from desire in the physical sense, but from deeper aspects. I totally agree with this approach and I feel that sexuality, in the physical sense, needs to be explored, not necessarily completely in the sexual way, but at least in an intimate way, where the body has the ability to express its feeling of love to someone. So unlike other spiritual traditions perhaps, I do not see sexuality as a taboo. I see it as very important.

Even though sexuality seems free in the West, in my opinion it is not. It has just become a form of entertainment, disconnected from feelings but more connected to the ego, to the looks and desires which are very external to deep feelings. I am generalising here, but with young people, this is the drive. You go to a club and it is all about meeting a pretty well dressed person. It is the sexual attraction rather than the depth of the attraction to a person that seems to be the main focus. This is so out of context with the native societies where – when the marriage is not arranged, which is also another strong trend of group relationships – the goal is to feel something with a person and to see if the body corresponds to that feeling. So what to do in the modern world?

We do not live in a tribal community where things are different. We are individuals. We live mostly in the cities and meeting more appropriate people is not so obvious. It is not like a community where you grow up with people you see and you know and where everything is much simpler. We have reached a point where it is very complicated to connect sexuality to the spiritual path because we are normally caught up in the physical infatuation with beauty.

On the other hand, Osho is known for having said, "Fulfil all your sexual desires and go into sexuality completely". This is not the correct approach for me because if you do this then you go into another dimension of your being and you get lost in that dimension. What really matters is to bring consciousness into what you do. It is not to bring guilt or whatever else into it but to bring consciousness and wonder, "How can I feel more deeply, beyond just the picture of desire that I may have with that person? How can I go deeper?" In doing so, the physical communication becomes more than just a physical communication. I consider this important because sexuality is a gift that the divine has created between man and woman to experience that union. When we honour that gift in this way, we honour what the divine has created in man and woman. If we just treat it as a physical entertainment like we do in the West, we are not honouring sexuality.

Real sexuality is seeing where the sensations lead us and where they come from. That has a different focus and a different intention as it brings us closer to the person that we really want to be physically intimate with. Physical intimacy is essential. Without it people create a barrier and a form of neurosis, even when they are intimate. A lot of women say that even when they are physically intimate with someone, on some level they are not because some part of them holds back and they are not able to completely be open to the physical sensations.

This is notably the case with people who feel that they are liberal in sexuality. Many women say, "I have no problems in my sexuality. I have been in twenty relationships and I am totally free with my body". But is it really the case? It is only in the physical and not in the intimate sense. I feel that people who have relationships after relationships do not have any clue what real physical intimacy is. A relationship that is physically intimate involves much more than just the physical. It is beyond feelings, it is a physical aspect that can only be communicated when you love someone.

For example, it is easy to be physically intimate with children, not sexually of course, but physically. You can hold them, you can be free with them, you can tickle and play with them because there is no physical barrier. Yet it is much more difficult to be intimate in that way with an adult because there are all the walls. Deep physical intimacy goes beyond sexuality because you know each other, you trust each other, and you feel comfortable with each other.

Most often women, especially if they are attractive, expect men to just see their physical beauty and they close some levels of their being because of that. This is a dilemma in modern society because this is a game a man and a woman play together. It is not just a man thing. When men and women are only intimate in a physical sense, their relationship loses the quality of intimacy because they are not loving and embracing the person deeply, it remains superficial. This is basically how western sexuality has developed.

Physical sexuality is essential and I remember a woman asking me at the end of retreat, "Now what should I do with my partner when I go home?". I answered, "You need to be physical. Every day you need to be physically sexual with your partner!" That woman looked at me and said, "What? You are telling me to be physically sexual?". I said, "Yes! Every day!" Her partner was of course very happy because he was a bit suspicious and not really open to my teachings but they needed to explore their physical being to really be intimate beyond what is normal in the current belief systems. After a month they understood this and of course it was not just the sexuality that was missing, it was the intimacy between them, the physical intimacy that holds a relationship and is vital for it.

Without physical intimacy, a relationship loses a quality. The intimacy can be as simple as holding your partner's hand. I find it amazing and beautiful when I see old people who have been married for fifty years still holding hands – and therefore the same space – as if they had just met. For me this is physical intimacy and sexuality because really when you go beyond the fulfilment of a personal biological impulse, sexuality is what the universe is doing all the time. It is intimate, very intimate with everyone all the time, so it has the form and quality that is very sexual.

There is an attraction when you see someone that is beautiful. There is an attraction to that person that has that quality of wanting to be in union, and of course it is beyond physical sexuality but it has that same quality. This is why when someone asked me once, "How can you say that your love for your family is the same as your love for someone who you do not know and comes to a retreat?", I answered, "In essence, intimacy, when it goes beyond the physical, the emotional and the social sense, connects us and has that quality that is universal. It is not just a separate or distant love. It is a very intimate love which embraces and goes beyond the personal into the impersonal".

This is almost like the breath. When you take a breath, that breath is more intimate than anything but we do not see that intimacy until the moment where you feel the sensual breath in your body and you realise, "The breath is an expression of intimacy, of connection and union!". I do not want people to misunderstand because I am totally distant from the normal idea or sense of sexuality. I am not in anyway saying that this is good or bad because it is not my way, but I do not believe in open sexuality or free love as some people call it. I believe that a relationship needs to be between two people.

This understanding of using a physical relationship to enter a divine one with everything is very similar to what ancient Tantra is about. Do you relate to this approach in which an intimate relationship with anything – not only a human being – is a mean for Union?

I do not really know Tantra because I have not read or learnt about it so my concept of Tantra is very limited to the very basic understanding that is popular. I would say that if the little I know about Tantra is true, then what I speak about is quite different, because for me, physical relationship is totally unimportant. It is important but totally unimportant because the physical has no meaning without a deeper connection to a person. I do not know if this is Tantra.

Intimate relationship does not have to be physical. Intimate relationship is based on union and the union is not in the physical sense, the union is in the consciousness. This is not to belittle the physical aspect but it is just to highlight where the energy needs to be. It is the connection in the consciousness which is most important, but what does this mean in a practical sense in relationship? Some people in relationship will rely on emotional aspects, like in the West. An emotional relationship is normally seen as the major constitute of a relationship and I think this is OK but it is out of balance because it forgets other parts of ourselves. Maybe Tantra, as I understand it, is the physical which helps the consciousness come back into union. To me it is not through emotions nor through the physical but it is in remembering the divine aspect of yourself. In that remembrance, it brings that aspect of your being, the vibration of your whole being, to a level which is much easier to connect to intimately with the person that you are with.

It can be done in the physical sense but it is not the way I usually encourage. I encourage more remembering yourself, not the aspect that is selfish but the higher aspect of yourself and always relate that higher aspect in relationship to the intimate person that you are relating to. This avoids having to rely on something that is temporary and what is temporary is the physical and the emotional bodies because they are not same as consciousness. Consciousness lives forever. When you bond on that level of relationship, then the physical and the emotional get fed from these higher aspects of consciousness and of union instead of being the feeding organs, the feeding energy of the relationship.

The physical and the emotional then carry consciousness within them. This of course creates intimacy in that aspect and it is important because intimacy is expressed on all levels. If you are a human being, you have a body and you have to express it in the physical sense. When you hold a baby, it feels natural to hold it and you do not just emotionally relate to the baby, you actually physically touch a baby and tickle and play and it is the same in relationship that is intimate. It is important to remember the physical expression of consciousness coming back into union.

I feel that Tantra got lost on the way and that the physical became very important. It may be because in India, people spent days, months and years working on themselves so they had time to do this in some of the settings like ashrams and other specific situations. They had more time to develop these aspects through what may have been Tantra at that time, but today, Tantra as I see it is really just using the physical body. It has become a bit like Hatha Yoga, using the physical body through postures to come back into a remembrance of a higher aspect of yourself.

I believe that it is being done in the opposite way of how it needs to be done. The physical could be important for some people because maybe it is traumatised. Maybe there is a karmic remnant that needs to be worked through, an emotional disturbance or a sense of not being able to communicate, but if we focus too much on it, then we pull the energy away from consciousness. The physical then has all our attention and intention and that means that we are unable to really focus on what is, for me, of benefit in relationship.

This goes with what you said before but it seems that the focus on this physical aspect is a reductionist version of Tantra. In ancient Tantrism the idea is apparently close to what you said: to relate to the consciousness not only through the physical or through a human being but also through an object or through nature. In this case would you relate to this ancient form of Tantra?

Yes perhaps, because consciousness is not only about a relationship, consciousness is with all life.

Intimate relationship with an aspect of all life is a way to access the Unity?

Of course! In some countries, people wanted to be intimate with all life because it was not separate. It was not as individual as it is now. You went in a place and you wanted to have an intimate relationship with a mountain or with the trees because it is a beautiful thing to have, but maybe we have closed it to be just a physical thing with a partner. There is of course a lot of energy in the physical sense but the energy is not from the physical. The energy is from consciousness.

The importance of intimacy in spiritual awareness is understandable but why then are so many well-known spiritual sages single men or women?

Because it is much easier! To have a family and be totally open and free with the family is a lot of work! People manage everything because it all falls into control

mechanisms, the children are socialised, they go to school and watch television…
In contrast, to be a free family in the sense of being open, intimate, and allowing
the unfolding process to happen not just for you and your partner, but also for
your children and for the whole dynamic of family life, is a full time job! It is
difficult to do. This is why if someone really is willing to focus on spiritual work
with other people, like a teacher, he or she sometimes decides to say, "My family
is not as important as my work".

However, I understand that for some it is possible to embrace everything, the
mundane world, the family life and the spiritual world, all as one experience. It
is definitely much more hard work, but that work is much more fulfilling because
it gives you compassion and a deeper understanding of what it is to be a father,
what it is to be in a relationship with a partner, and what it is to be facing all the
things that families have to face.

The Heart, the Centre & the Essence

You systematically invite people to come back to "the heart", to "the centre", to "the essence", to "the love inside". What do you put exactly in these notions? What is the centre? What is love for you? Is it a feeling we can develop?

When I say "the heart", I do not mean the physical heart or even the heart located in a specific area of the body. It is almost like when you use the word "heart" in English, it means the core, the middle, the depth of an experience. It is the consciousness that we have of our experiences.

Do you see the centre and the heart as the same?

Not really, because the heart has more to do with your consciousness being able to recognise the experience and translating it to the senses. It then becomes obvious in a way where you can say, "Yes, I feel this", or "I can think about this", or "My body recognises this". It entails a form of recognition and a form of knowledge that becomes understood. This is why the heart chakra that we find in the Hindu yoga system, and also quite common in the New Age circles, is important. Your heart can understand love for example. It can understand that love is very deep, but how does it understand love? It is because that depth is translated to a form of consciousness, perhaps through the senses or perhaps through the emotions or the feelings. That then becomes a space where the heart recognises something.

But what is "the heart"?

The heart is the consciousness that recognises. It is more personal and it has a sense that you can relate to. The centre is different. It is still that same space but it is more impersonal. It is going deeper. When I say "go deeper", I am not asking for the heart to recognise anything. I am asking for the person to go deeper into that experience. Going deeper is being present to the experience that the heart can translate into something more personal. The centre and the heart are different in a way but they are the same experience, although we are much more related to who we are as human beings or as individuals.

As for the centre... You could go to the centre and then you could recognise the centre from the centre. It is like when you go to sleep. You do not lose consciousness but in the sleep you recognise sleep from sleep. When you wake up slowly, you recognise from your heart that you were in a very deep space and having a profound experience during the sleep. The centre is more impersonal in that sense, at least in words.

... and love?

I am not sure in what sense I use that word. If I am talking about love in the more profound or the more personal sense of love, that is selfless service. The heart recognises something and then it is not enough that the recognition is there. That recognition gets acted upon through intention in a way that becomes an external action of giving, because the heart knows that this is of great importance. When you recognise that you love someone, of course you want to manifest that sense of love by giving love and not just receiving it. The heart recognises love and wants to give more of that experience to everyone around. For me that is love. It is the extension of that experience not just to humanity but to all that is present in your life, nature, everything, even cars! If you love your car, it works better!

The problem with the concept of love is that it is overused and it loses its meaning.

The word love is abused because it has no real meaning anymore. It does have a meaning but it does not capture the imagination as it could because it is used in a type of language, in advertising and in religion where love is not felt in the heart. The concept is an alien one that is not tangible so it loses its meaning. In this way, I totally agree and this is why sometimes I use different words.

Like "essence", "substance" ...

Exactly, because then people do not automatically go to a concept but have to think a little bit.

So the centre, the essence, the substance are equal?

The centre and the essence yes, but not the substance. Yes and no actually, because the substance is even more impersonal. The centre has its different degrees. It has some form of recognition, so when you are sleeping the centre recognises itself, but the substance does not die when you die. It is there. It has a form that never changes.

Is that substance unique?

No, it is not unique, it is part of everything. It may seem unique because it is your experience. It is not like in Buddhism where everything dissolves into nothing. The substance has a sense of reality to itself.

Is it awareness?

I think it is a form of awareness, yet it is much beyond the senses of awareness that we normally relate to. It is an awareness that we are born with. This is why a child has awareness. People used to believe that babies did not have awareness and they did painful things to them, like operations without anaesthetics and it was quite painful. Now it is recognised that children have a nervous system giving them feelings and pain.

When you have awareness, when you are connected to this awareness that I am speaking about, then you realise that people can recognise things beyond many forms. Even a tree has a sense of awareness that recognises things beyond the senses. We now reach a deep and profound level where language is not helpful. Normally I avoid these things, in words at least, I demonstrate it in actions but in a book you cannot, you have to use words...

Is working with the "substance" that animates people the whole purpose of your nightly "energetic work"?

It is! Working with the energy, the substance or the atmosphere...

Can you explain this work?

It is difficult to explain this work. I really do not know how to explain it. This is not to make it sound easy but I do not even think about it. When someone teaches me how to work with a computer I think it is fascinating and complicated and I really wonder how anyone can do this. The work I do is a bit like breathing, you do not think about it.

It is not entering into another dimension or reality?

No, not at all. For me it is not, but of course, if you are in the mundane, you have to enter another dimension otherwise you are not connected to anything but the senses that cannot see what I do. Trying to understand this through the senses can work because it can help to navigate you to certain bridges that reach to that point, but it is much beyond and this is why people sometimes think it is really strange. Some people have asked, "How can you be working with this or that person while you are talking to me, or cooking food, or doing whatever?". I do not have to stop anything to do that. I am doing one thing with the senses, I am talking and using my brain, and the other thing is not from that space. I do not have to stop this space to function from another space. It is like when you are feeling love for someone, it does not mean you have to stop everything to feel love. You could be feeling love and driving a car, you could be talking, and still your heart has that sensation of love. This is the closest I can get to describe how you can function on the different levels.

... and working with someone else's substance can be done without this person being conscious of it?

All the substance is the same. People do not even have to have consciousness because what is connecting everything is beyond that consciousness.

The substance beyond the personality...

It is the same. Normally people not even know that it that exists. They only have awareness of that in a few moments of their experience maybe in a day or in a year. Normally they do not have that connection because the mundane is there all the time. It is impossible to have awareness from the space of the mundane. To reach the profound, you have to jump over it and that jumping over is the work that I do with people on the conscious level. Yet, when the conscious work is over, I am still working but people do not have to be aware to understand or to feel what I do. They could even be angry with me and think I am the most horrible person, stupid or clever, this or that. It makes no difference because the work is beyond all those things.

It is a space of connection between substances?

Exactly. It is the space that is beyond the spaces. If you look at particles, it is not the space around the particles but the substance that holds the energy of the particles. If you could squeeze everything, what you would get would be the substance, and the rest is all the other things that create the known dimensions, the brain, the senses, and the physical experiences. What is holding all that together is like what the essence of the particle is. That is what I work with, but to get to that you have to go beyond the spaces. It is like what shamans do.

Another dimension?

Another dimension, a journey into another world.

Which is right here?!

It is like the table. We see the table as it is because it has that form, but if you went through you would see that the substance is totally different.

In this other dimension can two substances communicate together independently of the substances around?

They are always communicating together.

How? If everything is connected in this whole dimension, is there still a one to one communication of substances?

Of course. It is just like heating water, the fire changes the substances that are interacting with the water and makes it hot. I am trying to explain how but it is very difficult to put into words. They are not communicating through physical means. When people say that they see ghosts and spirits, it is again a fragment of imagination that projects into what could be on some level real but it is not real to how I understand things because if you were to put everything into particles, minute particles, even consciousness – which it is not, it is beyond particles – then the vibration of these particles moves. They are excited by the understanding that they are one with everything and this sense of oneness is the bond or the passage of communication between the different aspects.

Are we some specific type of particles?

It is not really particles. I am using the word particles to define the space that creates you, but you is not as you understand "you". It is another you. It is a You beyond the ego, or beyond the mind. It is a You that is really You. That is why it is difficult to conceptualise and say "I am working with you" because I am not working to change concepts in the mind, to change your feelings or to even change a physical structure. It is deeper.

When we are born into the physical realm of this world, human beings have a love of coming back to the divine inside of themselves. In the end, this is what we are doing in every action, whether we are conscious of it or not. Even a baby's first words to communicate are not really to communicate the language of communication like English or German for instance. It is rather to find a method of coming back to addressing this oneness. This is how the essences communicate. It is from a feeling but it is not an emotion. It has a quality similar to the emotion because it is a communication that could be said to come from the heart, meaning the centre of the heart, not the emotional heart or the heart which feels. This is how the essences or substances communicate with one another. On some level, this also creates conscious communication in the world between people beyond language and even beyond distance. It transcends physical boundaries. If there is a mother in Iceland and a child in China, there is a communication that happens and it happens through this substance, which can be seen if you are able to see it and if you are, what you see is one dimension of it.

I call this the etheric, which is around the body. It is the invisible body which is around all the physical senses. It is visible and you can see when it is wanting to communicate, it has the quality of feeling, which is love or joy. It expands and moves outwards. When there is the opposite quality of fear or negativity, it contracts because love cannot be communicated so then it is not communicating. Then our memory is to come back to a sense of love so that this ether, which is the external aspect of the substance, begins to communicate to all aspects in the world. This etheric body is the end product of the essence, which is the substance, and the substance communicates like this.

It is not a matter of metres...

It is not even connected to time or to space because it does not follow those laws. Consciousness is beyond that. It communicates on a level that can only be grasped and caught through the etheric body. The understanding then comes through this etheric body into the physical body and the understanding in the physical sense then sends a picture to the mental sense. In the end we have a little picture but it is very far removed from the reality of the communication. It has gone through many levels of trying to understand something that cannot be understood from that level.

Are physics too limited to understand this communication between substances in this dimension? Since particles are not the right word to describe what you are saying, is there no current explanation for this in words?

Today's physics cannot explain this. Particles are there but that has more to do with quantum physics, and consciousness is of course beyond quantum physics.

The ether is the closest, because through it, consciousness begins to touch the particles. This is what some people call the aura around the body.

And outside this everyday physical dimension, in this other dimension, do the substances communicate together by the simple fact of being? How do they communicate?

Their communication is not in words, actions, memories or any such things. It is simply love being expressed beyond those words or concepts. Love can carry a multitude of meanings within itself. It is like poetry, you can have two sentences that express so much more than two sentences because they are inferring and touching upon things that are invisible.

Simply love…

Yes!

Why is this awareness not in the conscious mind of the person with whom you are in contact with in this dimension?

It can be if they are in touch with themselves enough, but the problem is that most people are not. Even if they are, it takes a lot of neutrality and energy because most people are always projecting themselves to other moments, to either their past or their future, so it is difficult to have that sense. Yet, if someone really takes a deep breath, lets go of everything and is able to be present, there will be no doubt that this awareness is present. Babies and animals are more able to recognise this than adults because, they are more able to focus here in this experience. If you are conscious, I am sure that not only will you recognise this but other parts of your body will also acknowledge what is going on. If you could measure, I am sure you would recognise that the body goes through biological changes. I am not a scientist so I do not know how they would do these things, but like with meditation I am sure there would be an obvious sign that something is happening in that moment.

You said that in this dimension the person, or the person's substance, communicates back to you, yet the person holding that substance has no memory of it when waking up. It sounds like being in a magical world…

It is like a dream. You have many hundreds of experiences in your sleep and in your dreams. Then you wake up and…

Is it human fate not to remember what we really are?

If you remember everything, all at once you would be very overwhelmed because it would be too much for the brain, so I think it is useful to take things step by step.

Is it healthy not to remember?

It is a survival mechanism that the brain has adapted to filter certain experiences and to translate other experiences to memories, feelings or other senses … and to prevent certain things from being obvious.

Can't the memory of the spiritual experiences during sleep be a way of tuning into our spiritual dimension during everyday life?

It is a goal to come back to understand what is wisdom but we have to be ready to embrace that wisdom in its complete sense. We cannot embrace wisdom if the part of us that is trying to understand wisdom is not wise enough to comprehend the wisdom! It is a bit like asking someone who only reads English to read Chinese, it will not work because we will not see. We look at it and we know that it is there but we will not see the meaning of what is there because it makes no sense.

It is a matter of different dimensions…

Yes. Part of why we are here in this world is to remember who we are, but we have to bring that memory into our whole consciousness, not just into the mental concept. The consciousness is in the moment, remembering everything. It is consciousness related to this dimension that we are living in now, which is the dimension of the physical and of the intuitive senses. This then creates completeness inside of ourselves. Consciousness does not have to remember anything because it is always remembering. Only parts of ourselves, like the mind, need to come back into harmony with that wisdom but they cannot come back in harmony with it because they are so limited. They are attached to all the experiences in this dimension so you cannot just say, "Stop! I don't want to have that experience! I want to have another experience now!", because it does not work like this. There is a whole process of coming back to your real self and it would be wonderful if it were very quick, but we have so many parts that need to transform in order to hold on to the space where consciousness can live that it is not quick.

So if we would remember, it would be the mind, not the consciousness which is already there because the consciousness does not need to remember?

Consciousness is always remembering but we remove ourselves from it as a survival mechanism. Some people are born enlightened. They are gifted with the fact that consciousness then dwells in their mind, in their body, in their emotions and in their actions but this is very rare! It does not happen every day. Most people have to go through a stage of understanding, slowly getting to the place where they remember why and how consciousness can be integrated into their physical senses like the mind. If the mind were to remember everything at once, it would explode because it would be too much energy. It would be like pouring boiling water into a paper bag, it just would not hold it!

Consciousness is there. What has to change are the other parts of you, like the mind who is trying to understand. It goes on like this, "You are consciousness and

I want you to be inside of me and I want you here so that I can be conscious!", but this is not how it happens. Consciousness is everywhere. We are walking in consciousness as individuals. We have a physical realm in which we say, "I can see this and I can see that but I can't really integrate it because I'm here and I'm dealing with what is more energetically present to me, which is the physical reality of eating, sleeping, relating and survival". All this is essential, we have to do it, you cannot leave it behind. But when you are not attached or you do not have to deal with this, then you expand to a point where consciousness is integrated into your actions because you are not walking anymore: you are part of the consciousness that is there.

When people ask, "Wouldn't it be good to be conscious?". It would be good but it also means that some parts of us have to be changed and those parts do not like to change. If we are attached to the desires of loving someone for example, and we get upset with that person, it is very difficult to change the "upsetness" because we feel like we have to deal with it. As a human being, we have to allow consciousness to slowly come into the space that is "upsetness" by letting go of it first. If we hold on to it instead, then that is the space that we live in, within our physical senses. It is a desire. It is almost like the heart wants to be at home but cannot because it is at home in other places. It has to let go of these other places to come back to the real home.

When we sleep, we let go of the physical senses, to a certain degree. We come back to the intuitive and core aspects of ourselves so we are much closer to consciousness, but it does not mean we are more conscious, because in sleep we are still asleep in the same way. We cannot actually transform many things in the same way as we can in everyday life because when we are not sleeping, we have a world where we have the gift of freedom. We also have freedom in our sleep, but not in the same way. It is more automatic and it relies on a level of consciousness that is happening to deal with whatever situations arise. If we are angry in our sleep, then the anger carries on as a bad dream or carries on as a nightmare and we are very much caught in that consciousness. It is much more intense. Well ... not always ... because sometimes people can be very intensely angry even in waking life! But usually in waking life we have many other things that distract us from dealing with it, unlike in dreams where it becomes the focus of our consciousness.

There is no control so in a sense that is good but in a sense there is not as much freedom because we do not have the level of awareness to change things. Even so, dreams will take you to parts of yourself that will transform much quicker than in waking life if you are able to do so. In waking life, we can keep repeating the same thing over and over again, whilst in dreams we do not have that freedom to suffer in the same way, because when we suffer in a dream, we really want to move out of the suffering, there are no other games.

We are more true?

Yes, we are more like a child, having to deal with the moment of what is going on, so sleep is a very useful way. It is actually one of the ways with which I work a lot, working with dreams, so that we work with the consciousness that is more free of the mundane. I think that this is a very useful way to bring consciousness back.

Is your point that we do not need to remember because the consciousness is there in the awake state?

Exactly. It is but we just do not know.

If we remembered, it would be the mind working with ideas and not a state of consciousness.

Yes, and many people who say they remember do not actually remember. What they remember is a concept of consciousness, images or feelings, which may have a sense a reality so they put these images in realities to a point where they become so overwhelming and powerful that instead of being consciousness they become dogma. They become mental concepts and limited ideas of what consciousness is, which then creates people getting fanatical about something and saying, "I have found the way! I'm sure this is the truth or I am this...". Maybe they have found a certain aspect of the way but the limited concept of I, which is the ego, is still controlling the picture so it is not consciousness. It is a mirror of consciousness through the filter of the mind.

But at the same time it seems to be a goal in life to consciously express this substance, this essence of who we are.

I do not know if it is a goal but I think the goal is to transcend our attachment to what we believe to be reality, so that we can see the complete reality. I am not saying the mind and the mundane need to be pushed aside or that we need to get rid of them. I believe that they are important. They simply need to be in balance with all aspects, just like feelings needs to be in balance with the mind.

Again, the work is more pulling off the psychological and cultural layers covering our being than getting something new...

Yes.

It seems easier to get to the past because we know it, or to the future as it just needs imagination at work. Why is being fully in the present moment so difficult?

People feel that if they let go of what they know, they will disintegrate and they end up in a space that is unknowable. It is like death. Everyone is afraid of death, at least on some level, and will do everything to prevent that, sometimes in a clever way and sometimes in a very strange way, which makes no sense if you look at it logically.

You talked about "the Path of the Heart". How would you define this path?

Many people ask me what I mean by "The Heart". Some think it is about being good, being nice, being more kind. To me that is not exactly what I imply when I say "The Heart". The heart is the centre. It is the essence. It carries the emotional, loving, and compassionate aspect of your essence, but it is much more. The heart is the space that is closest to your essence, to who you are. It is the seed that can grow beyond the ego to encompass acts of humility, compassion, intelligence and creativity which come from a space that is totally different from simply feeling or sensing something good in the physical heart. Many people say that if this is the path of the heart, they need to feel good, happy and free, but in actual fact, this feeling good and free is only a by-product of coming back home. It is not what you have to do to be working in this way.

When you go back to the essence, one of the things that happen is that you become more compassionate. You become more centred in the space that normal people see as the heart, which is being good to others and doing nice things, but it is not exactly what I mean by "the Path of the Heart". This path is going back to the essence of what is most divine inside you and what is most divine is beyond the mind, beyond the body, beyond the knowledge that is in books and beyond belief systems. It is deeply ingrained in what created who you are as a personality, and that can be manifested in action, in things that you actually do.

So what is the path of the heart? It is a path that most people refuse to take because it seems so confusing. For example, one of the things I talk about is coming back to this present moment. When I say this, most people cannot comprehend what that means. As soon as I say it, the mind is thinking, "What it this present moment?" and tries to figure it out. Then of course, it is already gone into a concept that is related to your past and your future, and you are trying to make sense of what this moment is.

Why is it so complicated? Simply because you have to let go of those concepts related to all your experiences in the past and all your pictures of the future to taste what it is like to be in this present moment. To translate it into a language that makes more sense, you have to let go of the concepts that have been inherited culturally or personally to be able to communicate and explain beyond them in a language that people can comprehend.

This language needs to transmit the essence of what it means to come back to the space of the heart rather than just intellectual words. This is complicated in books. Normally you can see it or you can sense it because our perception opens to that. Certain well known people have come back to a space of the heart. I now think for instance about the Persian poet Rumi. I read a little bit of what he wrote and I understood that he realised many things about the heart. He could have remained silent of course. This is actually what many spiritual teachers do: they remain silent because they say that as soon as we utter things in language, it gets corrupted. For me that is an easy way out because whatever happens, we have to communicate. We are part of humanity, we need to say, "Hello, I am part of you", rather than withdraw and sit somewhere quietly. Someone like Rumi is able to express concepts that touch the space that, in a moment, stops all those concepts that were used to define what this moment is. Those concepts drop because he invites other aspects of you, usually feelings, to come into the picture. That is basically what I do. I work with the heart and the deeper feelings that are part of the heart. It is not just the empty space or the space of nothingness, like in Zen Buddhism.

I work with what it means to activate the space of the heart. It is almost as if there is a feeling that expands and becomes strong. This feeling is beyond just feeling morally superior or feeling good. It is a feeling that drives you. It is an emotion that becomes like a light that shines through your body and gives you strength to continue to explore the world from the heart. It is not just in quietness or in senses but also through emotions.

I work very strongly with emotions because, of course, we are emotional human beings. Let us look at babies. If you have babies, you know that they are totally emotional and express their emotional aspects in a complete sense. For me babies do not need to stop being babies but need that communication to be carried on deeper as they grow in the sense of language and in the sense of action. Later, people understand that communication directly. Then it is not to stop being a baby, but to be a baby in an adult form, so that this communication does not stop, as it happens to most of us.

We give up our heart and we lose faith that the world is exciting and has magic. Instead, we get into a cultural depression about the world and its state as well as our own state. The enthusiasm and the action of the heart, the vibrancy of the heart, which the baby is born with, are then not transmitted in language. Rumi was able to transmit this as he said that part of himself caught fire and was made alive in a way that was not before. This is part of the work I do. My work is not to sit quietly and become nothing. It is actually to become more who you are, more who the baby needed to be as an adult but just got lost in the process of self-development. This is for me the path of the heart.

Your teaching seems very close to the kind of Sufism Rumi taught, as it is a call to experience in direct and physical contact with what you call "the Divine". Yet, you do not suggest much dance, prayers and songs...

I do not know about Sufism very much except that I grew up in a place where they were many Sufis. Rumi initiated a special type of Sufism with the dervishes and I think it was him who started the whirling dance, which is related to just one type of Sufism. There are many other schools and the dervishes belong to one. It is interesting, but like all traditions, it has become coloured by many things. For me the historical background is often more interesting than the modern practices that we see today.

Dervish people still reunite and gather in groups, looking for a divine personal experience. This is what I find most attractive in any spiritual tradition: the directness of this experience. This is why Zen Buddhism and Shamanism appealed to me before.

Experiencing Reality

Would you say that some states, deep states of perception people could have in ceremonies – the connection between everything, the material world and people seen like a vibration, with atoms in motion like a filter – are somewhat similar to what can be experienced during meditation by yogis in India?

Yes, of course. I do not know how many yogis actually experience this today, yet I think the ancient yogis could see things, in what I call the invisible world, or the work that is not so easily seen. I think they saw exactly the same as what everyone experiences: the connection.

It is interesting that for many people, one of the first things that happen in a ceremony is that you begin to see beyond the visual senses. You look at an object but it does not remain as an object. If you look at a tree, it is not just green leaves and the shape of a trunk and nice branches. You actually begin to float into the tree, to see and connect to the tree. Some people may think, "I am just hallucinating. It is only the *San Pedro* changing my visual idea of what the tree really looks like. The tree does not really look like this". But it does! What we are doing is seeing the molecular structure, the atoms, the particles and the vibration of the tree, and yogis described this thousands of years ago.

They did actually see atoms and particles even though it was not explained in today's scientific language. It was explained in a way that people could use at that time. They saw that the universe, which we think is so solid and has such strong forms, is actually not that solid. Its particles have a different structure and they are floating into another dimension that quantum physics is recognising nowadays as something much more important than we ever realised. Yogis realised this thousands of year ago – not just yogis of course, but they were the ones who explained it in literature.

During deep spiritual experiences, you are opening the brain structure so that it can see beyond what is normally necessary for survival, such as seeing the wild animal that is coming towards you rather than its particles, to run away and hide in a cave or wherever. This is what people believe evolution is about – and I am joking a little bit about it – but in the end, when you see the structure of a tree, you can actually go to different points in it, which are the particles and their structure, and you can realise how it is very interchangeable with other things. You realise that the particles are not a structure. The tree is not separate itself. The particles can actually flow and connect, not just as roots connecting to the earth, but on different dimension.

This then shows us that the cycle of life is much more complex than the simple picture that scientists have put forth as being the reality for us to understand. We realise that reality is much deeper and has many more levels than the simple solutions that philosophy or scientific dogma dictate as being the reality that we have to believe in.

Of course, when you do this as an individual, it is very scary because you are breaking the pattern. You look at the tree and you think, "This not a tree because this is not what everyone has told me a tree looks like". Then, instead of seeing the particles, we touch upon our fear of what we are seeing because it seems too strange, too unknown and too deep to be what it is. In doing so, we connect to the emotions and to the programs that resist this openness to life, which is interesting. The whole structure of our vision changes and goes to a different point. This is what yogis realised and this is why they created certain paths for working through the different layers that come out with these aspects, such as yoga, *mantras* and many other techniques.

It may be useful to distinguish Hinduism, which is the religion, from spirituality in India...

Exactly. Hinduism now as the religion has created a structure that is different from the spirituality of ancient India, which was a more personal and real experience.

These people do not talk about the many Gods and this form of Hinduism is somewhat apart from what they experienced...

Exactly. These spiritual people are sometimes not accepted when they are alive. They only are accepted and respected once they die and become perhaps less controversial to the Hindu religion that may have felt threatened by their presence when they were alive.

Apparently, at least in ceremonies, when people open their perceptions and can see these vibrations and filters of atoms, they have this feeling of rediscovering something that they knew before and of acknowledging how obvious it is. That totally goes with what you keep repeating. Is that the sign that we already know things and just have the chance to open to another dimension for a moment?

In a ceremony or in meditation, there are two things that are interesting to note. One is that what we often see are just images that come to the surface and we know deep inside that they are not reality. We see images and the mind creates pictures that are almost like layers being released. We see it, we become conscious of it and we let it go. The other thing is that we go deeper. Once those layers are released, we go deeper to a point that recognises reality not from the intellect but from the recognition that it is part of what we understand. Then, as you say, we see something and it is not with the feeling of discovering something totally new but rather like recognising something we knew. Yet, the amazing sense of recognition is so compelling that it becomes overwhelming. It is not the fact that you are seeing but rather a sense of, "Gosh, it is so amazing to recognise this!"

At other points, when we are doing spiritual work, something that I call the "mind rubbish" is released and it has nothing to do with recognising anything. For example if we begin daydreaming or sitting and it is almost like when you sit in meditation, it is not going deeper. It is just floating around in ideas, drifting from one thing to another. It is recognising superficial aspects of the mind but not really going to this point which recognises the depth of what is around.

There are two kinds of experiences that happen in deep meditation and in ceremony. Sometimes we are releasing programs, silly programs – and we cannot confuse that with what I call enlightening experiences – because often the mind will need to let go of rubbish. Some people ask me, "What is the purpose of going through all this? Why do I need to see all these silly things if they are not real?". The purpose is to recognise that if they are not real, there is no need to keep the thoughts, the feelings and the visions that are just nonsense, or have no profound meaning, as part of your reality.

This happens in the deep meditations. Sometimes you get to a point which is coming home, which is understanding something that is so real that there is no doubt that its reality has validity. The experience is so profound that we are overwhelmed by it, but it is not what we are seeing. When we go through deep meditation, sometimes what we see is the letting go of layers and this is quite superficial because those layers are just the limitations that we have and that we need to let go of. This is why the inner world is as complicated as the outer world. It is as difficult as living life outside. Maybe even more so because we do not know the inside territory as well as we know the outside territory.

During ceremonies some people can have a glimpse of this reality – the intensity of life, the vibration, the light around the trees, the connection with the environment, etc. What should a wise person do with these experiences? Is the goal to keep this state of perception awake twenty-four hours a day or is it rather going back and forth between the material world they live in and this very deep reality?

There is no goal. In the end, if you try to go back to something, you are not going back from the space where you touched that reality. You are going back from another space. It is almost like you have to use another aspect to get to that point, so that aspect would be for example that it was very clear for you in that moment. But that clarity then gets remembered in the mind as a picture and then you hold on to that picture, so you are going back to it rather than being in this moment.

Even if it is a remembrance, that picture helps to be aware in the present moment that there is something beyond the everyday life situations we are in. So, with the emotion related to it, this picture is still essential...

Of course, and this is very important, but there no need to go back to it. Actually there is, but there is no need to go back to it in the sense of reliving that past experience because we are still living that experience. We just do not recognise it. However, to remember that experience is essential because it puts everything into perspective. When we are lost in whatever the mundane takes us into, it becomes like an anchor to another reality that we forget about. Rumi referred to this when he said, "Once the heart has tasted eternity then it gets more thirsty", or something like this, I cannot remember his words exactly. That thirst becomes almost like fire and in a way, it is very good because it then becomes our intention to live life in a different way than just being like a robot, without the acknowledgement that there is more to life than just what we see. Still, to get too caught up in a remembrance can also be another process of forgetting this present moment. In this present moment here, whatever that moment is, if you are in relationship with someone or if you are walking in the forest, there is something else that is as important to recognise.

So the point is not to have this intense perception of a vibrating unity continuously?

You have it.

We have it but we do not see it very often...

We do not see it because we are in the future.

If we are not careful and we go to the future, to the idea of something, then that can become a game that keeps us from the present.

Wanting to see it again is like a trap as it can prevent from seeing what is already there?

Yes. It can be a trap because it is almost like the mind will then go to that moment. But what about the breath here if the mind is over there thinking about that? What about the breath coming and filling what is actually happening right now? I am not at all dismissing this vision as something unimportant because this is actually the whole purpose of the ceremonies I am familiar with, that people taste this "other world", and then, once that taste is deep in the body, it can never be forgotten. That taste is our driving force. Yet it is important to do something to keep that alive in all experiences, rather than going to the past or to the future.

Often people will want to have another ceremony and may say, "Ah, but this was not as profound, or it was not as deep as ceremonies that I've had before. Why? Am I doing something wrong?". It is almost as if the whole situation had been focused on one thing, forgetting all the rest. It is almost like falling in love with one person and then just remembering that person who stays in the back of the mind, holding the energy there and forgetting that this love can be expressed in many different ways. When people say this about a ceremony, "Ah, the ceremony, it was interesting but it was not so profound", it shows that something was forgotten in that moment. In reality, everything is profound. Every moment is uniquely enlightening. We cannot say that this is good and this is not so good. The vision that someone has can never go away. It is there, not there in the future or in the past, but there as a present experience.

It is always there but not seen consciously...

It is not seen consciously, but that experience can never go away. It is like if a child is born, that birth is present in eternity. It can never go away. No matter what happens to the child in the future, that birth is there forever. Life takes us on and we get old, forgetting that experience, but it is us who have forgotten. It is not that this birth is less powerful than it was in the moment it happened. That moment is never ending, never stopping.

For me, the present moment has the quality that we attribute to the future and to the past. It is total in its essence, in its completeness and in that moment there is no future and no past. When our mind goes to the future or to the past to try to bring an experience to this present moment, that is precisely the whole process that prevents that present moment from expressing its beauty.

To put it in a more practical sense without being too esoteric, some people say they have a *déjà vu* experience where they sense that they relive a sensation or an experience. This is so strong that it shakes the person for a split second. We hear remarks such as, "Oh, I have been here before", but they have not been here before. What they are experiencing is there all the time. It is just that their mind has allowed them to drop into that space for a split second.

How can you put this in words? Words are language and language is communication. This is why we use language, but it is difficult to put into language something that is unlimited because language is limited by time and by its whole built-up structure. It is difficult to communicate what I really mean in words. This is why I try to approach it from different angles.

Going back to that experience, it is like Romeo and Juliet who have fallen in love. Some people consider that their love is dead, but for me, Romeo and Juliet live forever in the atmosphere. That love can never die. It is actually similar to what Christians think when they say Jesus is alive in your heart. It is symbolic of course but I believe this means that the mystery behind the whole work that Jesus created two thousands years ago never died, because its beauty is alive now, and we can experience it now. When people believe that they have a mystical Christ consciousness, or a "revelation", they feel it because that moment that happened two thousands years ago never stopped. We believe it is history but it never stopped.

This is the thing with compassion and love. It does not stop. It simply expands. It never goes to a point zero and then comes to a point one. It comes to a point one and then adds another dimension. It transcends that one to go the mystical union of oneness, giving birth to another aspect which starts at zero and then goes to one, so to speak. It is an ever expanding experience in this moment. It is not that this moment is limited or stops. It is not that any profound experience that you have, and that some would call enlightening, ever needs to be seen as part of the past. The idea that it is past is what is preventing us from being present.

This is a very personal question: do you personally access at will to these visions of reality, like Roshi or Ramana Maharshi did?

No, not at will, because "at will" means that the ego wants something. If you want something, then it comes from a limited perspective and the divine cannot fit into that perspective because it is beyond that whole sense of limitation. What has to happen is a total letting go.

So putting the ego and its will aside means that this state of reality is simply being in the present moment. Is it a continuous state of being or "flow" for you, as it was for Jesus, Buddha, Ramana Maharshi and Roshi Sazaki?

"Being in the present moment" is a very popular expression but being in the present moment is not as people understand it to be. It does not mean being present to the ego or to the will. It means being present to a part of yourself that is beyond the ego or the will because the ego does not live in the present moment. Instead it almost always lives in the future even though it is connected to past experiences. It is always trying to find something, it is running ahead of yourself. If you have the ego and the will being fed from the space where there is something to reach or something to catch up with, having the ego repeat, "Next step, next step, next step", then you are running after the ego. In this way you cannot be in the present moment because you are present to a space that is a little bit in the future. You can, however, be more present to what is going on. You can see the interaction of what is going on much more clearly.

The present moment for me is actually letting go of the whole game that the ego and the will play. When you let go of it, then the ego and will do not disappear but they are fed from the space that is feeding everything in the present moment, which is consciousness. The present moment is being present to consciousness in the complete sense. The ego and the will are still there because without them it is difficult to maintain a physical presence in this dimension, but they will play. They begin to enjoy the game of life from a space that is much more child-like but it is not childish, it is quite serious. Yet it is not so serious in the sense that you do not get hurt yourself, do not hurt other people nor do you try to achieve something. You are not trying to limit the experience through the picture that the ego is creating for you to chase.

Instead you are playing and then it is like the ego becomes an invisible body that you accept along with its form and structure. It does not disappear because the ego cannot disappear. It always remains in the physical realm but the quality of it disappears so you still have an ego. It is not like you turn into a divine angel that cannot not say anything that relates to the level of human experience. You still have the human experience, but the quality behind – which is what feeds the ego and will – is invisible and comes from a space that is divine. This is very different than being caught up in the limited picture that the ego is feeding you. This means that if you are in this real present moment, you are present to much more than ego and will. You are present to everything, the whole big picture.

Do you "enter" the present moment?

You cannot "enter" into anything. You have to be in that space. It is not like, "Now I am here and then I don't really like being here because it's difficult so

I choose to be here so I enter at will or I want to be in that space". It does not work in this way. If they are or were enlightened – and who knows until you are in that space where you understand what enlightenment is? – Jesus, Ramana Maharshi, Buddha and Roshi Sasaki would never, in an enlightened state, choose to not be in that state for one minute to stay in the ego and the will, and then in another minute, go to a space that is flowing. They always are in the space and it does not mean that the ego is not there, it just means that it has another quality and so does the will. The flow is always there but the flow is there for everyone. To picture someone as higher and having reached a flow that is more flowing or more conscious is to miss the whole picture of consciousness. It is conceptualising it into boxes, which then creates another mind game.

Some people conceptualise Hindu terms such as *moksha*, *nirvana* or enlightenment. It is like something out there. For me, it is not out there to go and collect at will or with the ego. It is there all the time but the thing that is stopping you is your attachment to the mundane because the mind and the physical aspects of yourself do not have free will. They are so connected to what is happening in the mundane that they cannot open up beyond the limited picture, but you are it. How can you be something that you are not? The question is saying: can you access enlightenment at will? But enlightenment is not something that you achieve. Enlightenment is something that you are. There is no access to it. It is more a letting go of the concepts that prevent you being in that space. It is the opposite of your question because when you say, "If you are", you have gone into the thought of the western culture, which is based on heaven and hell, "Heaven is an enlightened state and hell is a place I don't want to be in". We try to leave our mundane world and think that there is something beyond it that is better and that some people have – me, or Buddha or whoever. Then we are running away from what has to be done, which is actually the work, which everyone does, whether they like it or not, they have to.

We have to deal with the mundane. You cannot say, "I don't want to deal with the mundane, I'll just sit here and wait". It has to be dealt with. If you are alive in the physical sense, you have to deal with food, hunger, anger, frustration, sadness, grief, death, birth, life, relationships... And that is an enlightening experience if you are present to the consciousness that is there. When we say, "I just want to run away and find an enlightened space", this is a bit like heaven and hell and it is not dealing with what is here. It is not honouring the space that is a gift to humanity, which is this present moment. In the end there is no flow and there is no will. The will is usually controlled or determined by the limited concepts that you have in the mind and so the actions that you put forward using willpower usually are actions that are negating reality. In actual fact we have to drop will and instead we have to trust. We have to forget flow and instead be in the flow, not trying to find it because the flow is our experience of life in this moment, it is not something alien to what is happening now.

The only advantage of people like Ramana Maharshi and Jesus is that through words, through actions and through presence, they bring a gift to people that awakens their desire to understand things away from the limitations of will and ego. It is not that you have to be enlightened or even look at the picture of enlightenment. It is rather that you have to integrate that trust into yourself so that this picture allows for the bigger picture to open up more deeply. People follow or followed Jesus literally, even when they were alive during his time, and just followed the words and the big picture of, "What a wonderful person and it's so nice". They are or were not listening to the energy that is being conveyed in a deeper sense, which allows the person to remember who they are. That is why Jesus found it very difficult to speak to people because they were listening to his words, they were not listening to the energy that was being transmitted. He never said, "You have to follow me", or at least I do not think he ever said it. In Aramaic, it is not, "You have to follow me", but actually, "What you have to follow is the consciousness that I am expressing to you in this moment". That consciousness does not live in me or in you. It is beyond me and you, it has nothing to do with will, it has nothing to do with flow, it is everywhere all at the same time. Jesus, and others like him, are just a reminder, not of what the will wants, but of what is possible.

Are you?

People have got an image of who I am and that picture has nothing to do with the reality unless you understand who I am. Who is Tony Samara? And how do you understand who I am? Only by being who you are. Otherwise it is just a game... As I said before, you have to let go.

Letting go with no desire?

Yes, no desire. That is why I was somewhat explaining time. Desire comes in the perspective of linear time, with the idea that something begins at one point and ends somewhere else. When we have that linear time, it creates the idea that something has to be reached outside of itself. This is why I was also saying that love expands. It never stops. If you open yourself to that expansion, to that union, then it is not will. It is just that you are letting go of everything that stops that union from being seen. Otherwise you just see what everyone is seeing without seeing the divine and everyone.

For some who do not have that attachment to certain limitations that prevent that vision from being actual in the physical, in the mental or in the emotional experience. This is where the intelligence of the heart moves to the mind, moves to the body and moves to the emotions. It speaks to those aspects rather than letting the ego connect to these aspects. It is so because the ego always comes from a space where it believes that reality is individualistic and divided into segments. Yet, that love is there, everywhere. The ego tries to make sense of the whole thing and on some level it can do so. This is why it is important to have science, philosophy, intellectualism and logic, but beyond a certain level, it stops and this is where mysticism then bridges that understanding to something more profound than just logic.

So compassion and love come from these feelings, these experiences of knowing unity. If it is just the awareness of unity, does it need to be developed?

It cannot be developed but it can be replicated, so we can force ourselves to be compassionate. For example, if the ego says to you, "It would be very nice to buy this car because I need something nice and people would think it is wonderful", then you can work with that desire. When you work with it, you can develop compassion so that you go beyond the need and see something more profound instead of focusing on this need to have a car. I do not mean this in a moralistic sense, but we cannot just sit and do nothing.

My philosophy is that you cannot just wait and hope that everything is going to change, that the ego will disappear and that the divine will enlighten you, just by doing nothing. Our actions have to bring us closer to this point and those actions are not really external: they are internal. Internal in the sense that if we see that we are creating barriers and points which we cannot go beyond, the activity is to remove them. In doing so, we open to other things. If we have a desire, it is not enough to say, "All right, I can see the desire is there". We have to work with the desire, see what it means and what we can do with it. This is very different from simply waiting for the desire to extinguish itself.

Desire will never extinguish itself. It will always attach itself to more and more forms. In Zen Buddhism this is called the "hungry ghost". The hungry ghost has an appetite that can never be satisfied because its throat is so small that it cannot eat enough to fill its belly and its belly is very big. The hungry ghost will feed the desire to no end, so what we have to do is to make sure that it does not latch on to a desire and create a path for us that we blindly follow like robots, without seeing what this ghost is doing. We have to be active and say, "The hungry ghost is a part of myself, but I do not need to acknowledge this part of myself to the point where my actions are living and acting out of that part. I can work with it but I do not need to actively be the hungry ghost as a person, because then my desire will never be fulfilled and I will be as hungry as the ghost". To have a car and to want another car, to have love and to want love in a different way is not coming from the point of union that can be satisfied. It comes from the emptiness of the belly which needs more and more and more.

You have a specific relationship to time, the past and the future, and you seem to apprehend reality in a different way than in a linear perspective...

This is a very important issue because this is a point where a lot of people find it complicated and somehow disagree with me. I am aware I have made a few people upset by talking about time in a non-linear form as you say. I do not see history or evolution unfolding from nothing into a sudden big bang as a beginning. I find the quality of time much more spiritual because if you look at it deep inside, time is the divine. It has no beginning and no end. In our linear way of thinking, we cannot understand this because of course there must be a beginning and there must be an end, at least scientifically.

When I address time, people find it very difficult because I explain it from a point of view that does not make any logical sense. When people talk about reincarnation for instance, it fits into time, but as I mentioned previously, reincarnation for me is not like some traditional belief systems where there is a beginning and you start as a plant, you develop and become an animal and then you change to another animal, then you develop as a person and you become a better person, etc. Even though this may help to clarify and simplify certain perspectives of time, I see this as another illusion.

I do not see time as a movement that is the subjective picture that we put upon time. For me, time simply is not moving at all. When people say, "The past happened yesterday", I say, "No. It is just that in that moment, we have entered a different dimension of time and have categorised that moment as yesterday". Then they ask, "So have we lived tomorrow?" and I say, "Yes. It is just that we are not in that dimension so we cannot see". I use the word "dimension" because language – at least the English language – is very linear and it is not easy to put this meaning into words. People then ask, "Is everything this moment?" and I say, "Yes. Everything is this moment. Nothing has actually changed in this moment. You are being born in this moment and you are dying in this moment, you are a child and you are an old person in this moment". All is in this moment and that is very difficult to see.

When I say this, it sounds very odd and I know people get very confused and think that is not possible. But it is possible. It is just that if the mind were able to see that there is no time, it would not be able to exist as a mind. We cannot see it from that perspective of limited logic, but mathematics would probably help us to understand what I am saying in a formula that uses logic to go beyond logic. I am not a mathematician and I was never good in mathematics so I do not know exactly how you do this, but I am sure it is possible to explain the non-linear dimension of time. This would change the quality of culture, society and everything.

How does the non-linear time connect to linear time? How do these dimensions relate to each other?

This relates to what I was speaking about earlier. Linear time and non-linear time... What is non-linear time? It depends. In my understanding, linear time is based on the whole western civilisation of time, beginning, end, first, last, one and zero. It is a way of understanding and it is useful to get things happening and things moving. On the other hand, non-linear time has linear time taken away so that it is valued in a different way. Time is valued using other concepts and so for me, non-linear time is more related with the cycles that are natural. These cycles are natural to being a human being rather than wanting to be a human being in a certain way, so for example it could have the cycles of a child growing. In linear time this is, "OK, you're eight, so because you're eight, this is what has to happen, ok, you're nine...". That is measuring in linear time but cycles can go in completely different ways and it takes the internal rhythms and the external rhythms as the guidelines of how to measure time. This is more related to the moon, to the seasons and to cycles within oneself depending on the age, depending on time of society's development.

Also, if you are putting the non-linear as an important aspect of your life, then the linear becomes less important. Sunday or Monday or 5 o'clock is not the guiding principle in your actions anymore. Your actions come from a different space and I think that is what is natural for most people anyway, but because it was changed and because we live in a modern society that has to perhaps function differently, we forget. I see that sometimes we forget simple things like when to eat correct food because we are not connected to the cycles of growing and seasons, we are connected to linear time. "It's nine o'clock I'll go shopping in the supermarket and I'll buy my apple, it doesn't matter where it comes from". It is the same with work, it is the same with relationships and it is the same with many other things. This is not an integrated holistic picture of what non-linear time is and it is difficult to live in both worlds, but how can we connect both? I think we can say that if non-linear time lives in the heart – heart meaning the feelings – and linear time lives in the mind, then we bring them both somehow to meet somewhere. We honour them both, but at the same time we listen to the heart as the guiding principle.

Everything you understood and explain in your teaching obviously does not come from books. It seems that you have developed an intuitive knowledge connected to different dimensions...

It is very interesting because I do not always try to understand where anything comes from. In a way I am like a child because I do not see what I know as very important. Yet, when I sit with someone who does mathematics or does something on the computer, I am always amazed. On the other hand, what I know seems very obvious and unimportant, because for me, intuitive knowledge is very simple and very easy to comprehend. This knowledge is not unique. It is so present that on one level there is no need to try to understand it like a computer because a computer involves another part of my brain that seems mysterious and difficult to use. This is why I am fascinated with it.

What I know appears obvious to me. This is why I do not usually say very much or I do not explain things in details until a situation like now where you ask me questions. This way of thinking is unusual for me, as I have never really used words to describe this experience or to describe how I know these things. The knowledge comes naturally and this is actually quite a job to describe it in words, to connect things together and make them comprehensible, because I have to use this other part of my brain that I find very difficult to use consciously. When I need to learn practical things, like how to go shopping or how to do mundane activities, I need this part of the brain that is working automatically for most people but not for me.

Sometimes people offer me books to read about spirituality, but I am normally reading books about science and other mundane topics. This is because I am trying to understand these things. Whenever I need to know something about spirituality – spirituality meaning this moment – it comes naturally. I do not have to do anything.

How does this happen? I do not know, but I know it began at the age of twenty-seven, where a flow of energy came in. That energy contained knowledge and wisdom connected to spiritual teachers that I began to embrace and understand without really knowing how this was happening. It was like an opening that I cannot explain as it took over everything in me. Since then, I have not been trying to explain how I know things and I have carried on down that path for many years. It has been quite a few years now and I never questioned this. I accepted and embraced it with amazement and fascination, but I am now beginning to understand it to explain it to other people.

I remember one day you spoke to me about a rosemary plant beside us, telling me that it is good to help cure cancer. I asked you "How do you know?" and you just answered almost apologetically, "I just know" …

Yes. This is what I say but it is not good enough for most people to make sense…

Would you consider that it is a way to connect to a world of knowledge that is beyond the mind and can only be reached through intuition?

Intuition is a key but I also think that knowledge is useful. Sylvia would read a book for example and say, "Tony I have read this. Can you please tell what you think about it?". I read it and sometimes I say, "They are really nice words, but I do not really see anything here", but I also sometimes say, "How fascinating!", and I get very interested in understanding how someone else sees plants in such and such way for instance. I read more and more and get fascinated by it, but I never have enough time to go deeply into any of it because there is always something else. It is not that I do not like knowledge, but I am only interested when it has some meaning to me and has some connection to something that matters.

When someone asked me to read a few books from Ramana Maharshi, I read and found it fantastic. The words were exactly what I think but his ideas were very eloquently expressed to describe things. I said to this person, "Wonderful, read the book, this is great for you", but I never completed reading the book myself because there were too many words for me. It is not that I am putting down books or knowledge. I am fascinated by it but I find there is too much out there and unless it has relevance to you and inspires change, healing, or something deeper in you, it is not relevant and it is just filling the brain. I feel that people do not go directly to the point and therefore read and keep reading more and more…

There is a trap in reading too much about spirituality?

I do not know how they can do it because for me it is a headache.

It can be a game we play with ourselves, to keep reading and reading…

It is much more interesting for me to go out for a walk. Books can be great to read to your children, and I also like books as references, because when someone for instance says, "What you are saying is totally untrue", I really want to find out if it is untrue. Then I look at new scientific knowledge. This is what I am the most interested in when it comes to books, so I tend to have books with many references.

The Aim of Life

Your itinerary, your involvement, the fact that you do not create a school and that you are always on the move, your modest way of life impresses people working with you as it expresses what you teach through your own life. That makes your point very clear. If we look at Krishnamurti and Ramana Maharshi for example, their dealing with knowledge was a little bit different. Krishnamurti just talked and did not want to imply anything, explanations or help or anything that would prevent the person to understand by him or herself. Ramana Maharshi just irradiated the state of awareness he had attained. He inspired people, but personal involvement with them was absent. All these ways make me think about a Native American story of a humming bird, which is often quoted by ecologists to make their point. The story is that one day there was a big fire in the forest and all the big animals where running away for their life. Only a hummingbird was not escaping and kept flying around, getting one drop of water in its beak and going back and forth with it to let it fall into the fire. A bigger animal, seeing that scene exclaimed, "What are you doing? Are you crazy? Do you think you are going to extinguish the fire with these little drops?" Continuing his task, the little bird simply said, "I am just doing my part" ...

Exactly. This resonates with me and it is a wonderful story. In the end, I think this is not just what I am doing but what everyone is doing. Whether we recognise it or not, we are all doing our little part. For some reasons that are beyond understanding at times, we are doing our little part. Sometimes mothers will ask, "I had children and I did so much for them. I did all I could. What was the purpose of this? What is my part in the whole picture?", but we do not really even need to understand our part in the picture. Like this story demonstrates, the humming bird loved the forest and he was just doing what it needed to do. It did not come from an expectation or wanting to do anything. It just came out of pure love.

When you do something out of pure love, like a mother does with her child, there is no meaning beyond that pure love. It is the same. We all sometimes question life and ask, "Have I done enough?", "Could I have done more?", or "Is there any more meaning than just the little that I have done in this world?" We all do a little bit and in the end, that little bit is enough. Mothers will often think something like: "I could have done more for my child. I could have given more time and not been so busy working or cleaning up the house, not being so busy doing this or that". Ultimately, the little that they did is that they added more love, more expression of them to the world than was there before. So that little action, just like the little water that was being dropped onto the forest, is their part and it makes a big difference beyond what can be understood.

The difference is to do things with love...

Everything. In the end, human beings really need to do thing with love. If not, they get so lost and destructive that they not only destroy themselves but they destroy everyone around. This is the problem with alcohol and drug addictions and of course, it can go further into crazy materialism and desires that never get fulfilled. In an obvious sense, alcoholics and drug addicts get so lost that they only destroy themselves. From the outside, that seems terrible and painful, like any person who loves someone who is an alcoholic or a drug addict can observe. But even that action of destroying oneself cannot be seen as completely negative, because within that space, only the alcoholic and the drug addict are conscious that there is still a sense of love. If that love is completely extinguished, there is no more possibility to be a human being. All your human aspects disappear and there is no humanity inside of you, but there is humanity even in the drug addict. It is, however, so destructive towards itself that it is of course not obvious like a mother who is caressing her baby where that expression of love is there, easily seen from the outside. It is hidden inside the addicted person but it is still there, so they are also doing their little part.

The moral statements from the Church or from society for example, that a person is very bad, the loss of faith in him or her and telling children that we must leave them or we will end up in a horrible situation, are in themselves misunderstanding the complexity and the complete picture of what is going on. They are not relating to the humanity that is present in people and this is why they are destructive towards themselves. With love we can see the person's disarray and their humanity. In the end, everything that is going on has a little bit that creates much more than we see. Your story is a wonderful story that can also be understood in this way.

What is your part, what is for you the aim of life – yours and for other people?

When I think, "What is the aim?", I realise that I do not really have an aim. Having an aim would mean that I want something to happen, and I do not really want anything to happen.

But all of us wonder why we are here? Why do we have to go through all these experiences of love, joy, pain and sorrow? What is this life journey about? To find who we are? You said we are spiritual by nature...

Why are we here? That is a very good question. Why are we here? Often people say if we understood why we were here, it would be like a cosmic game. Once we understood it from the real sense of understanding, we would just laugh because it would seem so insignificant to everything that we thought. It would be so funny, not comical but funny because it is so beyond that question, it is a cosmic joke. I know this is very esoteric but I also say this because often when we have an outburst of spontaneous laughter, this is close to the aim of life. Sometimes we have this, not really often as an adult, but sometimes we have this even as an adult where something is so funny that we lose our sense of identity and we come to the space where we just let go. For me that is closer to the aim of life, to let go of everything, of course, in the philosophical sense of the ego.

By letting go we realise that everything is just a theatre. This also sounds philosophical and easy but it is not. We are going through an illusion, as if we were watching a film but identifying with the film, thinking that the film we are watching really is who we are and forgetting that who we are is actually the aspect that is watching. Yet because we have forgotten that aspect, we get completely caught up in the film. What I mean by film is our experience of life, why we are here, and what is the meaning of this experience that we are undergoing. There is no solution. There is no explanation. There is nothing that can clearly open our understanding of this because we are not the film. This makes answering the question of the aim of life almost impossible with words.

So what is my aim? From this logic, my aim is for people to be free of that identity that they believe they need to identify with. This is a whole process that is actually quite enjoyable because as we become free, we connect to something more real inside of ourselves, which in turn gives us and our emotions more joy and a more spontaneous happiness that comes from the space of pure freedom. Then we understand that the aim is to go more into this, at least for the emotions. It is not be detached, because detached sounds cold, but rather to not identify with this circle that we are going through in the world, in the mundane sense. It is not to switch it or turn the film off, because that is not good, but instead to watch the film with another sense. In some cultures, they have meaningful words for all these things but I can only use the limited English words...

The aim I have for other people is freedom. I explain this when I say that the evolution of human consciousness is ever expanding. What I mean by that is that our consciousness of who we are becomes clearer as we realise why we are here in the world. We do not realise it through negating the world and saying that the world is bad. We do not realise it through going into deep spiritual trances either. We realise it by actually being free of everything, so my aim is for that freedom to be more accessible for people in the real sense, in an emotional sense. Most of our suffering in the Western world is emotional and of course there is physical suffering, without a doubt, but the strong experience for people is usually emotional and mental.

How to free that space? We then come back to *karma*, which is also part of the whole situation. I use the word *karma* in the sense that I explained before; it is often part of this movie that we identify with because we identify with our *karma* rather than with the whole situation that is behind the *karma*. Our *karma* cannot in anyway explain or make sense of the world we are in. What we need to do is move away from this karmic circle that we are creating.

This is my aim with people but my personal aim… What is my own aim? I have to think about this because I have not really given much thought about why I do what I do.

You see, I am not looking for results, meaning it does not really matter to me if nothing happens, if everything I say gets forgotten tomorrow, if all the years – forty years now – I have spent working just disappear, like a leaf falling off a tree disappears on to the ground. I will not wonder, "What has this work been for?" or "Why hasn't it achieved something more concrete?" It is not that I do not care but I simply do not attach any importance to this. What I attach importance to is the immediate experience in that moment with the person, because I know that when something is touched in that moment, it can never be forgotten. It is like a camera taking a picture. Even if it does not make any sense to the whole world outside, that picture remains forever in the universe.

It is as if the expansion of other people's consciousness were also an expansion of my consciousness. In the end, it is an expansion of the consciousness of the divine and the consciousness of every aspect of the divine, whether it is a tree, a rock, a mountain, the sea, animals or other people. As we sail together through the oceans of the illusion of maya, this creates a sacred vehicle that becomes almost tangible, but on a level that is not here. It is not like we can quantify it and say, "This is the aim". It would then become religion rather than spirituality, with the aim being to convert other people to believe or to do certain things. For me, it does not matter if people believe or do whatever. In the end I do not really care. I do not have a method that is important to preserve in books and remember forever nor something to be passed on in a verbal way, as stories are for traditional people like the Aboriginals. In the end, everything that is true is registered in a space that goes beyond this worldly attachment to objects, thinking and feeling. It is beyond this.

That is where I am at. I am not here. It can be very difficult for people to understand. The comprehension of the work that I do is still so vague to the many who are connected to me, because they find it difficult to live in the moment when everything changes all the time. There is nothing concrete that they can hold on to, which is what people like to do. The only concrete thing they have to hold on to are the miracles, the love and the obvious things that happen around me. In fact, even that is intangible because there is no explanation to it. It changes from moment to moment.

Some people say, "My aim is to grow old and be happy, to have my pension, to have the children happy going to school and to have my life secure". With me, as soon as that security is there, I will drop it, just so that kind of form is not attached to. In New Zealand for example, when there were lots of people coming to a conference I did, it would have been obvious and logical for someone else to stay there and create something out of that, but I said to myself, "Let's move". The same happened in Portugal where things were working with a lot of people involved. I just moved. I do this kind of thing all the time.

Things have no concrete form and there is no aim. My aim is simply that people live in the moment and that is very difficult for everyone. Living in the moment is not just a philosophical idea. It has to be put into practice. The practice for me is to drop our attachment to everything, but most people like to attach that moment to something. It could even be that you attach the person that you love to a certain way of being or to love you in a certain way.

I can be quite a complicated person to attach that idea to because I can change it from one thing to another. People see me and they expect me to be in a certain way, which is generally as someone who is loving and kind, but I can be quite dramatically strong on the outside, so they say, "I thought the aim of your work was to be loving and kind?". You see, love has an attachment and an idea of what it means, but it is much deeper. It does not have that form. I do not have the aim of becoming kind or making it easier or expressing my love in a certain way. I just want to be in that moment as it is. That is what I see that people also want and this is why I never stop in that point of communication with people. I never fall into the trap of being something. Some people like to try to build things around me and that can be very confusing for them because it seems that what I am doing is aimless.

What is the aim of the work? To quantify it? To build a structure? To have certain courses, teachers or buildings? For me what is more important is the experience rather than the building. It can irritate people because all the energy is put in one thing and then, all of a sudden, the carpet is taken from under people's feet and they wonder, "But why am I doing all this?" and I answer, "Yes. Why are you doing all this? What is your aim? Is your aim the same as your spiritual work? Or is your aim now getting caught up into a form that somehow wants to contain the spiritual work in the idea of where it needs to go? Is your goal to reach a certain point?". The divine cannot be put anywhere except where it is. So where is it? It is obvious, it is not in anything that we think, nor in what we try to do or try to create, nor is it in an aim or a goal. Then why create that?

It simply is...

Yes. To build a temple for example, is a waste of time because the temple of life is not a structure. To build this wonderful structure and to put effort into it is useful for a little while, but beyond that little while, the structure becomes too solid to hold the miracle of life within it. This is what people do when they have an aim: they quantify things to make them easier to relate to, even though the miracle of life is everywhere. It is not in the stones that you build the temple with, that is not where the essence of spirituality lies. The divine simply is. Why try to create something else than what already is?

Glossary

Amrita (or **Amrit**): Sanskrit word meaning "that which is immortal", often referred to in texts as nectar. Associated to the Aryans' soma and the Greeks' Ambrosia, it is referred to as the drink of the gods, which grants them immortality.

Aramaic: A Semitic language, ancestral to both the Arabic and the Hebrew alphabets, that was the original language of large sections of the biblical books of Daniel and Erza, the language spoken by Jesus, and the main language of the Talmud.

Ashram: Sanskrit word to signify a religious hermitage or a locus of Indian cultural activity such as yoga, music study and spiritual instruction.

Aurobindo (Sri Aurobindo, 1872–1950): A poet and a yogi who developed his own vision and philosophy of human progress and spiritual evolution.

Ayahuasca: Sacred psychotropic herbal potion used for physical and psychological healing by shamans in the Amazon basin.

Ayahuasqueros: Peruvian shamans specialized in the use of *ayahuasca*.

Ceremony: In Tony's sense, it is an intensive spiritual and introspective work, also called the « San Pedro Ceremony », taking place at night and during which the participants drink the San Pedro cactus.

Chakra: Sanskrit name used to designate some points in the energetic body that concentrate energy and that can be activated through different techniques among which yoga. There are seven main chakras.

Curanderos: Healers shamans in the Peruvian Amazon bassin and north coastal regions of Peru.

Dharma: Sanskrit term close to "destiny" or "fate" used to designate a person necessary acceptance of his or her birth's status and duty (caste, gender, etc.) in relation to the Hindu caste system (the antonym of *dharma* is *adhamra* means "unnatural" or "immoral").

Gnostics: Refers to diverse syncretistic religious movements in Antiquity (Gnosticism) who considered that only revealed esoteric knowledge would allow humanity to remind their true origin and escape materiality.

Gurdjieff (1877-1949): Spiritual teacher originary from the Caucasus who distinguished the « essential being » from the « superficial personality » and taught that what someone knows is in direct relation to what he or she is.

Hara: Japanese word which means simply "belly". In Chinese and Japanese tradition, it is considered the physical center of gravity of the human body and is the seat of one's internal energy (qi).

Hawking, Stephen W. (1942-2018): English theoretical physicist, professor at the University of Oxford. He is well known for his work and contributions in the domain of cosmology, black holes, space-time and quantum mechanics.

Huachuma (also called "*San Pedro*"): A fast-growing columnar cactus (*trichocereus pachanoi*), native to the Andes of Peru and Ecuador and other places in South America, used by *curanderos* as a sacred plant during healing rituals.

Kabbalah: A discipline and school of thought and esoteric teaching concerned with the mystical aspect of Judaism notably the relationship between an eternal/mysterious Creator and the mortal/finite universe (His creation).

Kabir: A Mystic poet, philosopher, religious reformer and a Sufi saint of Northern India (1440—1518).

Karma: In the Hindu tradition, it is considered that all the feelings, thoughts, actions create a reaction in peoples lives, present and future.

Koan: A key aspect of the Zen Buddhist tradition consisting of a story, question or statement whose meaning cannot be understood by rational thinking but rather by intuition.

Krishnamurti (Jiddu Krishnamurti, 1895–1986): Indian spiritual speaker and philosopher who constantly stressed the need for a revolution of the psyche of every human being beyond religious, political and social dogmatism.

Kundalini: In Indian yoga, it is an energy coiled at the base of the spine of every being and symbolized as a sleeping serpent awaiting to be awaken and raised to achieve enlightenment.

Kwan Yin (**Kuan Yin** or **Guan Yin**): The Goddess of Mercy and an Immortal for the Taoists, she is also a feminine form of Avalokitesvara, the Bodhisattva of compassion in Indian and Zen Buddhism.

Mantra: A Sanskrit concept for sound, syllable, word or group of words, often repeated, to create spiritual transformation.

Maya: In Hinduism, Buddhism and Sikhism, it is the principal concept which manifests, perpetuates and governs the illusion and dream of duality in the phenomenal Universe.

Osho: Indian spiritual mystic and guru, born Chandra Mohan Jain (1931–1990) and also known as Acharya Rajneesh. He preached against religion and had a notable impact on Western New Age thought, especially from his creation of active meditations.

Overtone: A musical note from a voice or instrument that is part of a harmonic series above a fundamental note and may be heard with it.

Phytagoras (Pythagoras of Samos, 570-495 BC): an Ionian Greek pre-Socratic philosopher, mathematician, mystic and scientist, founder of the religious movement called Pythagoreanism.

Pineal gland: A small endocrine gland in the vertebrate brain that produces melatonin and plays a central role in the regulation of the biological rhythm.

Pituitary gland: A small endocrine gland, a protrusion off the bottom of the hypothalamus at the base of the brain, considered as a master gland that secretes hormones regulating homeostasis.

Ramakrishna (Sri Ramakrishna Paramahamsa, 1836-1886): A famous Bengali mystic and spiritual teacher who dedicated his life to the Goddess Kali in Calcutta.

Ramana Maharshi (Sri Ramana Maharshi, 1879–1950): A Tamil sage who maintained that the purest form of his teaching was silence, although he also sometimes gave verbal teachings in which he recommended self-inquiry.

Reiki: A very popular practice and technique among New Agers and alternative healers, commonly called *palm healing*. It was developed in 1922 as a spiritual practice by Mikao Usui, a Japanese Buddhist. It is based on the principal that the therapist can channel energy by the means of touch and therefore help with creating balance in the patient.

Rumi (Djalâl ad-Dîn Rûm, 1207–1273): A 3th-century Persian peot, jurist, theologian, and Sufi mystic whose teaching transcends ethnic borders. He is considered to be the founder of the Dervish order.

San Pedro: (voir Huachuma)

Santo Daime: A syncretic spiritual practice founded in the 1930s in Brazil that incorporates elements of several religious or spiritual traditions (Folk Catholicism, Kardecist Spiritism, African Animism and South American Shamanism) and whose ceremonies include the drinking of *Ayahuasca*.

Satori: A Japanese Buddhist term for "enlightenment" (the word literally means "understanding") in the Zen Buddhist tradition (the equivalent of *Nirvana* in the Hindu tradition).

Satsang: (in Sanskrit, *sat* = true, *sanga* = company) In Indian philosophy, it is a moment in company of a spiritual guide who delivers his or her teaching.

Shintoism: Traditional and ancient Japanese spirituality dating from the 8th century characterized by the worship of nature, ancestors, polytheism, and animism, with a strong focus on ritual purity, involving honoring and celebrating the existence of spirits or natural forces (*kami*).

Soma: A ritual drink of importance among the early Indo-Iranians, and the later Vedic and Persian Zoroastrian traditions. In the Vedas, Soma is portrayed as sacred and as a God (*deva*). Some theories consider it drink was actually extracted from a psychedelic mushroom (*amanita muscaria*).

Third Eye: a mystical and esoteric concept referring in part to the sixth chakra (*Ajna*) in the Hindu yogi tradition. Located between the eyebrows, it is considered as the gate that leads to intuition, clairvoyance and higher consciousness.

Thymus: A specialized organ in the immune system, located anatomically in the anterior superior mediastinum, in front of the heart and behind the sternum.

Vipassana meditation: One of world's most ancient techniques of meditation, it is a way of self-transformation through self-observation and introspection which in the Buddhist tradition means *insight* into the nature of reality.

Whirling meditation: A special meditation created by Tony Samara for spiritual transformation. It enhances the function of pituitary and pineal glands through a slowl and quiet rotating movement of the trunk while sitting cross-legged. The sound *hu* is also chanted on the out breath during this practice.

Index

P

Paulo Coelho 30
peace 17, 22, 23, 24, 33, 50, 129, 177, 197, 233, 245, 246, 249, 260
pineal 109, 110, 115, 135, 139, 140, 141, 149, 307
pituitary 109, 110, 115, 135, 139, 140, 141, 142, 149, 307
Pythagorus 134

Q

quantum physic 244

R

Ramakrishna 27, 305
Ramana Maharshi 101, 137, 287, 294, 297, 305
reiki 106, 305
reincarnation 221, 226, 231, 247
religion 14, 15, 16, 18, 22, 75, 76, 136, 199, 247, 272, 284, 305
responsibility 21, 37, 97, 115, 205
Roshis 108
Rumi 137, 232, 280, 281, 286, 306

S

saint Francis of Assisi 23
San Pedro 30, 62, 71, 76, 108, 283, 303, 304, 306
Santo Daime 75, 76, 306
satori 50, 130, 306
Sazaki 47
schizophrenia 195
sexuality 145, 204, 205, 206, 208, 263, 265, 266, 267, 268
shamanism 20, 77, 107, 281, 306
shamans 37, 56, 93, 122, 123, 131, 132, 167, 274, 303
shintoism 20, 306
silence 54, 190, 208, 305
simplicity 30, 31, 35, 166, 169, 190
Socrates 101
soma 303
soul 151, 152, 153, 202, 221, 230
sound 18, 41, 48, 85, 92, 93, 101, 114, 132, 133, 134, 135, 136, 149, 190, 201, 242, 273, 305
spiritual discipline 145, 163, 171, 175, 239, 260, 261
spiritual teacher 41, 45, 87, 97, 114, 135, 137, 165, 166, 188, 201, 202, 215, 243, 244, 305
Stephen Hawking 214
suffering 14, 15, 19, 36, 37, 42, 51, 87, 93, 118, 122, 140, 152, 165, 170, 172, 186, 209, 212, 213, 214, 215, 216, 218, 224, 225, 232, 234, 257, 258, 299
sufis 18, 41, 137, 281

Printed in Great Britain
by Amazon

66407466R00179